SCHOOLS FOR MISRULE

SCHOOLS
for
MISRULE
LEGAL ACADEMIA AND AN OVERLAWYERED AMERICA

by **WALTER OLSON**

Encounter Books   New York • London

First American edition published in 2011 by Encounter Books,
an activity of Encounter for Culture and Education, Inc.,
a nonprofit, tax exempt corporation.
Encounter Books website address: www.encounterbooks.com

Manufactured in the United States and printed on
acid-free paper. The paper used in this publication meets
the minimum requirements of ANSI/NISO Z39.48 1992
(R 1997) (*Permanence of Paper*).

FIRST AMERICAN EDITION

LIBRARY OF CONGRESS CATALOGING-IN-PUBLICATION DATA

Olson, Walter K.
Schools for misrule: legal academia and an overlawyered America/
by Walter Olson.
p. cm.
Includes bibliographical references and index.
ISBN-13: 978–1–59403–233–2 (hardcover: alk. paper)
ISBN-10: 1–59403–233–5 (hardcover: alk. paper) 1. Law—Study
and teaching—United States. 2. Law schools—United States.
3. Practice of law—United States. I. Title.
KF272.O474 2011
340.071'173—dc22
2010028814

10 9 8 7 6 5 4 3 2 1

contents

Contents

to Timothy

the hatchery of bad ideas

IF YOUR GOAL IS TO REACH THE WHITE HOUSE, THESE DAYS the place to start would seem to be the law lectern. Before entering electoral politics, both Barack Obama and Bill Clinton spent time as law professors, at the University of Chicago and the University of Arkansas respectively. Earlier, both men had made their mark in the nation's most famously elite law school environments—Obama at Harvard, where he was elected the first black president of the *Harvard Law Review*, and Clinton at Yale, where he joined forces with the future Hillary Rodham Clinton. Both men used their time in Cambridge and New Haven to develop the sorts of connections of which students at lesser institutions can only dream; in later years both drew on these networks of movers and shakers old and young for advice, campaign and financial help, and as staff in their administrations, not just in lawyerly parts of the government like the Justice Department but across many other subject areas. And both men—at least in the opinion of many of their campus colleagues—went on to govern in ways shaped by their law school experience.

The United States is conventionally said to have no equivalent to France's *grandes écoles*, the exclusive, inbred educational institutions that train the country's ruling elite in technocratic fashion. But that is not quite true. We have our law schools, and in particular the dozen or two of them generally ranked as best—Yale and Harvard, Stanford, Columbia, and so forth. To a remarkable extent, the members of America's governing class and, perhaps more important, the received ideas that inform their views of government are products of these institutions.

Tocqueville noted long ago that in America those who rise to the political top tend to be lawyers. If anything, the rule has been confirmed in recent years: lawyers now hold nearly 60 percent of the seats in the U.S. Senate and nearly 40 percent of those in the U.S. House of Representatives. But politics and the law are just the start. Nowadays expensively trained lawyers are key players in many other sectors of society as well, including higher echelons of journalism and commentary, many categories of business management, and so forth. If you wait long enough, it has been said, any public issue in America—from Hollywood to Wall Street to Madison Avenue to K Street—eventually turns into a legal issue. When that happens, more often than not, lawyers will get to decide it.

Which brings us to the wider importance of law schools: they shape what the general community thinks about law, which in turn shapes the law itself. The work of legal scholars, as we will see, has revolutionized (or created from scratch) whole fields of law, from product liability to sexual harassment to class action law. Judges draft their opinions with one eye on the law commentators, most of whom are either in the legal academy or one jump away from it. (They also hire clerks who reliably import into their chambers the attitudes and presumptions of legal academia, year in and year out.) Anyone who takes part in the world of public controversy, from Capitol Hill staffers to radio hosts, is swayed directly or at a remove by the climate of opinion in legal academia. "[W]hat is taught in the law schools in one generation"—so a celebrated law professor once put it—"will be widely believed by the bar in the following generation"—and, by way of the bar, will come to be believed by many of the rest of us.

So what *is* being taught in the law schools these days? And what is the climate of opinion in which the Barack Obamas and Bill Clintons of tomorrow are being formed?

THE LEFT-LEANING LECTERN

America's top law schools have a very distinct ideological profile, one that, as Chapter 2 of this book relates in more detail, fits comfortably with the liberal-left wing of American politics, more specifically its affluent *New York Times*-reader wing. "As the Anglican church was once described as the Tory Party at prayer," John McGinnis and Matthew Schwartz have noted, "the legal academy today is best seen as the Democratic Party at the lectern." Certain opinions are expected as a matter of course on everything from the death penalty (overdue to be abolished) to fast food (why isn't there more of a crackdown on it?). Meanwhile, positions held by very many well-educated, civically minded persons in the outside world—that immigration laws should be enforced, or that pain and suffering awards should be limited in tort cases, or that government should not engage in racial preferences—are infrequently encountered, occasionally even beyond the pale, in legal academia. As a result, persons who are used to the narrowly circumscribed dialogue afforded by the one context can be ill prepared to cope with the relative freedom of the other, and only the most agile—such as Clinton and Obama—are up to the challenge of switching back and forth without a gaffe.

The consensus can be all the more tight and hermetic for going unacknowledged. As one professor has put it without apparent self-consciousness, for judges to extend constitutional law in new directions, "there must be a broad consensus among members of the elite, thinking class and like-minded folk that some institutionalized practice is systematically depriving individuals of constitutional rights." Who counts as being in "the elite, thinking class and like-minded folk"? From the inside, the answer can seem satisfying and natural: people like us.

To outsiders, on the other hand, ideas that pass with little objection in the law school milieu can seem, to put it diplomatically, badly mistaken—daffy, eccentric, or bonkers would be less diplomatic ways of putting it. "I don't see a difference between a chimpanzee and my 4½-year-old son," said one high-profile specialist in animal rights law who has taught at Harvard and Vermont, drawing gasps from some onlookers, but none that were recorded from his faculty colleagues.

—⚏—

Bad ideas in the law schools have a way of not remaining abstract. They tend to mature, if that is the right word, into bad real-life proposals. Bad ideas in university French departments are of self-limiting importance, given that people on the outside are likely to go on speaking French in the usual way. Bad law can take away your liberty, your property, or your family.

One fount of bad legal ideas is the nation's law reviews, whose content, despite their gray and dull appearance, often turns out to be madcap, terrifying, or both. Surveying contemporary law review scholarship, the formidable Richard Posner is struck by "the many silly titles, the many opaque passages, the antic proposals, the rude polemics, the myriad pretentious citations." The *Harvard Law Review* published an account of the supposed impact on judges' constitutional interpretation of Einstein's theory of relativity, space-time curvature, and quantum physics. An article in the *University of Pittsburgh Law Review* proclaims the need to banish from the legal system "sanism," defined as being the "irrational prejudice" held against the ideas and contributions of persons who happen to be mentally ill. French-derived high theory reliably engenders such marvels as "The Black Body as Fetish Object" (*Oregon Law Review*) and "Lacan and Voting Rights" ("Our wounds speak of rituals of scarification that are codified as law and made into memories of future behavior.")

Many law review articles teeter on the boundary between funny and alarming by advancing proposals of a can-this-be-serious nature. Thus one feminist law professor got a sober hearing for her proposal that companies sued by "less-empowered" individuals not only should have to prove affirmatively that they are innocent, but also should have to fork over claimed damages at the start of the controversy and then sue to get their money back. (Asked to respond to this and similar theories, an evidently stunned practicing lawyer told one practicing reporter, "It's just so far from the way the legal system currently operates that I—I just don't have a reaction to it.")

Trouble is, many of the can-this-be-serious proposals in the legal academy are hailed as entirely serious. Thus a Northwestern law professor, building on the undeniable fact that many persons behave badly on the dating market, proposed as a remedy the development of a new tort of "sexual fraud," which would allow lawsuits for cash damages against persons who use lies or insincerity to get others to sleep with them ("You're really special to me," "Of course I'm not married"). It was one of the year's most widely applauded and talked-about articles.

Alas, the can-this-be-serious legal essay not infrequently leads to can-this-be-serious developments in real-life law. One lengthy piece in the *Harvard Law Review* argued that the law should do more to address the allegedly dire problem of lookism in the workplace; what with employer bias on the basis of physical appearance running rampant, face-to-face job interviews should be seen as the "prejudicial" affair that they are, permitting "illegitimate appearance evaluations" of the disabled, elderly, or just plain homely. The suggested solutions? Expanded use of telephone interviews and interviews held behind screens. While the idea of interviews behind screens has not yet caught on, the article was if anything ahead of its time; Washington, D.C. and other jurisdictions have indeed passed laws banning "appearance-based discrimination," and a recent survey found that litigation raising such claims is spreading fast around the country. As for the student author of the Harvard article, he went on to jobs with the *New York Times* editorial board and *Time*, writing commentary for those publications about law, and a professor's position at Yale.

SCHOOLS FOR SOCIAL ENGINEERS?

Law schools were not always considered idea-hatcheries for social reform. As Chapter 3 explains, their origins were humbler, if still useful. Influential though lawyers were in early America, their actual training was mostly an unprestigious affair out of the public eye based on apprentice-like work assisting more senior lawyers. True, some persons—among them great philosophers, judges, and statesmen—had won fame for profound thinking about law and jurisprudence, but few of those persons were associated with the university teaching of law. Aptitude in training novice lawyers was one thing; insight into what the law should ideally be was another, and the two skill sets did not necessarily overlap in any great degree. When it came to shaping the future course of the law, it was taken for granted that the primary actors would be elected lawmakers (who might or might not have legal training), other public officials, and of course judges, aided by the bar.

By the late nineteenth century, the success of the pioneering Harvard Law School had led to a new public image of law professors as persons of scholarly heft whose views on jurisprudence were to be listened to. With the arrival of the Progressive Era and the twentieth century, the law schools began to feel an ever stronger calling, and eventually a sort of entitlement, to prescribe the law's direction rather than merely to analyze where others were taking it. The eminent Roscoe Pound had described law as "continually more efficacious social engineering," and weren't law schools therefore akin to great schools of engineering? If so, why shouldn't they begin lending a hand at designing the engineering projects? Since then, American legal education has been torn between the not always easily reconciled goals of filling a public role as intellectual leaders and eminent authorities on the law and providing future lawyers with the practical skills and information needed to make a success of practice, or at least get past the bar exam.

Following the New Deal era some influential members of the Legal Realist school came to argue that law schools should see it as a primary part of their mission to drill their students in how to develop and evaluate public policy, even if it meant spending less time on skills useful in everyday legal practice. Elite lawyers themselves were beginning to develop a new self-image at around the same time, less as waiting upon clients' needs and instructions, and more as free to act on their own initiative on behalf of (what it was hoped would be) the public interest. By now law professors had become Authorities with a capital A, and it was not unheard of, as Chapter 4 explains, for the treatises and casebooks they wrote to reshape whole areas of law, with results that include the modern tort revolution. At the same time, they enjoyed wider scope to assert their authority in other ways—as litigators working for love or money, as hired expert witnesses, or as popular authors and television celebrities. How well (or poorly) they have used this new prestige and authority is explored in Chapter 5.

—⚉—

One could argue either way about whether the Sixties brought us the modern law school. What seems undeniable is that the modern law school helped bring us the Sixties. In particular, it was central in advancing the so-called rights revolution that was the signal achievement of the courts in that era. From judicial takeovers of schools and prisons to widened environmental standing to due process for welfare recipients, the Warren Court heeded academics' urgings by devising a host of new legal rights, often of constitutional dimension. Rather neatly, one of the law professors most involved in laying the intellectual groundwork for the rights revolution, Yale's Charles Reich, leapfrogged the legal-cultural divide to write a 1970 bestseller (*The Greening of America*) which stands as a period-piece monument to the flower-child-shall-lead-us school of Sixties dream-spinning.

Much of the well-organized courtroom campaign that brought about the rights revolution was managed from within the law schools, as professors coordinated strategy with outside litigators, legal services programs, funders, sympathetic journalists, and other players. Law schools directly housed many key legal services programs supporting landmark suits, and provided assistance to others by way of the student-staffed legal clinics that sprang up on dozens of campuses.

A powerful influence in all this was philanthropy. As early as the 1950s the Ford Foundation had begun sinking large sums into the revamping of law school curricula, much of it aimed at reorienting law toward the cause of "social change"—an ill-defined term that included but was not limited to the championing of the poor and racial minorities. As it became evident that dollars invested in law school-based activity could go a very long way toward reshaping the law itself, other foundations followed, setting a pattern that continues into our own Soros-and-MacArthur era: many high-profile law-school centers, programs, and initiatives are funded and often originated by donors interested in influencing law beyond the campus gates.

Chapters 6 through 8 look from varying angles at the movement that resulted, which sometimes flatteringly (and question-beggingly) refers to itself as "public interest law." A new cadre of public interest lawyers, it was imagined, would help rectify age-old gaps between rich and poor, powerful and powerless, effectively serving as lobbyists for the poor and other traditionally underrepresented groups. Judges would step in directly and force government bureaus and agencies to live up to the promise of their charters. Idealistic litigators would tie down the Gulliver of bureaucratic government and force it (at last) to heed the interests of its constituents. It was a heady time, in which law and cutting-edge lawyering took on an almost unheard-of glamour as ways of remaking society. Law schools would not merely serve as visionaries anticipating the new developments, but—in another of the Ford Foundation's most successful and durable initiatives—would take part directly, through the student litigation clinics that sprang up at more than a hundred law schools over this period.

Things didn't work out quite as planned. The new way of doing law was rife with unintended consequences, which often proved hard to correct. Litigation in areas like welfare, education, prison, and environmental law bogged down in what came to be termed paralysis by analysis. Court decrees extending over decades demoralized the loathed Establishment and drove up the cost of government yet failed to produce the advertised revolutionary results. Public opinion reacted sharply against much of the handiwork of the new rights revolution, from school busing to prison overcrowding release orders to the deinstitutionalization of mental patients. Congress and other key players began to distance themselves from the new trends, while the courts increasingly declined to create the new rights urged on them by the legal academy and the public interest litigators. The litigation didn't cease, by any means; indeed, it became a premier way of gaining and exercising power in battles over government. But its glamour did fade, and with that came an end to what has been called the heroic period of the American law school.

—⟋⟍—

After an interval marked by a lurch toward obscurantism and high theory, as symbolized by the brief ascendancy of the more-radical-than-thou Critical Legal Studies (CLS) movement, the mood in law schools shifted toward identity politics. The movements that resulted—Critical Race Theory, legal feminism, and a half-dozen others—changed the atmosphere within law schools and also had an impact on law outside the walls. Chapters 9 and 10 take up two case histories of identity grievance: the slavery reparations movement, in which support from law school activism played a surprisingly big role, and litigation over Indian land claims. While the slavery suits got more national attention, the Indian land claims, sparked by a pioneering 1971 law review article, actually got much further in court. Eventually they came to dispute the ownership of tens of millions of acres, including the land beneath cities as large as Syracuse and Denver.

Both the slavery and the Indian-reparations movements invoked implicit challenges to national sovereignty. But the greatest such challenge was yet to come. In recent years the hottest flavor in legal academia has been the suddenly ubiquitous international human rights movement. Dozens of schools have launched centers, programs, and professorships to advance the new specialty. Along the way, all sorts of old controversies—not only in defense and foreign policy, and in the treatment of minority and indigenous populations, but also in such far-flung areas as gender inequality, prison conditions, environmental, labor, housing, and welfare law—have been redefined as international human rights matters. Busy litigation centers at leading law schools now promote the view that the United States is a systematic violator of domestic human rights and should yield to the corrective authority of such transnational bodies as the United Nations' Committee for the Elimination of Racial Discrimination (CERD) and the new International Criminal Court. That raises the prospect that elected U.S. officials could face reversal by international tribunals—or perhaps even personal liability, arrest, and prosecution—over questions that earlier generations would have seen as purely for domestic U.S. law and politics to settle.

DISCONNECT AND SOUL-SEARCHING

A few years back the legal academy went through a certain period of soul-searching, not so much about its ideological out-of-touchness as about its disconnect from the world of practical law. The perceived uselessness of High Theory and ambitious interdisciplinary work had brought on a serious backlash from the bench and bar. Law review articles deploying the latest in game theory, or fictional narrative, or the study of urban slang might be (often) original, (sometimes) clever, and (occasionally) entertaining, but they were usually remote from the needs of lawyers grappling with real-world cases. "I haven't opened up a law review in years," the Second Circuit chief judge Dennis Jacobs told the *New York Times* in 2007. "No one speaks of them. No one relies on them."

There has followed a reversal fraught perhaps with both positive and negative promise. Younger faculty in recent years have been disengaging from unfruitful theory and purely inter-academic disputation and moving back to engage with real-life legal controversies. Blogging has caught on among law professors, encouraging such once-scarce writing qualities as clarity, timeliness, force, and accessibility. One consequence is that the practical influence of law schools on the law appears to be once again on the upswing. But will that be a good thing?

—ɯ—

The problem, this book will argue, is not just that law schools generate so many bad ideas—mistaken and benighted ideas, impractical and socially destructive ideas—but that those ideas follow a predictable pattern. They confer power on legal intellectuals and their allies—at least the power to prescribe, often the power to litigate. The movement that results—whether couched as public interest law, as minority empowerment law, or as international human rights law—is in fact a bid for power, whether naked or cleverly disguised.

On occasion one hears that the legal academy these days is chastened in its ambitions, that it has learned its lesson from the last time it tried to remake society, that it no longer looks to the courts to act in "transformative" ways. In a 2009 *New Yorker* article, the writer Jeffrey Toobin presents President Obama himself as emblematic of this new sobered-up breed of legal academic, who is careful to avoid the hubris of the Warren era and agrees that elected officials rather than courts or litigators inevitably will and should set the main contours of public policy.

Are the would-be social engineers of legal academia indeed chastened and sobered? Or have they rather been nursing their ambitions, saving up new theories and rationales, while they wait for a more favorable moment to strike out again in quest of heroic and transformative legal interventions? As we will see in the pages ahead, the signs are not reassuring.

chapter TWO

the forces of unanimity

THE NOMINATION TO THE U.S. SUPREME COURT OF AN identifiably conservative figure tends to set off a flurry of noisy opposition from the ranks of legal academia and that of Judge Samuel Alito in 2005 was no exception. Rallies were set up, petitions circulated, and more than 500 law professors signed a letter urging the nominee's defeat. A particular hotbed of opposition emerged at Yale, where faculty organized something they called the Alito Project to furnish the nomination's opponents with ammunition. There was a bit of a human interest angle on this last, because Alito, a fifteen-year veteran of the Third Circuit who had garnered the ABA's highest recommendation, was himself a Yale Law graduate. For that matter, an earlier Court nominee who had also drawn frenetic opposition at Yale Law School, Clarence Thomas, had been a Yale grad too. On many campuses a running campaign against the Supreme Court nominations of the institution's own alumni would have been considered an unthinkable lapse of school spirit. Not in New Haven, though. You might even say that by leading the charge against ideological turncoats and traitors, the professors were embodying Yale's own special kind of school spirit. The U.S. Senate in any event proceeded to ignore the profs' efforts, confirming Alito by a 58–42 margin, as it had earlier confirmed Thomas 52–48.

One moment in the affair did occasion a bit of eyebrow-raising, however. It came when renowned liberal Professor Owen Fiss explained to the *New York Times* the link between the two nomination battles: "The one lesson for the law school [of the earlier fight] was that we didn't work hard enough to oppose him [Thomas]." "We"? A lesson "for the law school"? After some confusion, the Yale administration altered its website to distance itself a bit from the Alito Project and to clarify that Professor Fiss had not actually been speaking for the faculty as a whole; on the question whether its alumnus should be confirmed to the Court, the school instead preserved a studied neutrality.

Not to say that Yale Law did not think of itself as an engaged sort of place. In a welcoming speech to incoming students a few months earlier, Dean Harold Koh (like Fiss, a famously liberal figure) had recounted at length the school's courtroom fight to avoid having to admit recruiters from the U.S. military as a condition of taking federal funds, a battle that later emerged as an issue in Elena Kagan's Supreme Court nomination. The long controversy illustrated, Koh said, how at Yale "the human rights tradition runs deep. . . . There is only one Yale Law School and it is us. We are not just a law school of professional excellence, we are an intellectual community of high moral purpose." After that rhetorical wind-up came the not un-self-congratulatory pitch: "Ladies and Gentlemen of the Yale Law School of 2008, Citizens of the republic of conscience, Welcome to the Yale Law School!"

A ONE-PARTY REPUBLIC

Citizens of the republic of conscience. If the modern elite law school really counts as a republic of conscience, it is very nearly a one-party republic: Democrats at last count outnumbered Republicans 28 to 1 on the Stanford faculty, 23 to 1 at Columbia, while Harvard is said to have gone thirty years without hiring a single Republican (even as it formed a panel to fret about the need for more faculty diversity of other kinds). In 2008—admittedly a year in which one of their own, Barack Obama, was running for President—law professors donated somewhere between ten to twenty times as much to Democratic as to GOP White House contenders. Reporting on a study with similar results—an 81–15 percent Dem-Rep split among top law school faculty—Adam Liptak of the *New York Times* noted that only the presence on the list of the University of Virginia, which had a relatively even balance, kept the figures from being even more lopsided, as they were at Harvard (91 percent D), Yale (92 percent) and Stanford (94 percent): "Whatever may be said about particular schools and students, professors and deans of all political persuasions agreed that the study's general findings are undeniable."

From time to time this ideological imbalance occasions wider discussion, with some commentators within the academy perturbed about it, others not. Professor Peter Schuck of Yale Law, whose self-described "militant moderate" politics place him well to the right by the standards of fellow faculty members even if not by those of the nation generally, has written that while the schools invariably claim to "cherish robust debate, iconoclasm and arguing issues from all sides," the truth is that "they care much more about diversifying their skin colors, genders and surnames than about diversifying their points of view." Sloganeering about the need for a faculty that "looks like America" is at best inconsistently applied; a study by Northwestern's James Lindgren found that the most demographically underrepresented group on law faculties, relative to the pool of available legal talent from which faculty might be drawn, are white Republican women.

Of course others have proposed that if conservatives do not fit well into modern academia it's because—well, because they're not all that bright. "We try to hire the best, smartest, people available," Duke philosophy chair Robert Brandon said of similar findings at his institution. Brandon went on to cite John Stuart Mill (not quite accurately) for the proposition that "stupid people are generally conservative." (As Lindgren points out, conservatives and liberals score similarly on intelligence tests; Republicans show markedly higher rates of educational attainment overall, for whatever that's worth, though Democrats are more likely to stick it out through graduate study.) Some voices in the legal academy take a Brandon-esque line. "Not all ideologies have merit," offers the left-leaning Chicago law professor Brian Leiter as a reason for the shortage of Republicans among his colleagues. Leiter has dismissed calls for wider ideological diversity as pleas for "affirmative action for conservatives who can't make it on the merits of their work."

—⚏—

The imbalance is especially strong in constitutional law, the legal specialty with perhaps the highest profile and highest stakes: "every casebook, treatise, and handbook used to teach constitutional law in American law schools is the product of Democrats writing from Democratic perspectives," complains one writer. One might tour a dozen elite institutions without running into a single constitutional specialist well disposed toward, say, Rehnquist or Roberts Court jurisprudence. Opinion is scarcely more divided on such areas as employment or consumer law: pick fifty law review articles at random, and you are unlikely to find one that argues for reducing as opposed to expanding the scope of liability. Environmentalism? Feminism? Disabled rights? Gay rights? Immigration? Topic after topic rouses lively controversy in the rest of the country, but not in the legal academy.

Some fields are more open to a spectrum of views than others. Leiter, the Chicago law professor, has compiled lists of the most prominent law professors in various specialties, as measured (however imperfectly) by citation counts. They confirm the Left's near-total dominance in constitutional law, where outspoken liberals occupy all the half-dozen top spots and no well-known conservative appears until around position #18. International law, labor/employment, legal ethics/legal profession, environmental law, and procedure are others with strong liberal concentrations. A few areas—intellectual property law, tax, and inheritance—appear to lack much of a political charge one way or the other. In only two areas—business law and law and economics—does a noticeable concentration of conservative or free-market-oriented scholars appear, and in both cases it is as part of a decided mix of left and right voices. (Contrary to what some imagine, many highly regarded law and economics scholars have politics to the left of center).

Unsurprisingly, the range of permissible opinion is at its narrowest where identity politics is at stake, a set of topics often associated in private faculty conversation with terms like "minefield" and "career-ending." Many schools have launched law-and-race centers and projects, which without exception situate themselves very much to the left of center. Thus it is with the Chief Justice Earl Warren Institute on Race, Ethnicity and Diversity at Berkeley, the C.H. Houston Institute for Race and Justice directed by Obama's mentor Charles Ogletree, Jr., at Harvard, Florida's Center for the Study of Race Relations (recent lecture topic: "Reactionary Colorblindness"), UCLA's Critical Race Studies Program, the Structural Racism Initiative at Ohio State, or the similar centers at Chapel Hill, Northeastern, and so on.

Many topics with no obvious identity politics dimension, however, command almost as much consensus. Thus pretty much every labor law specialist with a national profile favors expanding the distinctive legal powers of labor unions; all but a few land-use experts favor giving government more powers to regulate private landowners; and so forth. Where there is an exception, it is often named "Richard Epstein," the libertarian-leaning polymath called on to serve as a voice of near-lone dissent in a half-dozen or more far-flung areas.

COME FOR THE EDUCATION, STAY FOR THE ACTIVISM

To be sure, there is these days a haven and refuge for dissident students and faculty in the form of the declaredly conservative/libertarian Federalist Society. Successful as they are, however, the Federalists are by design an outsider's debating group, not a part of the institutional law school, and utterly unrepresentative of faculty opinion at most schools. Even more recently, a couple of schools have experimented with opening up more of an institutional home for right-of-center scholars, notably at the George Mason University School of Law, a state school in the Virginia suburbs of Washington, D.C.

But such programs are outnumbered 30-, 50-, or 100-to-1 by projects and programs of an opposite view, which often make no effort to conceal their ideological mission. Yale's Legislative Advocacy Clinic attempts to move the state of Connecticut toward "a more progressive agenda in taxing." Georgetown's course offerings include "Organizing for Social Change: Anti-Subordination Theory and Practice," incorporating "the strategies of professional organizers" in a class "designed for the lawyer as change agent." George Washington's program in animal rights law "attempts to change attitudes about the relationship between human and non-human animals." Choices for students at Pace include the Social Justice Center ("Supported by a grant from the Ford Foundation, the Center is engaged with various communities in exposing police abuse of minorities and facilitating civilian oversight of the police") and the Energy Project, long engaged in the campaign to close a nuclear plant on which Westchester County relies heavily for its electric supply. Santa Clara's Center for Social Justice and Public Service "builds a community for students, faculty, lawyers, and others who share a commitment to marginalized, subordinated, or underrepresented clients and causes."

Students who seek a law school with an even more explicit ideological commitment to the "progressive" side have many choices. Since the 1970s a number of schools have sought to define themselves in reference to such an ideological mission, including Boston's Northeastern; Queens Law School, a unit of the City University of New York, which has served as a home base for many radical Gotham lawyers; and the former Antioch School of Law in Washington, D.C., which pioneered such novel pedagogical techniques as having law students live with welfare families (the last-named institution eventually found the market for its offerings too weak and was absorbed into the city run University of the District of Columbia to form its law school). Most recent, and most significant, the University of California—ignoring cautions from an official panel that public and private law schools in the state already offered more than enough spots to serve demand—chose to found a new law school at its Irvine campus dedicated to activist approaches to law, selecting as its first dean the famed liberal constitutionalist Erwin Chemerinsky. With financial help from a local plaintiff's injury lawyer, the school got off to a bang-up start in the fall of 2009 by offering students their first year's tuition free. Left mostly unasked was why a new law school with overt commitments to "social change" was needed when students could get so much of the same experience by going to a regular law school.

—m—

The farther shores of leftism are amply populated as well. Among the renowned career successes of the modern law school is that of the former Weather Underground terrorist Bernardine Dohrn at Chicago's Northwestern. Given her past as an FBI Most Wanted List long-timer, Dohrn couldn't practice law and had never held a teaching position, but that didn't stop Northwestern from hiring her to run what developed into a high-profile national clinical project in juvenile justice. Dohrn's presence on the faculty provoked some dissension—"I thought that what we were doing was participating in the laundering of evil," Professor Daniel Polsby, then on the faculty, told the *Chicago Tribune*—but the school's dean vigorously defended her. Notoriously, the *New York Times'* profile of Dohrn and her equally unapologetic husband and former underground colleague, Bill Ayers, ran in the paper, under the headline "No Regrets for a Love of Explosives," on the morning of September 11, 2001.

Then there's the remarkably friendly reception accorded to Lynne Stewart, a New York lawyer from the farthest fringes of left-radicalism, who was convicted and disbarred in a high-profile case for unlawfully helping one of her clients, the Islamic terrorist Abdel Rahman, pass messages out of the country to his followers. (Despite the ideological differences between the two, Stewart apparently admired the "Blind Sheik" Rahman as someone at war with the capitalist U.S. government.) Free while her appeal was pending, Stewart embarked on a tour of law schools and other campuses organized by admiring supporters. (Others who've made the rounds on the radical law school speaking circuit include Kathleen

Cleaver, a former high official of the Black Panther Party and now a senior lecturer in law at Emory; the former Ten Most Wanted fugitive and terror acquittee Angela Davis, given a standing ovation at Harvard as part of the inaugural program of Professor Ogletree's new institute on race and law; and Laura Whitehorn, a member of a Weather Underground splinter that bombed the U.S. Capitol and seven other buildings.)

The key to success on this particular speaking circuit is to come across as entirely unrepentant and even more radical than the audience dared hope. Stewart did not disappoint, explaining in one interview that yes, she did look favorably on violence when it was "directed at the institutions which perpetuate capitalism, racism, and sexism, and at the people who are the appointed guardians of those institutions, and accompanied by popular support." Her words on another occasion confirm that Stewart is no namby-pamby practitioner of let's-be-nice civil libertarianism: "I don't have any problem with Mao or Stalin or the Vietnamese leaders or certainly Fidel locking up people they see as dangerous. Because so often, dissidence has been used by the greater powers to undermine a people's revolution."

When Stewart's campus visits took place under the sponsorship of like-minded student organizations, as was mostly the case, they hardly registered as more than the screech of ideological background noise one gets used to hearing on campus. But people did notice when Stanford Law School, which vies with Yale as the most prestigious and competitive of them all, invited Stewart to serve as a "Visiting Public Interest Mentor." Even at Stanford, this was enough to touch off a furor, and Dean Kathleen Sullivan—much to the outrage of some in the school's "public interest" community—stepped in personally to see that the invitation was withdrawn.

Lesson learned? Maybe at Stanford itself, but not at New York's Hofstra Law School, which proceeded to invite Stewart to lecture on *legal ethics* as part of a major annual conference, on a program studded with vocal supporters of her case and bereft of vocal critics. This time the outcry was bigger and broke into the national press, at which point the school hurriedly revamped the program to ensure that critics of Stewart would have a conspicuous role as well. It also was obliged to drop continuing legal education (CLE) credit for

Stewart's panel, after it was pointed out that a New York law forbids the awarding of CLE credit for courses taught by convicted felons.

TUNING OUT MAIN STREET

The fact is that Hofstra's administration seemed to be genuinely puzzled and surprised at the public outcry provoked by its invitation to Stewart; it really didn't seem to have anyone on hand who was enough in touch with national opinion to warn them. And indeed the ideological isolation of today's legal academy, the virtual pride it takes in being out of touch with Main Street ways of thinking, often winds up undercutting its effectiveness in the causes it seeks to advance.

Consider the long-drawn-out series of battles that came to be known as the Solomon Amendment affair, and which resurfaced at the Elena Kagan hearings in 2010. The conflict began because law schools had enacted policies forbidding visiting employers from using official facilities to recruit unless they promised to pursue nondiscriminatory hiring policies. This had the effect of banning recruiters from the U.S. armed services, given the military's ongoing policy (ratified by President Bill Clinton) of excluding openly gay servicemembers. Congress responded with a series of enactments popularly known as the Solomon Amendment, providing that colleges could not continue to receive federal dollars for research and many other purposes while excluding the military from recruiting on campus. Schools challenged the amendment in court, and the case went up to the U.S. Supreme Court.

The most ironic thing about the struggle was that the universities had prepared the ground for their own defeat by declining to assert a case for academic independence on many previous occasions. Years earlier the federal government had begun to attach strings to the money it gave out for education. Often this was done in the name of antidiscrimination principles, and bore a very loose nexus if any to traditional federal objectives, as with Washington's insistence on closely regulating men's and women's college athletic departments to equalize coaches' salaries and other sports resources. Some colleges, particularly small religious and conservative institutions, had resisted these conditions and in particular had tried to fight the government on its ambitious assertion that a scholarship student's receipt of a single federal dollar should open the door to the full panoply of institutional regulation from Washington. Liberal academia, including the best law schools, had extended precisely no sympathy to these colleges. In the absence of any resistance from the prestige institutions, the courts had found it easy to reject the small colleges' position in favor of the contrasting precept that to take the king's shilling was to place oneself at the king's service. No wonder the precedents were unfavorable when the law schools finally discovered a cause which made their own independence seem worth defending. Moreover, the Solomon Amendment did arguably advance a core responsibility of the federal government, by assuring the military had access to talent for its own corps of lawyers and judges.

Had the Harvards and Columbias been in closer touch with the wider society, they might have realized that their position drew less sympathy than they imagined. Outside the walls, most Americans believed the recruiters should be let in. That included plenty of people who had sterling liberal credentials, people who had long been on record against the military gay ban, or who were themselves gay. Some saw the conflict as one that the public's representatives in Congress were within their rights to resolve, imperfectly or not. Some didn't think the university should push away from engagement with a vital American institution just because it disagreed with one of its current policies. Some even shrewdly calculated that if the goal was to modernize illiberal service policies, recruiting more military lawyers trained at places like Yale and Stanford would hasten the day when that happened. Some even might have harbored pangs of—apologies to Dean Koh!—conscience about the appearance of insulting and shunning uniformed personnel to whom even law faculties might be thought to owe so much.

Instead, leading law faculties outdid each other in their zeal for Solomon-resistance. At Stanford, Georgetown, NYU, Fordham, and Minnesota, to name a few, the school itself or its faculty lent official support. Individual professors from virtually every top school submitted amicus briefs. It was the most florid display of academic support for a Supreme Court cause seen in many years, and the voice of the American law school came across as well-nigh unanimous.

The voice of the U.S. Supreme Court was unanimous too, but in the other direction. In *Rumsfeld* v. *FAIR* (2006), by a vote of 8–0 with Alito not participating, the Justices agreed without exception in upholding the amendment as constitutional. For all their florid display of talent, the schools couldn't muster a single vote for their position from the Court's liberal wing—not from John Paul Stevens, not from David Souter, not from Ruth Bader Ginsburg, not from Stephen Breyer. The bounds of the Republic of Conscience, it seemed, stopped at the hothouse walls.

—m—

Even on a pedagogical level, schools can be hurt by their estrangement from Main Street opinion. Alienating students planning to enter military law is just one danger. More broadly, the atmosphere at many schools radiates us-and-them disdain for the sorts of everyday law, often in the representation of businesses or affluent individuals, that many or most students are likely to wind up practicing. Dave Hoffman of Temple University laments that law professors "continually push out the message that corporate lawyering is a less moral and desirable career path than 'public interest' lawyering." This can in turn, he says, make it more difficult to train students to behave as ethical lawyers in a business context. When Hoffman asked his students in a corporate law class whether they would be willing to draft ethically troublesome documents, most said they would. "Why? Because by going into big firm practice in the first instance, they'd have already decided to be ethically gray. When deans (and well-meaning liberal professors) reinforce the idea that corporate practice is 'corrupting and essentially random and beyond your control, and there's not a whole lot you can do about it,' students are more likely to let the situation corrupt them." A better view, according to the UCLA corporate law specialist Stephen Bainbridge, is that of one professor who emphasizes the constructive social contributions of business law when handled in the right spirit:

"If his corporate client was doing the right thing, he helped him do it, thus creating better lives for employees and customers. And if his corporate client was doing the wrong thing, he told him to stop it and do the right thing, thus also serving the public interest."

CONSERVATIVES AND COMFORT LEVELS

Other academic disciplines such as sociology and political science show ideological imbalances similar to those of academic law. There is reason to believe that the barrier or deterrent to conservative entry is not so much in acquiring the requisite credentials (such as advanced degrees) but in converting them into a durable career in academia. At *Minding the Campus*, the economist Daniel Klein describes a study of scholarly association memberships:

> We found that Republican-voting members of the scholarly associations were significantly more likely to have landed outside of academia. For example, in Anthropology/Sociology, 43% of the Republican scholars were working outside academia, compared with only 24% of Democrat scholars. In History, it was 47% versus 27%. In all six disciplines overall, it was 41% versus 25. The individuals we are talking about here are members of the American Anthropological Association, the American Historical Association, and so on. Most had PhDs. So we find that Republican-voting members of such associations are consistently more likely to be working outside of academia—in government, private sector, independent research, or other.

In law, much more so than in anthropology or history, jobs outside academia (in private law firms, for example) offer many extremely attractive options for persons with the relevant qualifications. And in fact the ranks of high-end practicing lawyers—many with stellar academic training in law—are far more balanced politically than those of legal academia. If promising young conservatives are disproportionately attracted to private practice, bias or discouragement alone might not fully explain what Richard Posner has called the "self-selection of leftward-leaning lawyers into academic law."

When conservatives do make the attempt, however, the clubbiness will be an obstacle. And the temptation will be to keep their head down, suppress views known to be unpopular, and either stake out some topical specialty where they happen to share in the liberal consensus, or one like securities or estate law that is mostly off the political radar screen.

To succeed in academic law, most younger scholars need to publish widely and network at conferences with like-minded colleagues in a position to advance each others' careers. Candidates with acceptable politics have an advantage on both fronts.

Where to publish? Conservatives and libertarians looking for a like-minded outlet may choose between the Federalist Society's *Harvard Journal of Law and Public Policy*, the *NYU Journal of Law and Liberty*, the *Texas Review of Law and Politics*, and perhaps a few others. On the left, to start with Harvard alone, the array includes *Unbound: Harvard Journal of the Legal Left*, the *Journal of Law & Gender*, the *Civil Rights-Civil Liberties Law Review*, the race-and-law *Black Letter Law Journal*, the *Environmental Law Review*, the *Human Rights Journal*, the *Latino Law Review*, and several others of similar hue, all aside from the *Harvard Law Review* itself. And that's just one school. The broader menu of publishing options affords many dozens of choices in the race and gender categories alone, from the *Iowa Journal of Gender, Race and Justice* ("Feminist inquiry and critical race analysis are the touchstones of our endeavor. . . . We include all struggles against oppression within this conception") to the *Georgetown Journal of Law & Modern Critical Race Perspectives* (founded by students "inspired by their experiences with critical race theorists here at Georgetown and who saw the establishment of a race and identity law journal as a meaningful kind of activism)." Given this superabundance, a young scholar working in the right vein will have very good chances of placing his or her output, all the more so since a well-executed article on gender, international human rights, or public interest law is something the "regular" law reviews may be more than happy to publish.

When hiring time arrives, a key threshold question is what kind of hires the target school wishes to make. KC Johnson has observed that a school can utterly transform the political tenor of its history department simply by deciding to stop acquiring new scholars in military and diplomatic history, rightly or wrongly perceived as redoubts of conservatism, in favor of identity-history specialties. Similar effects are seen in academic law now that every forward-minded school needs a specialist in gender law and race-and-law. And if you want a reputation as diversity-friendly, why stop at one? Once you add in a few politically engaged exponents of education, health, consumer, police-misconduct, environmental, or housing law, the inevitable international-human-rights specialist, and especially clinicians, a critical mass quite likely begins to form that can set the tone on many issues, even aside from their co-thinkers among those who teach old-line legal subjects.

UCLA's Bainbridge, one of the higher-profile conservatives in legal academia, says conscious political opposition to right-leaning candidates is a less important factor in screening them out than shared assumptions, connections, and comfort levels. "In other disciplines, there are more objective standards for quality of work," one dean told the *Times*'s Adam Liptak. "Law schools are sort of organized in a club structure, where current members of the club pick future members of the club." "I think blacks want more blacks, women want more women, and leftists want more leftists," adds Harvard's Alan Dershowitz. "Everybody thinks diversification comes by getting more of themselves."

ACCREDITORS, LITIGATORS, AND DONORS

At least three kinds of pressure from the outside push the law school leftward. They are accreditation, fear of litigation, and—surprisingly or otherwise—donor influence.

—⁓—

The ongoing process of law school accreditation is reliably rumored to have been a leading torment for law school deans inclined to vary from prevailing Left-friendly management for-mulas. Most schools of any stature find it unthinkable to do without a clean bill of health from the two major accreditation agencies for legal academia, the American Bar Association and the Asso-ciation of American Law Schools. To pass muster, all law schools must submit to periodic site inspections and undertake what the ABA calls "self-study" (sometimes nicknamed "self-criticism"). For starters, self-study requires the school to confront the adequacy of its diversity efforts; tougher language adopted in 2006 provides that schools "shall demonstrate by concrete action" their commitment to this goal. Thus a sample question from the 2007 ABA site evalu-ation questionnaire:

> IV 15. Describe and itemize how the law school has demon-strated by concrete action during the past two years a commit-ment to having a faculty and staff that are diverse with respect to gender, race and ethnicity.

In practice, even schools that have pursued diversity with much vigor often feel pressure from site inspectors to do more: it couldn't hurt, in satisfying them, to add yet another Latino law journal or feminist conference series to the mix. A professor at one well-known school in the Northeast, who has taken part in two reaccreditation self-studies, explains:

> Like locusts, they come every seven years. The folks who accredit law schools are left-liberal academics in the service of the ABA, with an occasional member of the practicing bar thrown in. They not only threaten the accreditation status of schools that do not have clinics, but actually [demand] that clinical professors be integrated into the life of the law school on general terms of equality with the research faculty, leading to a left-tipping bloc in most faculty votes. And don't even get me started about "mission statements," each of which must be more self-abasing in terms of service to the underserved than the one before it.

Resisting the zeitgeist can also place a school at a disadvantage in lawsuits. Denials of tenure to feminist scholars have repeatedly led to high-profile discrimination claims, and more than one case has contended that an unwelcoming attitude toward feminist or minority-focused scholarship is part of the pattern or practice for which a school should be held accountable. One such lawsuit was filed against Oklahoma City University School of Law following a memo by four female professors complaining of harassment, unequal pay, "insensitivity," and "discriminatory attitudes and behavior that are harming and have harmed our professional careers and quality of life." Among the bill of particulars, according to one news report, was an all-male panel for a Constitution Day program in 2007:

> The female professors also complained the OCU law school has no regular civil rights course, criminal law classes don't cover rape, and the landmark abortion case Roe v. Wade is only covered sporadically in constitutional law.
>
> The memo notes the lack of women on a faculty appointment committee, which regularly included two university professors who are "openly hostile" to the idea of giving special consideration for women and minorities.

One of the four women subsequently filed a federal lawsuit contending that school administrators had brushed aside the concerns in the memo.

Note that some of these complaints go to the heart of professors' discretion on how to teach their subjects, as with the constitutional law professor who chose to cover *Roe v. Wade* "only . . . sporadically" rather than treat it as central and iconic. As threats to core academic freedom go, you might even think this would stand higher than a mandate to let the armed services in with everyone else during recruiting week.

—∭—

From early days, universities have been known to trim and adjust their operations in search of philanthropic support, even altering their principles of theology as needed to preserve the health of the institution. And while most deans are expert at fending off garden-variety negative donor influence—the stereotyped crotchety alumnus who disapproves of a controversial program—they are not necessarily immune to the positive blandishments afforded by funding availability. One reason some academic careers outpace others is that some candidates are highly "fundable"—that is, have the backing of key grantmakers outside the institution. Consider, for example, Bernardine Dohrn, and how she got ensconced at Northwestern despite her lack of ordinarily expected teaching and practice experience. One factor that can't have hurt: both Dohrn's father-in-law and her former employer sat on the Northwestern board. But another was that her program reliably raked in major grants from the high-profile MacArthur Foundation and other grantmakers. Observers say the grants were widely read as a vote of confidence in Dohrn personally, and might not have been assured had the program been assigned to someone else.

But not every proposal can get past the university committee. "They won't take money just from anyone for anything," says Daniel Polsby, dean at George Mason and previously a Dohrn colleague at Northwestern. "There is a very ideological screen." Columbia, Duke, UCLA, and Stanford were among schools that accepted $7 million in grants from a foundation established by the TV personality Bob Barker to endow programs in animal-rights law; Harvard established the Bob Barker Endowment Fund for the Study of Animal Rights, while Georgetown launched a clinic that it said would give students credit for working with Humane Society litigators. Would the resulting projects pursue research findings and court action that might displease the followers of Barker, known as a passionate advocate of animal rights who intended for his foundation to advance that cause? It's hard to say for sure; but one can speculate whether the schools would have been as likely to accept millions to establish animal-law programs named after Fred the Furrier.

Some funders are pushier than others. Perhaps the most famously pushy of all is the Ford Foundation, which pioneered high-stakes law school philanthropy in the 1950s and has remained a key donor since then. Over the years Ford has endowed many a blue-ribbon panel, countless graduate fellowships and faculty positions, and—probably its most successful initiative—the modern development of clinical legal education. Among its constants has been the goal (to quote an early Ford-sponsored panel) of "developing the social conscience of law students and professors." Ford has also aggressively sought to introduce new topics to the law school curriculum, beginning with a largely failed Sixties effort to establish poverty law as a new subject, and later through generous patronage of women's studies, race studies, and other identity-based studies programs, which it also supports in other parts of the university. More recently it has turned major attention to promoting international human rights law.

Even by the standards of legal academia, Ford's Left-tilting style of philanthropy is something special. For one thing, it is frank in emphasizing movement-building in contrast to a spirit of inquiry. Whatever their political leanings, most faculties pride themselves on the kind of regard for the life of the mind that values research for its own sake and for its potential to reveal unexpected things about the world that might call on us to revise our current thinking. Ford, on the other hand—as reflected in its policy document on legal philanthropy, *Many Roads to Justice*—hews to an official view of research as purely instrumental, providing ammunition for causes and crusades already settled on as desirable. "Research can be a powerful tool for social change," it concedes. The resultant findings can "support policy and law reform, provide the factual basis for litigation," and, as it explains at another point, help grantees "galvanize public support for policy reform." But it goes on to caution in all sternness that research "does not constitute a stand-alone strategy." The mere elucidation of a social problem for purposes of understanding it more deeply, in other words, is not a good enough reason to open the foundation's ample checkbook. Which makes a sort of sense, on the assumption that they're not expecting the findings of new research to change their *own* minds about anything.

—⟊—

Frequently the funding of a law school project serves as a key strategic step in planning a longer-term campaign toward some desired breakthrough in the real-world courtroom. Thus generous foundation support enabled the founding of the Harvard Civil Rights Project in 1996 with the aim of laying the groundwork for the (successful) defense of racial preferences in university admissions before an ambivalent Supreme Court. Dohrn's juvenile justice project at Northwestern "played an integral role," in its own words, in advancing the long campaign of legal and public advocacy that culminated in 2005's 5–4 Supreme Court decision in *Roper* v. *Simmons*, declaring the death penalty unconstitutional as applied to crimes committed before age eighteen.

In 1995 there was founded the Brennan Center for Justice, at New York University School of Law, to serve as something of an overall academic headquarters for the Legal Left. Brennan, which bills itself "part think tank, part public interest law firm, part advocacy group," has roared to an $8 million budget in its short existence. (Supporters include Soros, with more than $3 million in start-up grants, along with Carnegie, Ford, Pew, Joyce, Rockefeller, and so on.) To name just one of its many activities, its "Living Constitution Project" describes itself as "a comprehensive public education initiative" aimed at countering the "pinched and narrow view of the role of law, the Constitution, and government" purportedly held by conservative thinkers.

The Federalist Society has been in existence twice as long as Brennan, but its budget is at a comparable level ($9 million nationally). And if the Federalists are expecting to be welcomed into a top-ten law school like NYU as part of its official university structure, the way the Brennan Center has—well, they are likely to wait a long time.

chapter THREE

careerism saves the day

ONE LEVELING SIXTIES INNOVATION THAT REALLY DID change university life is the student-written evaluation, which gives the put-upon learner in the back row the anonymous chance to exact revenge on (or, as the case may be, heap praise on) the remote figure behind the lectern who assigned the 500-page readings and then humiliated the unprepared. Evaluations submitted to the university itself will ordinarily not become public, but one can get something of their flavor at the public RateMy-Professors.com, portions of which recall sites like Bitter Waitress in which restaurant staff trade stories of their least satisfactory customers. Thus if we check on the reviews for one famously self-promotional Washington, D.C. law professor, we find him extensively warned against as "rude and obnoxious," "biased," "a horrible professor who enjoys embarrassing his students and then tries to use his students as props when he gets publicity for his cases," "self-absorbed in the extreme," and "terrible." Of a torts specialist at a state institution in the Northeast: "She is mean, vindictive, and generally unpleasant. Papers are rudely graded and absurdly late;" "easily the worst teacher at [the institution]. . . . Arrogant, condescending, and a poor instructor. . . . Stay away, and be much happier." And this zinger: "pretty much sums up why the public hates tort attorneys."

Others inspire grudging praise. Of a left-wing firebrand at Indiana University: "Unapologetically infuses her politics into most classes, but is open about it." "She is extremely frightening and intimidating, pushes a very liberal agenda, but besides that beats the law into you and makes you a better student." (In the law school setting, it is worth noting, "beats the law into you" passes for praise.)

One-sided, malicious, grossly unfair? Clearly the reviews can be all these things. Yet when read in bulk, they do reveal wider patterns. One is that students complain if a teacher fails to get across the "black-letter" law they feel they need to know. If the course goes beyond that, great, but the rules of the existing game need to be in there. Hence the edge of exasperation in one comment from Harvard: "teaches whatever she feels like, even if that means you take family law and never learn about DIVORCE."

From the professor's standpoint this all relates back to one of the frustrations of classroom teaching. You've just steered the discussion around to a point where you've managed to drop in a particularly droll anecdote about rivalries on the Supreme Court in 1937, or the customs of plural marriage in the ancient Near East, or a case you worked on when you clerked on the appeals court, or the role lawyers play as characters in Henry James novels, when some student will pipe up, "Will this be on the bar exam?" and you have to concede that, no, it won't. And then the fear hits you again that at some level you are passing these hours not in the life of the mind, but in a kind of vocational training akin to instructing future electricians in the proper patterns of wiring. For all the Socratic pretensions, much of the law school experience by necessity is spent drumming into young ears year after year the prerequisites of federal jurisdiction, the manners in which title to real estate may be held, the principles of unitary taxation of corporations, and so forth, most of which can be grasped without much exercise of the higher intellectual faculties and many of which would be superseded in a moment, rendered of purely historical interest, if lawmakers undertook some broad overhaul of the area in question. Do students care only about the stuff they'll need when they go into practice? Are they really nothing more than careerists?

BEYOND VOCATION

If teaching about law as an intellectual matter and training newcomers to practice law seem to be in tension with each other, it's no wonder: through much of American history, and in many countries to this day, the two sorts of education proceed on different tracks with little crossover. In early America, prosperous families often sought liberal-arts instruction in law for their sons to help shape them as future men of affairs who might hire, though not necessarily be, lawyers. In 1777 Yale's president Ezra Stiles unsuccessfully proposed establishing a professorship of law at his institution, "not indeed toward educating lawyers or barristers, but for forming civilians," who in due course would "return home, mix in with the body of the public," and become "useful members of society, as selectmen, justices of peace, members of the legislature, judges of courts, and delegates in Congress"—judges in those days being like other officials routinely drawn from the ranks of non-lawyers. The tradition lives on at colleges like Princeton and Amherst that offer high-level courses in law and jurisprudence even though they do not house law schools or award J.D. degrees.

Meanwhile, until long into the nineteenth century, the well-established vocational track for entering the practice of law had little to do with universities or liberal arts. Aspiring lawyers could enter the field without an undergraduate degree or indeed, like Abraham Lincoln, with little schooling of any kind, and acquire their craft in effect as apprentices, studying as clerks alongside established lawyers. A few shrewd practitioners had the idea of organizing freestanding law schools to assist in and systematize the learning process, as with Tapping Reeve's pioneering Litchfield Law School in Connecticut in 1773. But no one was obliged to patronize these schools, any more than aspiring lawyers are obliged to patronize a bar review cram course today.

The acknowledged turning point in the development of the modern law school came with Christopher Langdell's development of the case method beginning in 1870, which made Harvard Law School a national sensation and was soon imitated elsewhere. Many of the distinctive aspects of American legal education, from the Socratic questioning of nervous students to the divisions of the curriculum, date from this period. In the half-century that followed, newly confident universities carried out a thorough and sometimes sharp-elbowed takeover of the field of legal schooling.

The Harvard model held out the promise of combining the instructional effectiveness of the freestanding law school with the scholarly heft and broadness of inquiry of the liberal arts university. To add to the excitement, treatises that soon achieved classic status and other high-quality work began to pour out of Harvard and its imitators during this period, helping to spur talk of law as a sort of science that could be given the rigor of more senior scholarly disciplines. Other prominent universities founded law schools on the Harvard model or annexed existing law schools whose teaching they revamped along more academic lines. The new law school, it seemed, could do almost everything well at once, from drilling students in the requisite language of contract formation, through forming future statesmen on the Ezra Stiles model, to carrying out quasi-scientific research into law. Significantly, Harvard went on to hire as dean a scholar (James Barr Ames) who had never spent a day in the conventional practice of law.

The Progressive Era, roughly 1890–1914, was a great age for professional licensure, in fields ranging from medicine and law to barbering and chauffeuring. Advocates both in and out of the affected professions and occupations promoted licensure as vital in protecting consumer and client interests. Later critics have discerned less praiseworthy motives: excluding informal and low-cost providers, raising the prestige and income of incumbents, and cartelizing (in effect) once competitive lines of work.

One favored model was for educational institutions to be entrusted with the role of front-line gatekeeper for admittance to a profession. Medicine led the way, with the American Medical Association campaigning for laws requiring that medical schools be certified and regulated and that only graduates of certified schools be allowed to enter practice. Many old-timers complained, but the profession's leadership triumphed by arguing that it was vital to protect the public from untrained or ill-trained doctors, and by 1900 most states had fallen in line with the program. Beginning in 1904 the AMA set forth school accreditation standards that included mandatory four-year courses of instruction, minimum rates of exam passage for graduates, periodic inspections of facilities, and so forth. Over the next twenty years, about half the nation's 160 medical schools proceeded to close down or merge, with schools not affiliated with universities having a particularly hard time.

Many in the field of law eyed these developments with interest, yet lawyers' training was less easily herded into the accreditation mold. A large share of existing lawyers, including revered figures of the then-not-too-distant past like Lincoln, had been trained under the old apprenticeship model, and it was not so easy to argue that the public was better off dispensing with their services. Even so, there was a push of legislation and rulemaking, and by 1922 most states had been persuaded to block the apprenticeship road to practice and restrict the granting of law licenses to law school graduates. Working through the American Bar Association, reformers began to tighten the screws on schools, requiring that they accept only candidates with undergraduate training, provide three years and no less of instruction, and so forth. As with medicine, there was no outright ban on freestanding law schools not attached to universities, but life was made harder for them. Legal education now began to provide a scarce and valuable credential, and its principal positions of leadership would henceforth be occupied by those who, like Harvard's Ames, thought of themselves primarily as academics rather than members of the bar.

—◆—

In his 1918 book *The Higher Education in America*, the gadfly sociologist Thorstein Veblen warned universities that they were making a mistake in their rapid expansion to include professional schools and related departments. These essentially vocational extensions of the university, he argued, put at risk "that disinterested intellectual enterprise which is the university's peculiar domain."

He reserved special disdain for the new vogue for academic business schools, which dealt in ideas that were "unscientific and unscholarly" and of a general "uselessness to the community." To impart skills in a field such as marketing was (he imagined) simply to give some clever members of the community an edge against others in the competition for wealth and power. What had that to do with the university's search for useful knowledge, beauty, and truth for its own sake?

Mortifyingly, Veblen dismissed law schools on similar grounds, as both intellectually unserious and of doubtful benefit to the wider public. A school of law, he declared, "belongs in the university no more than a school of fencing or dancing." *Fencing* or *dancing*? The insult can still sting after nearly a century, touching as it does on lasting insecurities felt in the legal academy. Has one somehow failed in seriousness if one's main accomplishment is to send people into the world trained very well in a certain set of skills? If graduates end up as ordinary, competent, comfortable lawyers conserving the wealth of affluent clients or helping the wheels of commerce spin, are they just as "careerist" as the business-school strivers Veblen so despised? Or was there some flaw in the sociologist's scornful logic?

—✦—

Veblen's criticisms were not enough to reverse the trend, and after the Depression and World War II the accreditation agencies resumed their ratcheting up of requirements. "Soon after the war," writes Steven Teles, "the [Association of American Law Schools] and ABA began to increase their standards for accreditation, requiring the appointment of a full-time dean in 1949, a minimum student-faculty ratio and faculty size in 1952, and gradually restricting admission to students with college degrees." Some of the most significant changes increased the pressure on schools to hire more full-time faculty and cut back on moonlighting practitioners, the latter a resource particularly valued by urban schools with a less affluent student body. ABA standards instead pushed a model of tenured full-time instructors with summer stipends and other common academic perks, the overall effect being once again to select for those whose loyalty was not to the world of everyday practice.

One might have expected the tightening of standards to reduce the number of accredited schools, students, and professors. Instead the ranks of ABA-accredited law schools rose from 111 in 1947 to 163 in 1977. (It now stands at around 200.) "Between 1962 and 1977," notes Teles, "the number of full-time professors of law in the United States increased from 1,628 to 3,875, the great bulk of which growth occurred in the five years between 1967 and 1972." To put it differently, the constituency on the ground for academic law abruptly doubled in the five or so years to 1972. This was bound to have far-reaching effects, and it did. And in no small part because of the accreditation process, law schools would be increasingly standardized and homogenized along many of the dimensions that matter most.

THE CONSTITUENCY FOR ACADEMIC LAW

In a law school fully oriented toward an academic model, certain things are expected. Not only will full-time faculty members be needed, but those faculty will need to engage in scholarship. So the rapid rise in the ranks of faculty was sure to lead to a boom in research, conferences, and the output of law reviews, of which no self-respecting law school could afford to be without a few.

"Law reviews are unique among publications," explained Northwestern's dean Harold Havighurst half a century ago, "in that they do not exist because of any large demand on the part of a reading public. Whereas most periodicals are published primarily in order that they may be read, the law reviews are published primarily in order that they may be written. . . . Large subsidies are therefore provided." As early as the 1930s most of the characteristic vices of law review scholarship—circumlocution, elephantine attempts at humor, overuse of footnotes—were on recognizable display. Yale's Fred Rodell skewered them all in a celebrated attack:

> [I]t is in the law reviews that a pennyworth of content is most
> frequently concealed beneath a pound of so-called style. The
> average law review writer is peculiarly able to say nothing
> with an air of great importance. . . . it seems to be a cardinal

principle of law review writing and editing that nothing may be said forcefully and nothing may be said amusingly. . . . The law reviews would rather be dignified and ignored. . . .

[I]t is not surprising that the law reviews are as bad as they are. The leading articles, and the book reviews too, are for the most part written by professors and would-be professors of law whose chief interest is in getting something published . . . because the accepted way of getting ahead in law teaching is to break constantly into print in a dignified way.

Meanwhile, Rodell noted, the students who slave away on the reviews "are egged on by the comforting thought that they will be pretty sure to get jobs when they graduate in return for their slavery," since making law review was one of the key credentials to be obtained in a law student experience. Little has changed since.

—ℳ—

With the triumph of the university-based model there came to prominence a new breed of high-level scholars who doubled as visible public intellectuals and even mentors of wide social movements, men such as Roscoe Pound, Felix Frankfurter, Zechariah Chafee, and others. In his 1914 address to the Association of American Law Schools, Wesley Hohfeld foresaw the day when a new elite of university jurists would have "a far greater share and influence than at present in prescribing for our [social] ills," a prospect unlikely to have displeased his later audiences.

Indeed, the series of movements in academic law that got rolling around this time had in common a guiding societal role for legal intellectuals. Pound's "sociological jurisprudence" set them up as evaluators of whether old legal rules fit emerging social policy. The Legal Realism movement, on the rise from the 1920s, added a sharp critique of Langdell's generation for its supposed "passive" and "formalist" view that judges should and could ignore underlying policy considerations and instead resolve cases solely by way of precedent, mechanical application of rules, and other purely legal grounds. Gradually, the prescribed role of law schools was coming up in the world. Law professors of the more self-effacing sort had long taken for granted that their main task was to lay out accurately what the current state of the law *is*—since their audience would need to deal with that for now—and only incidentally treat the (presumably less well-settled) question of what the law ought to be. Even if commentators disagree strongly with the direction the judges have taken, on this view, they need to keep close to the line of cases, like a ballroom partner who follows closely with each step even while convinced that the lead is headed off in the wrong direction. Legal Realists favored a more frankly adversary relationship, pulling back from the embrace of a hidebound judiciary in favor of more openly poking at its errors. To borrow the Veblen imagery, they were beginning to make law school less like a school of dancing and more like a school of fencing.

In the Thirties, progressive-minded law professors mostly backed the Roosevelt Administration in its expansion of the power of the public sector as against the private—Yale dean Charles Clark, one of the best-known New Dealers in legal academia, famously proclaimed that "the corporation lawyer of the past decade must give way to the public counsel of the next"—as well as in its series of spectacular confrontations with the Supreme Court. And after many pitched battles, they believed they were destined to win on both fronts: by Pearl Harbor Day, government agencies had taken over the direction of much of the economy, while the Justices had meekly submitted to FDR to avert his Court-packing threats in the famous "switch in time that saved Nine." The stage was set for the thunderous reception accorded Harold Lasswell's and Myres McDougal's 1943 *Yale Law Journal* article, "Legal Education and Public Policy."

Harold Lasswell was a celebrated New Dealer and political scientist whose jobs under FDR had included directing wartime propaganda, while the Yale professor Myres McDougal enjoyed a long career as an authority on international law. Influenced by the Legal Realist movement, both believed old rules needed a massive new infusion of social planning and expert rationality. Their remarkable proposal was to reorient the law school curriculum of today toward the radiant new legal world of tomorrow—whether judges and lawmakers were yet on board with the details of that world or not.

Law schools, they observed, still drilled students in such humdrum and half-outdated matters as "Bills and Notes" and "how to replevy [regain possession of] a dog." What was needed instead was a curriculum "oriented toward achievement of democratic values," as determined "in reference to social objectives." That would mean de-emphasizing such bastions of private law as contract and property, which they sniffed at as "much-favored instruments of the laissez-faire society." If a course in property law were needed, they asked, why not take land-use planning or the development of public housing projects as its jumping-off point?

Even after the Supreme Court's capitulation, the constitutional law over which New Dealers had stumbled remained recognizably intact in the textbooks. Lasswell and McDougal complained that "the so-called public law courses are still organized with too much deference to 'separation of powers,' 'jurisdiction,' 'due process,' 'equal protection,' 'interstate commerce,' etc." Trusts and estates? Schools should realize that the emerging society would want to keep to a minimum the role of private inheritance, though it might tolerate some little portion of it as a supplement to Social Security and similar plans. Insurance law? A mostly obsolete specialty, since we moderns recognized that most forms of insurance should be absorbed into the public sector. Local government law? Time would be better spent instructing students on innovative forms of regional government, such as the Tennessee Valley Authority. And law schools should recognize the need to train lawyers in entirely new tasks that would fall to them in the new world, such as that of determining an appropriate division of income among different sectors of society. In sum, legal education should take upon itself the job of "conscious, efficient, and systematic training for policy-making."

One thing was flatteringly clear, if casually assumed. In tomorrow's world, lawyers were to be on top as society's natural decision-making class—as its technocratic managers, if not outright philosopher-kings. Unlike others on the scene—such as, for instance, the general run of clients—lawyers were the ones who would have been trained to recognize and evaluate higher-level policy considerations. And law schools, rather than wasting time on the rules concerning Bills and

Notes, would assume the invigorating role of shaping future rulers. In one of the more ingenious parts of the scheme, if the professoriate would just agree to stop *teaching* all the old concepts that stood in the way of progress by limiting the government's wise exercise of power—private property, inheritance, separation of powers, and the rest—a generation of lawyers would grow up who would no longer take the concepts for granted as mental furniture, and in time, hidebound though it might be, the judiciary would stop according these concepts such undue deference. The only thing missing was the phrase "dustbin of history."

Lasswell and McDougal's piece was destined to become by far the most cited law review article ever published on the subject of legal education. Even at Yale, however, no one made any serious effort to implement its program whole. Had a school done so, as soon became clear, it would have equipped students neither for a career at the highest levels of national policymaking nor for a conventional law practice. A quarter century later, Thomas Bergin in a *Virginia Law Review* piece explained some of the reasons why. "The plain fact is, though it may have become plain only after the publication of the article, that training in policy appraisal is an extraordinarily complex and demanding business. Indeed, it is so complex and demanding that it would be difficult to imagine any student emerging from law school with anything more than half-baked policy notions unless he had devoted his full three years of study to the acquisition of policy-appraisal skills." To go far down the policy-training road would require sad compromises in the thoroughness of training in more traditional legal skills and doctrine. Wrote Cornell's Roger Cramton: "The worst of all worlds would be to abandon what we do well for things we do only badly."

There was another problem, too: fashions in policy keep changing. Expertise in policy areas like regional government and public housing planning, to say nothing of the centralized allocation of income, were to become less salable job skills as time went on. Meanwhile, the various constitutional concepts that Lasswell and McDougal complained got too much emphasis in the study of public law, from separation of powers to equal protection to the distinction between interstate and intrastate commerce, stubbornly remained (and have remained to this day) vitally important in real-life applications of law. In other words, even were "policy" the sole concern of graduating lawyers, the law students of Lasswell and McDougal's era would still have been better off focusing not on the then-current policy preoccupations of Washington, D.C. luminaries, but on the principles the old-line professors had gone right on teaching from their Langdell-style treatises: the Constitutional allocation of powers, the protections afforded by the Bill of Rights, and the fundamental legal principles of ownership, exchange, and duty.

Parenthetically, there have been many other attempts over the years to base legal training on forecasts about which areas of practice would flourish in the future and which decay, most of which have met a similar fate. The 1950s and 1960s saw predictions that there would be less demand for lawyers' services in the coming society because of the development of social policies averting the need for litigation, such as no-fault divorce and accident-compensation schemes. That was a very bad prediction indeed. Nor has legal academia typically been prescient in forecasting booms in particular areas of law. Advanced thinkers in the 1970s predicted a boom in energy law, which never came, and failed to predict a boom in trademark licensing law, which did come. Respected authorities predicted that group and pre-paid legal services would soar in popularity (they didn't) and that most socially salient litigation would in future come to be filed in federal as opposed to state courts (it hasn't). The older idea of general-purpose legal training—teach students how to think like lawyers, fit them out with a general skills kit and a wide fund of diverse knowledge, and let the world of practice take it from there—began to look pretty good.

Even as its details were forgotten, however, the Lasswell and McDougal article helped set the tone for much of what was to follow at elite law schools. It comforted many professors with the idea that their students would be running the world, even as it emboldened them to make clear in the classroom which contemporary holdings of courts were progressive and good, and which deplorable and bad. Why be deterred by empty charges of indoctrination? Wasn't the older manner of law teaching, when you got down to it, its own form of indoctrination? Law-as-it-should-be was up, prestige-wise, and law-as-it-is down.

THE YALE MODEL

In the 1950s, Yale Law School announced a new policy: it would no longer require its students to take a course in Property. This was an almost unheard-of departure from the accepted law school curriculum: property law was a cornerstone of the bar exam; it figured vitally in many areas of real-world legal practice; and to top it all it was a notoriously difficult subject. But so smart and agile were Yale's students, it seemed, that if need be they could master its details in their spare moments or in last-minute cramming before taking the bar. And meanwhile more class time would be freed up to talk about truly stimulating and interesting things.

No other school followed Yale's lead, which actually served to confirm the New Haven institution's enduring place at the very top of the law school prestige heap. The paradox had been established: Yale was the most exclusive and desirable place to study law, and it was also the school where you might wind up learning the least law. It all prefigured the Yale Law School "anthem" composed by one wit at a later date, set to the tune of "Don't Know Much About History":

> Don't know much about Property,
> Don't know much about Bankruptcy,
> Don't know much about Secured Transactions,
> Don't know how to file legal actions,
> But I do know Philosophy,
> And I know that with my Yale degree,
> What a wonderful world this could be.

Famously, Yale law professors could come off as endearingly clueless when faced with actual legal problems to solve, as with the dean of the school who found himself needing a real-world temporary restraining order: "It may be a little late in the day to tell you this," he confessed, "but I have absolutely no idea how to get a T.R.O." Another Yale lawprof briefly made national news during a front-page nomination battle when he admitted (or at least took the public posture of admitting) that he had no idea one had to file federal tax paperwork when employing a domestic nanny. It was as if the professors at the most admired medical schools were the ones most at a loss when confronted with an actual sick patient.

—✺—

There is a limited supply of the sorts of crème-de-la-crème students who can engage in round-the-clock discussions of policy and political philosophy while also cribbing the standard law school curriculum in odd hours. And so quite evidently most law schools are destined to fall short if they try to be Yale. Yet powerful forces influence them to make a show of trying anyway. The upshot is that School #77 in the *U.S. News* standings feels obliged to do its best impersonation of a little Yale, complete with interdisciplinary centers, globetrotting star professors, and unreadable theoretical output. The accreditation pressure to adopt more academic models also played a role here, as did faculty's own wish to move up to more demanding and highly ranked institutions. (It's seen as normal for a law professor to pull up stakes after a few years to accept an offer from a slightly higher-ranked school halfway across the country— one reason America's legal professoriate tends to be a "national" corps, with surprisingly little in the way of regional flavor.)

As Veblen himself described in his famous theory of "conspicuous consumption," people will go to strenuous, costly, and even self-defeating lengths to pursue status in social hierarchies. He would have found much to recognize in the behavior of American law schools, much of whose history can be understood as a series of persistent, salmon-like upstream leaps in quest of prestige. To say that law schools behave like debutantes at a cotillion would be deeply unfair to debutantes, who generally do a much better job at keeping jealousy and competitiveness in check.

The underlying problem is that legal education in America— much more so than, say, medical education—arranges itself according to an exquisitely calibrated and widely agreed-on hierarchy of quality and status. The student with an indifferent record from a low Tier I school will come into opportunities unavailable to the student with a sterling record at a high Tier II, let alone a Tier III.

The decisions made by all the involved parties help reinforce the stratification process. Applicants tend to sort themselves among schools with great efficiency by following the oft-given advice to enroll in the highest-ranked school at which they are accepted, whatever its geographic or financial pluses or minuses. In turn, the ranking of schools depends heavily on the test scores of the students who attend, so schools that have recently done well tend to continue to do well. School administrators themselves, whatever their declared devotion to egalitarian ideals, are supremely aware of the status distinctions, and generally act as if their prime goal in life were to maximize their rank in the standings, with not a few of them engaging in rather grubby dodges and cheats to inflate their *U.S. News* standings. (Roger Cramton has noted that even law schools with religious affiliations, which "might be thought to have a special mission," nearly always behave on a practical level as if their goal were to compete for prestige.) A tiny slip in the rankings can spell heartbreak for administrators; a minor advance can help make a career.

The hierarchies among scholarly subject matters and approaches are less clearly defined than the hierarchies among schools, but real nonetheless. Interdisciplinary work, theoretical originality, and startling counterfactuals have in recent decades tended to outrank sedate "case-crunching," judicious synthesis, and treatise compilation. It is prestigious for a school to acquire recognized authorities on topics like the death penalty, constitutional interpretation, and the doings of the U.S. Supreme Court; it is not prestigious to acquire specialists in non-capital sentencing, statutory interpretation, and the doings of state supreme courts. There is little correlation between the prestige value of a body of law and its importance to the general public; most law schools shun traffic law as a subject despite its exceedingly high salience to the ordinary citizen and not inconsiderable intellectual interest.

—ᴡ—

The ventures into competitive prestige-seeking often run into diminishing returns. Take, for example, the seemingly endless proliferation of law reviews. Harvard can more or less get away with running fourteen student law reviews where it once ran one because its student body boasts an unusual depth of editorial talent and because journals with the Harvard name can have their pick of many outside contributors. The many humbler law schools that get into the act will inevitably struggle. As their verbal tonnage continued to mount, at any rate, the influence of the law reviews on actual lawyers and judges began declining asymptotically toward zero. Between the 1970s and the 1990s, a time in which the volume of opinions by federal courts was rising sharply, the number of citations to the *Harvard Law Review* in those opinions dropped by more than half, from 4,410 to 1,956, with a further steep fall-off in the decade since then. There is no reason to think other law reviews have fared better. Meanwhile, the paid circulation of leading law reviews has been declining steeply for decades, both before and since the advent of electronic publishing: between 1980 and 2009 that of the *Harvard Law Review* fell from 8760 to 2029 (though as late as 2009 its website was claiming 8000); Columbia, from 3795 to 1364; Michigan, from 2950 to 711; and so on.

One reason is that the target audience of the reviews has been reduced almost entirely to academic peers and no longer includes the practicing bench and bar. When law review authors deign to analyze recent court decisions it is most likely to be cases that interest colleagues, students, or reporters. As one lawyer complained in an online forum, the law reviews will furnish plenty of relevant commentary should one's case involve a transgender inmate assigned to the wrong-gender prison and improperly prevented from practicing the rites of Wicca there; but "if I want some assistance on the problems with offsets when multiple uninsured motorist carriers [are] involved, something that implicates 5–10 of my cases a year, there might be one or two [articles] out there, but [they] are way out of date."

The missed opportunities from the disconnect between the law reviews and the world of practice loom especially large on a topic like pretrial discovery. As practicing lawyers know, the discovery process, in which litigants seek to compel each other to hand over documents and answer questions, has become the great runaway cost center in litigation, far more expensive than courtroom practice itself. The anticipated costs and burdens of discovery often shift the outcome of cases well away from what are smilingly called the merits. And yet law reviews accord remarkably little attention to discovery as a topic; one might riffle through thousands of pages at a stretch without finding a mention of the subject.

A MOUNTING CRITIQUE

By the Nineties, critiques of the disconnect from practice were emerging from within the walls. In *The Lost Lawyer: Failing Ideals of the Legal Profession* (1993), the Yale law dean Anthony Kronman indicted legal academia for its infatuation with brilliance over deliberativeness, its "contempt for the claims of practical wisdom," and its dismissal of older traits and skill sets such as empathy, broadness of experience, and dedication to clients' goals and interests. With the advent of "law and" interdisciplinary approaches, once you had learned a little economics, or sociology, or gender theory, or semiotics, you could proceed to reduce the law of collateral estoppel or plea bargaining to a three-factor model, or a template of sexual oppression, or a word game—and "the vast storehouse of accumulated precedent, to the extent that it conflicts with the requirements of natural reason, is nonsense to be discarded with impunity." In *Beyond All Reason: The Radical Assault on Truth in American Law* (1997), Daniel Farber (Minnesota) and Suzanna Sherry (Vanderbilt) took aim at deconstructionist and identitarian fashions. As Sherry noted, figures like John Marshall had given way in the curriculum to theory-heads like Harvard's numbingly abstruse Roberto Unger, a favorite of the Critical Legal Studies (CLS) crowd; a "lawyer who reads Roberto Unger instead of John Marshall, however, is unlikely to be able to function as a lawyer." The Harvard law professor Mary Ann Glendon saw in many of her colleagues' work "a growing disdain for the practical aspects of law, a zany passion for novelty, a confusion of advocacy with scholarship, and a mistrust of majoritarian institutions."

Equally significant, the unmooring of law schools from the actual world of law was being noticed outside the walls. "Law schools and law firms are moving in opposite directions," observed the federal judge Harry Edwards in a widely noted 1992 speech. He added that "many law schools—especially the so-called 'elite' ones—have abandoned their proper place, by emphasizing abstract theory at the expense of practical scholarship and pedagogy." Practicing lawyers were losing the benefits of the ethical as well as operational guidance that a more down-to-earth legal academia might have offered.

Matters have improved in the decade or two since then, and the credit should go not only to highly visible critics like Kronman, Sherry, and Edwards but also to an unsung body of critics, namely students themselves. All along, in their evaluations and course choices, they had exerted a clear preference for the grounded over the airborne, for black-letter law over ideology, for mastery of useful skills and topics over arid metaphysics. Say what you will about careerism, but it just might have saved the day.

—ɯ—

Wise heads have advised book authors to keep a dignified silence rather than respond to bad reviews, and the same advice would probably be fitting for professors who draw negative evaluations from students. Perhaps what goaded Professor A.—an extensively published and frequently cited scholar at one of the West Coast's highest-ranked law schools—into defying this advice was that he had garnered so many negative student reviews, and that they were, well, so mean. "Extremely propagandistic and one-sided," "ramming his politics down the class's collective throat," "Marx, Marx, and Marx," "obsessed with his own political viewpoint," "a little too biased toward a communist point of view"—on and on they went. To be sure, he could take solace in some more favorable reviews here and there: two evaluations had described him as a nice guy, several found him to be smart, passionate, and well versed in his subject, and a couple of students (perhaps a bit backhandedly) praised his "stimulating discussion" and "provocative way of presenting material." But then it was back to the slams: "close-mindedness," "anger and impatience for those who disagree," "always advocating socialist society and marxist viewpoints," "should be teaching at Moscow U." And perhaps most lacerating: "A. could lecture on SEX and people would fall asleep in class—he drones on."

Had Professor A. stifled his yearning to strike back, we might never have learned a word of all this. Instead he decided to turn his feelings of outrage into a scientific hypothesis and back it up with a full-fledged scholarly project. He undertook a survey of law schools with the purpose of assessing and quantifying the unfairness of student evaluations of professors. And he proceeded to publish the results as a lengthy article—which itself has been cited often and respectfully by colleagues in the years since—in the leading publication of its kind, the *Journal of Legal Education*.

As an epigraph, Professor A. begins his piece with a perhaps not entirely happy quotation from Henry David Thoreau, about how he, Thoreau, took up lecturing but did not make a success of it because what he had to say tended to go over the heads of the average man. Professor A. then unveils the problem. Universities allow and invite students as well as faculty colleagues to evaluate professors' classroom effectiveness. Yet there is nothing to keep these evaluations from being based on "illegitimate biases." Despite this illegitimacy, or potential illegitimacy, the evaluations, depending on how administrators use them, might be derailing academics' careers.

Was there something personal in all this? Well, now that you ask, yes, there was. "I have suffered personally from student criticism. Although I cannot avoid the nagging suspicion that I have written this article to get back at my critics, I have tried to pursue broader goals as well."

As one who had written that "all law teaching is political," it was not exactly a surprise to him that his views might be controversial. Nonetheless, he had refrained from assigning students some of his "more tendentious articles," such as "A Socialist Approach to Risk" and "The Real Tort Crisis: Too Few Claims." The class did not always seem particularly appreciative of his restraint, though. "Some students see me as highly, excessively, indeed illegitimately, political."

But the question was not just whether his own particular evaluations were unfair, although he would circle back to that very point again and again through the article. It was whether evaluations more generally were harmful. Had other professors been victimized by the problem, and was it common or systematic? Professor A. drafted a questionnaire on the subject and a committee of the Association of American Law Schools obligingly "distributed it to all ABA-approved law schools, 84% of whom responded."

One big problem with evaluations, it seemed, was that they were inconsistent. Different student evaluators did not always value the same traits or agree whether professors had them. One student would complain of finding a given professor incomprehensible, another would claim to have had no problem understanding. Some complained of inordinate difficulty, others of an excess of easiness. Evaluations by fellow faculty members were far from consistent as well.

Then there was the sore topic of his own evaluations. Were they fair? Far from it! They were infected with "error and bias." Students often based them on "explicitly political judgments"—an interesting criticism, given that Professor A. was himself not exactly shy about dishing out explicitly political judgments. Besides, "satisfaction is not synonymous with quality." Not that his students claimed to be surprised by his politics—most had heard he was a lefty. And despite his expectation that objections would come more from conservative students, the evaluations were "not correlated with the [evaluator's] side of the spectrum."

One of the preoccupations of his questionnaire was whether professors who were female or members of minority groups got poorer evaluations. The contemporary campus, Professor A. claimed (on evidence others might have found skimpy), was beset by "open attacks—both physical and verbal—on women, members of racial minorities, and gays and lesbians." While conceding that "their authority protects most teachers from flagrant assaults," he managed to get across a fairly clear intimation that his own negative evaluations from students were part and parcel of this trend.

So, in fact, *did* female and minority professors tend to get exceptionally bad evaluations? Well, actually, no, in general they didn't.

Studies disagreed as to whether students tended to give lower ratings to women instructors, but it didn't look as if there was a big effect. You'd think that would have been heartening.

It was all especially complicated because he himself—whose feelings of indignation at unfair evaluations had prompted the whole project—was not a member of those groups. In fact, he was a middle-aged white male. But there was an answer for that too. "If students express anger at me, it seems likely that they feel much freer to do so against teachers who are more vulnerable because they are women, minorities, young, or homosexual." So his own bad evaluations *did* show that women and minorities were at greater risk after all!

And there was one more surprise in store. With intimations perhaps of martyrdom, Professor A. had expected that colleges had often dismissed professors or put them through ordeals based on unfair and politically biased evaluations. But both the questionnaire results and a survey of other literature showed differently. "Most schools make *no* adverse personnel decisions on the basis of teaching and the rest make very few."

And what a relief that must have been on many sides.

chapter FOUR

the
higher volumes

IN 2006 LAWYERS FILED A CLASS ACTION LAWSUIT AGAINST the Apple Corporation alleging that it had wrongfully failed to inform buyers of its popular new audio device, the iPod, that listening to music at too high a volume might harm their hearing. Apple's user guide actually did contain language warning of such a danger, but the lawyers said it was not prominently enough displayed to command attention: "Millions of consumers have had their hearing put at risk by Apple's conduct." The suit demanded damages as well as refunds on behalf of everyone who'd bought an iPod over the previous four years. The named plaintiff in the complaint did not allege that his own hearing had been harmed in any way.

The suit looked serious enough; at least, the big plaintiffs' firm that filed it had succeeded in extracting large sums from well-known businesses in earlier class action complaints. Still, its announcement provoked a fair bit of ridicule on talk radio and online forums, especially from tech and audio enthusiasts. Why, it was asked, should Apple be obliged to protect users from their own listening habits? It's not as if the device lacked a volume control. The risk of hearing loss was widely known and was common to many portable audio devices dating back to the days of the transistor radio; why single out the hit iPod? And even if headphone and earbud users were better off avoiding the higher volume settings, other users had perfectly legitimate reasons to choose those settings, as when playing music at an outdoor gathering. Why pressure Apple to re-engineer the device in some way so as to stifle its sound output at the cost of making it less useful to those other buyers?

It's been described as the "American disease": in this country, much more so than in Europe and other advanced parts of the world, we run to court early and as a first resort, with claims of injury that are often dubious, and as a result we have much higher volumes of litigation, particularly in categories like product liability. What accounts for this great national difference? Some onlookers vaguely cite a supposed national tradition of litigiousness; others point to our abundance of hungry lawyers and our lack of a loser-pays principle in allocating the costs of litigation. But on the issues raised by the Apple suit—as with innumerable other long-shot and creatively conceived suits—the trail leads back to legal academia.

THE PROSSER LEGACY

The revolution in consumer law in the United States is conventionally dated to the 1960s, and sometimes more specifically to a 1963 California Supreme Court case by the name of *Greenman* v. *Yuba Power*. The court in that case declared that it would henceforth hold manufacturers of products to *strict liability* for injuries to California consumers arising from defects in their goods, rather than inquire as to whether they had shown *negligence* in the course of making them. The justice who wrote the opinion, Roger Traynor, was a nationally prominent jurist, and also a well-known protégé and confidant of the man who wholly dominated the academic teaching of the field of torts in America for several decades, the Berkeley law dean William Prosser. Prosser was known for many scholarly accomplishments, but above all as the author of *Prosser on Torts*, a treatise that defined its subject as few have before or since. As a result, for thirty years and more, new graduates had emerged from the nation's law schools steeped in the tenets of what you might call Prosserism.

The general public almost never reads casebooks and other academic treatises on law. But as Judge Alex Kozinski has noted,

> future law clerks do. And future lawyers—the ones who will soon be presenting cases in court—do. Some of the people who are reading casebooks today will be working on my opinions just six months from now; others will be presenting cases in a few years. Sure, teachers in the classroom make a big difference, but ultimately what lawyers take away from their law school experience is what is in the casebooks. . . . [They] provide young lawyers with a fundamental outlook on the legal landscape, which in turn shapes their approach to cases. Eventually, lawyers may outgrow their contracts or torts casebooks, but it takes many years of practice. Some never do.

Today Prosser is best remembered for his successful crusade to replace negligence with strict product liability, which required getting courts to do away with a cluster of old rules whose effect had often been to insulate manufacturers from liability. Eschewing false modesty, he himself applauded this early-1960s revolution as "the most spectacular overturn of an established rule in the entire history of the law of torts." Writes Georgetown's John Hasnas:

> In his 1941 treatise, Prosser predicted that, due in part to the public interest in providing the maximum protection for consumers, strict liability would "be the law of the future in defective products cases." When this change had failed to materialize by 1960, Prosser published *The Assault on the Citadel* in which he claimed to find a "trend" toward strict liability for defective products. In 1965, § 402A of the Second Restatement of Torts explicitly applied strict liability to defective products. Interestingly enough, Prosser was himself the draftsman of that section. Then, in 1966, Prosser published *The Fall of the Citadel* in which he announced the victory of the theory of strict liability for defective products.

When Prosser came on the scene in the 1930s, torts—sometimes summarized as common-law legal causes of action between private parties not arising from contract or family relations—was a famously sprawling and intellectually unsatisfactory field, a hodgepodge of inherited rules, approaches, and precedents that tended, like other parts of the common law, to change at no more than a glacial pace. Prosser recast the subject as a thrilling "battlefield of social theory": laissez-faire versus progressivism, individual versus collective responsibility. Judges, he held, should not be afraid to shake off the past, infusing the field with deliberately considered policy and throwing off outmoded precedent as quickly as the times demanded.

Famously, Prosser pushed for a tort law that was more generous toward plaintiffs (and, of course, concomitantly less generous toward defendants). The hoary old rule of *contributory negligence*, for example, provided that you couldn't sue someone else for their negligence after an accident if your own negligence had also been to blame. Prosser helped promote the alternative rule of *comparative negligence*, in which your suit could go forward but the court might reduce your recovery to reflect your degree of fault. And he favored liberal recovery of cash damages for such nonphysical hurts as emotional distress ("no less a real injury than physical pain").

For many of its followers, Prosserism came to stand in shorthand for the proposition that society could and should remake tort law into a sort of surrogate social insurance to help accident victims. As early as 1944, in a famous concurrence in a California case called *Escola* v. *Coca-Cola Bottling*, his disciple Traynor had declared that there was no need for society to allow the cost of accidental injuries arising from product failures to fall on unlucky individuals: "the risk of injury can be insured by the manufacturer and distributed among the public as a cost of doing business." If one analyzed a case this way, the real question that often emerged was how to find the most suitable set of deep pockets on which to fix liability. Prosser himself occasionally (and not very convincingly) denied that this was his actual approach, and it is certainly true that he wanted tort law to perform much more than merely a deep-pocket-finding function: it should also discourage overly risky activities, for example.

To many admirers as well as occasional critics, Prosserism stood for the reconstruction of the field of torts as an exhilarating venture in social engineering.

—*m*—

The older tort law had perhaps not been so much pro-defendant as timid. It tried to steer the courts clear when possible of complexity, tangle, and guesswork. Toward that end, it disposed of many cases through simple, sweeping, rough-and-ready rules limiting who could sue and who could be sued, and it did not dispense particularly generous damages. These restrictions in turn kept countless disputes from landing in court in the first place.

In the field of product liability, for example, the courts had for quite some time been willing to entertain suits alleging *manufacturing defects*, as when a foodstuff is discovered to contain a contaminant, or a carriage is shipped with a needed bolt left out. A key 1960s advance came when they agreed to begin hearing cases alleging *design defects*, in which a product is shipped in exactly the intended and expected form but (so the lawyers argue later) should have been designed in some different way that would have reduced the risk of injury. The inquiry into alleged manufacturing defects—Had the bolt been left out or the foodstuff contaminated?—had usually, or at least very often, fallen within the plausible competence of the judge or jury. By contrast, the need to resolve allegations of design defects opened up enormous complication and guesswork. It meant courts would have to preside over a detailed inquiry into how and why a manufacturer had settled on a particular product design, whether in hindsight some other design (perhaps never sold by anyone or even produced as a prototype) would have been safer; and if so, whether that safety advantage would have been worth the trade-offs to consumers in added cost, inconvenience, or alternative sorts of hazardousness. Trials soon became expensive affairs, assisted by dueling expert witnesses and hundreds of thousands of pages of supporting exhibits, and with inconsistent results: three or four juries in a row might find the vaccine, auto, or aircraft design nondefective, but the next jury might well disagree.

The older tort law had tended to steer cases into two-party formats in which one injured party faced off against one particular defendant. Prosser and his followers were interested in exploring the potential for wider socialization of the process both on the plaintiffs' and on the defense side. On the plaintiff's side, they favored extending rights of recovery to family members and dependents of the injury victim, and sometimes to onlookers as well. On the defense side, Prosser aimed critical barbs at old doctrines that limited the range of who could be sued after a product-related injury—retailers but not manufacturers, for example. This was not because he wanted to get retailers off the hook for manufacturers' errors: his idea was that litigation should at least potentially reach the whole chain of businesses up and down the line: not only makers and sellers of goods but wholesalers, component-makers, and the like. Likewise, liberal concepts of *vicarious liability* and *successor liability* were helpful in ensuring that higher-ups did not walk away from a sales force's misconduct, and in roping in deep-pocket investors who might have purchased a business after the sales in question.

—⚭—

Prosser was particularly keen on limiting the venerable old defense known as *assumption of risk*, which worked to disfavor lawsuits by persons who had chosen to undertake hazardous activities—skiers, baseball fans who had reason to know of the risks of flying foul balls, or—to bring things back to the iPod —headphone listeners who were presumably in charge of their own ears. Prosser took the view, as one commentator noted, "that implied reasonable assumption of risk should not be allowed to reduce a plaintiff's damage in any way." Even when injury had arisen from someone's gross or even criminal abuse of a product, it might still be appropriate to let the lawsuit reach the jury on the theory that the business that put the product on the market ought to have *reasonably foreseen* the misuse. Any number of lawsuits resulted arguing that forklift makers should have foreseen that high-spirited employees would engage in "wheelies" and other horseplay, that manufacturers of painkiller pills should have foreseen that users would crush them for purposes of abuse, that gun makers should have foreseen that their wares would fall into criminal hands, and so forth. And even if a product served a necessary purpose and could not be made less risky, that still did not mean excusing the manufacturer or retailer from a *duty to warn* of hazards.

In general the old law had seen consumer sales as a species of contract, governed by the spirit of voluntarism: if the two sides agreed that one side would bear the risk, that was where it should fall. So it asked: Had the customer been promised some particular level of safety, in writing, orally, or by implication? Or had the provider disclaimed responsibility for the risk? In general, written provisions trumped both the oral and implied kind. But one of Prosser's most influential contemporaries in the legal academy, Yale's Friedrich Kessler, had the answer for that. Kessler argued that the traditional contract law treatment of such issues was an outdated relic of the past. The modern world of commerce, he noted, was full of standard-form contracts, which in a consumer context amounted to take-it-or-leave-it "contracts of adhesion." Drafted at the behest of the business, these contracts (Kessler argued) were often unfair and one-sided, and judges should pay no great deference to their provisions. Just as Prosser's articles were the most cited on torts in the postwar period, so Kessler's 1943 *Columbia Law Review* article assailing standard-form contracts became the most cited contracts article of the postwar era. Together they pointed the way: courts should impose liability and lock the door on companies that might try to escape via disclaimer.

It took a while, but the courts began to go along. The New Jersey Supreme Court went first with a 1960 decision which not only proclaimed new rights to sue over injury, but announced that it would henceforth ignore and treat as void any language in consumer contracts that purported to disclaim or contradict the new rights. Other states followed suit. Prosser of course cheered on these developments. It was not that he wanted to banish contract law entirely: it did, after all, provide consumers with some valuable rights to sue that tort law did not. But as for disclaimers of risk, he felt courts should announce that their new regime of product liability "does not arise out of or depend upon any contract, but is imposed by the law, in tort, as a matter of policy."

As these legal advances proceeded, suits that would once have seemed unthinkable—over the iPod's loudness, for example—began seeming more thinkable. Had the device reached consumers in exactly the form they wanted and expected? That didn't rule out a design defectiveness or failure to warn claim. Had buyers knowingly assumed risk? That old doctrine might get more or less respect depending on which court you drew. Had Apple put warnings and disclaimers in its product manuals? Again, courts might or might not see that as a reason not to let the case go to a jury.

Another important advance was the wider opening up of *consequential damages*. Consumer contracts often specify that in case of discontent the remedy will consist of the item's replacement or refund of its purchase price. Plaintiff's lawyers tend to prefer theories allowing for recovery of more open-ended damages based on the consequences of the negligence or the product defect. In the case of an audio device this might include hearing loss from prolonged listening, unemployment as a result of that hearing loss, depression as a result of that unemployment, loss of interest in sex as a result of that depression, marital breakup as a result of that loss of interest, and so on.

Some worried that an ever more energetic and speculative quest to identify, remediate, and assign legal blame to all sorts of injuries, consequences, and potentially responsible parties might lead to, well, a sort of litigation explosion. Prosser had little patience for such complaints, however. It is "the business of the courts to make precedent where a wrong calls for redress, even if lawsuits must be multiplied."

COLLECTIVIZED LITIGATION

What about the lawyers' hope of turning the case into a class action so as to represent millions of iPod owners who had never expressed discontent, asked for representation, or even knew the suit was going on? Like product liability law, class action law underwent a revolution in the 1960s. And again, the seeds that germinated had been planted two decades earlier in legal academia.

Class actions at mid-century were not new, but they were a specialized device confined largely to securities cases. In general, if lawyers wanted to represent a group of clients outside that context, they had to sign them up one at a time. That "opt-in" procedure resulted in the need for cumbersome litigation committees, if litigation went forward at all. In both committee litigation and securities class actions, a troublesome pattern had long been noted: lawyers sometimes organized and ran litigation on their own initiative and for their own benefit. In particular, they might line up token clients as cat's paws so as to maneuver themselves into the representation of larger, more passive aggregations of clients. Their payoff would come when the case settled and the court allowed them to keep a nice share of the overall proceeds as their fee. All this violated at least the spirit and often the letter of ethics rules, but it went on nonetheless.

In 1941 Harry Kalven, Jr. and Maurice Rosenfield published in the *University of Chicago Law Review* the article that was to lay out the rationale for the modern, far broader use of class actions. Both were practicing Illinois lawyers at the time; Kalven, a longtime fixture at the University of Chicago, was later to become one of the best-known legal academics of his day. At the time they wrote the article, the then-new Federal Rules of Civil Procedure (drafted by a team led by the Yale law dean and New Dealer Charles Clark) had greatly eased the procedures for getting into court with a lawsuit. And yet many potentially meritorious cases still did not go forward, especially where a questionable business practice might have inflicted relatively small harm on many persons. To advance the project of "revitalizing private litigation," Kalven and Rosenfield argued, more was needed. "It may not be enough for society simply to set up courts and wait for litigants to bring their complaints—they may never come."

The answer? To expand the use of the class action in unprecedented new ways. Instead of identifying class members and tediously persuading them to sign up, lawyers would step forward "unchosen and unasked" to lead the litigation charge, and class members would be counted as clients unless they chose to opt out. Clearly this would make practical the pursuit of many controversies individually too small to be worth lawyers' time. Yes, it would mean jettisoning the age-old ethical rules, as well as breaking with the practice of other legal systems. But it would also admit more honestly what had already been going on with committee litigation. Even the stage of lining up a representative client in advance might be dispensed with: "Why not permit the lawyer alone to bring a class suit without an initial client?"

Objections were easily answered. Defendants might squawk, but that is because they would be resentful "that justice has been made too quick, too convenient, too exact, and too complete." Maybe lawyers would do well out of the system, but so what? After all, "paying lawyers handsomely" is important in attracting talent to a field. As for absent members of the class, they surely had no grounds for complaint: "they are not asked to put up money or to give authorization, but are simply asked to 'come and get it.'"

As in the case of product liability, the older law had worried about taking on cases so complex or amorphous as to strain the courts' capacity. For example, what if members of the plaintiff class don't really have identical interests in how a dispute turns out? Thus buyers of audio devices fall into many categories. Some listen through headphones at high volumes, some at moderate, some not at all. Some read warnings and others do not; some consciously run risks for the sake of musical enjoyment and others never give the matter a moment's thought. To what extent do all of them want or need the same particular judicial "remedy"? Indeed, in what sense have all of them suffered the same injury, if an injury it is? And if remedies are to be somehow tailored to different kinds of buyers, how does one sort millions of buyers into the right categories after the fact? By relying on their own say-so?

Kalven and Rosenfield brushed off as highly manageable the challenges of establishing so-called common questions suitable for once-for-all resolution. "It should be emphasized that except for certain stockholder cases virtually every situation that is important socially involves nothing over and above common questions"—a sentence that after the lapse of decades looks as if it must be missing a "not" or "can't" or "aren't" someplace, to make sense of it. In early versions of the class action, courts had also found it challenging to enforce lawyers' loyalty toward their absent or inattentive clients, especially in cases where a settlement might be rich in fees but not in benefits to the class. Kalven and Rosenfield breezily dismissed the whole question: the safeguards of "notice and court approval," they claimed, would be "sufficient to regulate" the problem.

—⟆⟆—

We know in retrospect what happened instead. Once favorable rules were in place, a specialized class action bar arose to churn out group complaints on an industrial scale. Endless wrangling resulted over whether common questions predominated in the resulting suits; lawyers' tendency to trade off client recoveries in favor of fees for themselves became a standing scandal.

The selection of cases for filing often seemed to owe little to the public sense of what consumer grievances might count as substantial. Thus after it was revealed that the author James Frey had invented many details of his supposed memoir, *A Million Little Pieces*, lawyers sued the publisher Random House purportedly on behalf of outraged readers; one demanded compensation for the value of the lost time spent reading the book. Despite widespread ridicule, that action settled, including a tidy sum for lawyers' fees. So did an earlier suit against record producers following the revelation that the popular teen singing duo Milli Vanilli had been lip-synching its songs. The firm of Hagens & Berman, which filed the suit over the iPod, had launched dozens of other high-profile class actions, including a suit against Anheuser-Busch and other brewers demanding billions as recompense over beer ads with talking frogs and other motifs said to appeal to underage customers.

For leading tech firms like Apple, such suits had long been an utterly familiar feature of the legal landscape in America, if not other countries. The firm faced one class action suit over its innovative iPhone, for example, because the device's battery could be replaced only in a repair shop rather than at home by the user. As with the publishing and entertainment suits, lawyers filed many cases on the basis of grievances that seemed less than vital to most customers not involved in the class action business. Palm was sued after conceding that one of its handheld computer models in fact displayed only 58,621 different colors or color combinations, not the advertised 65,536. Many other computer manufacturers were sued following revelations that the actual available space on disk drives was smaller than the industry-standard declared size, although since consumers mostly used the numbers to compare models with each other, the risks of systematic victimization seemed scant. In the most sensational of the lawsuits, Japan's Toshiba agreed to pay upwards of $1 billion, including $147 million to class counsel, after it was demonstrated that its laptops could theoretically lose user data if you set them up to run simultaneous multiple functions just so; the company said none of its 5 million-plus customers had ever reported the problem happening in practice.

One might, of course, advise companies not to settle. But the discovery process in a class action can easily inflict millions in costs. And the automatic multiplication of legal exposure means that even a very weak case can expose defendants to "bet the company" liability should it somehow win on a fluke. Even before the law's liberalization in the 1960s and 1970s, collective litigation had produced a recognized genre of "strike suits" aimed at obtaining quick settlements.

YOU MEAN THIS COSTS MONEY?

Things weren't working out entirely as hoped in the realm of personal injury law either. The idea, as Traynor had outlined, was to spread the costs of accidents over the designated payors, those deep-pocket and insured defendants. Courts might create new rights to sue over more injuries, but they would be uneventfully absorbed as costs of doing business, as with gradual increases in a tax burden. But that's not how the process was experienced by those on the receiving end. To begin with, there were the overtones of recrimination and guilt. If you get sued, isn't it because you're being accused of having done something wrong? A tax you might write a check for, but an accusation of wrongdoing was something you needed to fight. Meanwhile, it was getting harder for businesses and other actors to predict the legal consequences of decisions even one year down the road, let alone fifty. Under design defect theory, it was anyone's guess which designs, warnings, or procedures would be found defective after an accident: different juries were all over the map in the answers they gave. Creative damage theories multiplied the chance that everyday risks would escalate into million dollar cases. Since the 1980s, the business community, as well as doctors and other professionals, have been in more or less continual revolt and protest against the new legal developments.

It is unusual, at best, for a topic of private law to make it onto the national political agenda as a hot topic, let alone remain there for twenty-five years and more. Yet widespread dismay at our rules of tort litigation has lasted that long, with no signs of receding. How has legal academia reacted? For the most part, with a shrug. To be sure, opinion is divided: prominent critics of the new tort law, like George Priest and Richard Epstein, can be found on leading faculties from Yale and Chicago on down. But they are in the minority. The more common response is to write off the discontent as the griping of sore losers, or even a nefarious Astroturf scheme engineered by businesses intent on maiming and otherwise harming the public. Prosser disciples had taught torts and class actions to generations of law students as glorious, shining examples of how academic thinking could profoundly reshape legal practice and, in turn, whole sectors of the world economy. The great experiment *had* to have worked well. If it hadn't—well, the implications would just be too depressing.

Besides, downplaying the costs of the new legal ventures was something of an old tradition. Kalven and Rosenfield, it will be recalled, had waved off fears that class actions might prove costly and unmanageable. Prosser himself, against the opinion of pretty much everyone else at the time, dismissed predictions that his strict liability proposals would lead to a boom in product litigation, arguing that in reality they wouldn't change the outcome in all that many lawsuits: an "honest estimate might very well be that there is not one case in a hundred in which strict liability would result in recovery where negligence does not." So everyone could relax: "The alarm of the manufacturers over the prospect of a great increase in liability under the new rule is not in reality justified." That did leave the question why he saw it as so important to win the battle if it was not to make a big difference after all.

To be sure, the new doctrines did not guarantee that plaintiffs would win, and cases routinely did lose. In 2008, after much expensive lawyering, the Ninth Circuit Court of Appeals upheld a lower court's dismissal of the case against Apple over the iPod's loudness. But there was nothing to stop the lawyers from trying again if they chose, perhaps on different legal theories or under the law of a different state. The emerging law found it very difficult to issue a firm and final "no" to any proposed novel theory of liability, or a firm and final "yes" to any challenged product. It was an article of faith that today's losing case might turn into tomorrow's winner, as famously happened in tobacco litigation.

COURT—AND LAWYER—EMPOWERMENT

As with class actions and product liability, so with countless other areas of the civil law. Legal academia was smitten with the idea of expanding rights to sue, with less regard, or none, for the shrinking right to go about one's affairs without being sued. The bigger and more intractable the social problem, it was felt, the more pressing the need for courts and lawyers to involve themselves. All the innovations—turbocharging of procedure, erosion of old defenses, wider damage theories, and of course the parade of newly proposed causes of action—had implications for other areas too: employment law, commercial law, environmental law, local government law. All were promoted as ways to empower courts to do more justice. All of them also happened to empower the emerging lawyer class as well.

One important development that owed much to product liability was the growing interest in whittling away at *statutes of limitation* and *statutes of repose*. It had long been the premise of the law that it was unfair as well as inefficient to entertain suits too long after an underlying occurrence: by then witnesses would have scattered and memories faded, a prospective defendant might not have saved evidence needed for its defense, and so forth. Besides, after a long enough lapse of time, is the "same" entity even really still around to sue? But the logic of the Prosser approach pointed toward keeping potentially solvent parties in the game.

So the search began for ways to relax or skirt the old limits. In cases arising from mishaps on, say, elevators and small aircraft, it is not unusual for a sued-over product to have been built fifty or even seventy-five years earlier. A straightforward reading of the time limits on suit might dictate throwing out a case. But why be so rigid and mechanical? Perhaps the court could suspend ("toll") the ticking of the limitations clock by citing the state of mind of the plaintiff, who could hardly have been expected to sue until the accident took place, or the defendant, who might have covered up incriminating facts or at least had not done enough to bring them to public notice. Or perhaps the interests of a child were at stake, and how could you expect a child to know about or act on time limits?

Eventually it came to seem perfectly natural for whole sectors of litigation—over cigarettes, asbestos, lead paint exposure—to spring up based on defendants' sales of products back in the 1950s, '40s, '30s, and occasionally even earlier. Such sales were clearly *not* legally wrongful under the law that prevailed over those decades, but that seemed somehow not to matter: what was important was that innocent victims win compensation, and bad guys be brought to justice. Indeed, it was accepted as a valid argument in California's and other courts that precisely because courts had broken sharply with earlier law, it was fair to reset the limitations clock to begin running as of the time of the new court decision, that is, the point at which the once-lawful conduct was retroactively declared to result in tort liability.

Where courts declined the invitation, there was still hope. Advocates began to lobby in legislatures with some success for special laws extending still-pending statutes of limitation or even reopening lapsed ones, a step that became popular as a way of assisting asbestos litigants and which was subsequently adopted in other areas as well, for example to enable suits based on "recovered-memory" recollections of abuse. (Suits of this sort turned out to be mostly spurious, but those revelations seemed to do little to chasten anyone.) A remarkable line was being crossed: both courts and legislatures had lost the old sense that there was something dangerous to the rule of law in retroactively assigning liability to once-lawful actions. Like so many of the other doctrines, that was to have momentous consequences in areas far afield from product liability.

—Ɱ—

Over centuries of common-law tradition, courts had long supervised some degree of change and development in the law, though ordinarily at quite a slow pace, sometimes so slowly that it was hard to detect that the law was changing at all. While it might sometimes be a good idea for the law to change in a more rapid and disruptive way, that should be accomplished (or so it was argued) by way of duly enacted legislation, thus giving fair advance notice to those who needed to comply, allowing broad airing of the issue among interested parties, and taking full advantage of the democratic legitimacy of the elected branches. But increasingly—and nowhere were the urgings stronger than in the academy—it was felt that courts could and should go ahead and liberalize liability rules simply on their own authority. Certainly Prosser felt so. He dismissed the claim "that only the legislature should make any such changes" as "the cry inevitably raised against anything new whatever in the law."

With the feeling that courts were best fitted to drive liability rapidly into new areas came a subtle, or sometimes not so subtle, contempt for the other branches of government, notably the legislative. If legislatures were not the most suitable actors for deciding whether new measures should pass into law, after all, what were they well suited for? And why should other groups go through the political stress and strain of petitioning legislatures for redress of grievances when faster relief might be obtained simply by asking the courts to change the law? The question would recur in areas far removed from personal injury law.

chapter FIVE

the
authority business

THE HISTORIC SETTLEMENT OF THE MULTISTATE TOBACCO litigation of the 1990s did many things. It extracted a promise from the tobacco industry to pay $246 billion to state governments, over and above the taxes they were already paying. It bolstered tobacco companies' profitability by putting the states' clout behind new restrictions on upstart cigarette companies. And it brought the biggest payday in the history of the bar to dozens of private law firms that had been representing state governments, typically under contingency fee arrangements. It soon became evident that something on the order of $10–20 billion in fees was going to flow to law firms around the country, the exact amount depending on (among other factors) the results of a series of arbitrations. A large share of this, estimated at the time at $4 billion, was to go to the two law firms generally credited with managing the litigation campaign, that of Richard ("Dickie") Scruggs of Mississippi, and Ronald Motley and Joseph Rice of South Carolina.

After the settlement was reached, quite a few disputes broke out around the country in which lawyers said they had not been given their promised share of the winnings. For Scruggs, charges of this sort were nothing new; other lawyers had repeatedly accused him of not paying up on agreed fee splits. (Eventually one such dispute was to bring him down in a scandal over attempted judicial bribery.) On the tobacco-fee carve-up, one of the more interesting claims against Scruggs came from a Boston-based professor by the name of Richard Daynard.

Daynard's name had come up regularly in press coverage of the tobacco litigation. Indeed, there were few if any law professors more regularly quoted on the subject. Usually press accounts identified him as a professor at Northeastern University School of Law and as director of something called the Tobacco Products Liability Project, based at his school, which encouraged the development of theories under which tobacco companies could be sued. Reporters called him regularly for quotes on new developments in tobacco litigation even though (or maybe because) his views were of a highly predictable nature: he could be counted on to assail tobacco companies in the harshest terms—"license to kill," and so forth. Daynard also tended to predict an anti-tobacco breakthrough in whatever court proceeding was pending at the moment, and hail any new revelation about the industry as a smoking-gun proof of guilt.

Daynard sued Scruggs with a startling claim: he'd had a handshake agreement in which Scruggs promised him 5 percent of the revenues earned by his and Motley's firms in the tobacco litigation. If the $4 billion estimates of what the two would earn were accurate, that stake would be worth a cool $200 million.

Things got stickier from there. Scruggs flatly denied making any such promise, handshake or otherwise, and sniped at Daynard as "a bit more mercenary than people think he is." Motley for his part described as "stupefying" the professor's claim to have masterminded the litigation. Notwithstanding these aspersions, Daynard proceeded to score strongly where it counted, before the bench. A court ruled he had offered enough evidence to allow his suit to go forward. The Scruggs camp proceeded to reach a settlement with him whose terms were not made public.

The *Los Angeles Times*, which had long identified him in its columns by way of his academic affiliation, registered surprise at his newly revealed role. "Daynard has been quoted in news articles hundreds of times—though always as a public health advocate, never as a private litigator," it noted. Reporters had trouble recalling anything being said about his having secured for himself a piece of the action. When Daynard went before the U.S. House of Representatives in 1999 to testify against class action reform, a year after the settlement, he once again identified himself merely as a Northeastern professor.

The brief flurry of headlines about the Daynard-Scruggs dispute soon subsided, and before long media outlets like Daynard's hometown *Boston Globe* and even the briefly skeptical *L.A. Times* were once again quoting him on the subject of tobacco suits as if his only stake were one of ideological zeal. The Associated Press blandly characterized him in one story as the "head of an anti-tobacco clearinghouse," and in another as the "director of a group that encourages lawsuits against tobacco companies." In 2000 the *British Medical Journal*, which follows what it describes as a strict policy requiring contributors to disclose "competing interests," ran an article co-written by Daynard promoting tobacco litigation in which the professor declared that he had no interest to disclose. After repeated inquiries by a Daynard critic the journal tardily ran a correction rectifying the omission.

A few years later Daynard surfaced as a prominent figure in what the *Boston Globe* magazine called "a national legal movement to make soft drinks the next tobacco" through high-stakes litigation. Was he a mere well-wisher and bystander on this one? Or had he taken some sort of stake in it? Did anyone ask? More to the point, did anyone care? At no point was there any particular record of tut-tutting from Daynard's fellow legal academics or his university administration. So far as could be discerned, nothing he had done at any point along the way was inconsistent with their standards and expectations.

THE "VOICE OF OLYMPIAN PRESCRIPTIVENESS"

If legal academics are wont to adopt what one observer has called an "authoritative voice of Olympian prescriptiveness," it is only partly owing to their command of specialized expertise. It is also because the public sees them as somehow more disinterested than others who talk about the law. Litigants and their lawyers, of course, are the ultimate in interested parties, and their word gets discounted accordingly. But somehow law professors and their schools seem above the fray.

Often they are. But they do face temptations. And while law professors have long been among the most vocal critics of the conflicts of interest that arise in the rest of society, their own competing interests often pass unexamined, or never emerge onto the public record at all.

—⁋—

One might start with that eternal temptation, the love of fame and recognition, as embodied in that recognizable modern species, the TV law pundit.

Truth to tell, most law professors make rather bad TV pundits, which is to their credit. They speak too carefully and insist on drawing too many fine distinctions to get invited back regularly to shows whose stock in trade is highly opinionated commentary dished out in confident tones. But there are exceptions. Wendy Murphy, an adjunct professor at the New England School of Law, is a former Massachusetts prosecutor who appears often on shows like that of hang-'em-high CNN pundit Nancy Grace, typically taking a strong pro-prosecution line in the aftermath of crimes against women or children. Murphy is undaunted by a record of having applauded some of the most retrospectively embarrassing prosecutions of recent decades, such as the pursuit on bogus rape charges of the Duke University lacrosse team and the child abuse charges against the Amirault family in Massachusetts. Even after elements of the Duke accuser's story had begun to fall apart and DNA tests had come back clearing the accused, Murphy on the Grace show called the athletes "rapists—and I'm going to say it because, at this point, she's entitled to the respect that she is a crime victim." On a later show Murphy added: "I never, ever met a false rape claim, by the way. My own statistics speak to the truth." Quoted by Rachel Smolkin in the *American Journalism Review*, Murphy agreed that unlike some other pundits who "voiced the prosecution position," she had not backed off as events unfolded:

> She notes that she's invited on cable shows to argue for a particular side. "You have to appreciate my role as a pundit is to draw inferences and make arguments on behalf of the side which I'm assigned," she says. "So of course it's going to sound like I'm arguing in favor of 'guilty.' That's the opposite of what the defense pundit is doing, which is arguing that they're innocent."

The Syracuse professor and veteran legal journalist Mark Obbie writes that Murphy's defense of her record points up "the utter show-biz meaninglessness of such 'debate' shows."

At a more elevated level, law professors can get in trouble because their names are sought for many projects, which can leave them (to put the best face on it) overextended. Consider the plagiarism scandals that struck the Harvard law faculty in 2004. First Professor Charles Ogletree, Jr., a race-and-law star and Harvard's vice-dean for clinical programs, was caught swiping six paragraphs verbatim from the work of the senior Yale scholar Jack Balkin as part of a new book on the legacy of *Brown* v. *Board of Education*. Then Joseph Bottum in the The *Weekly Standard* showed that Professor Laurence Tribe, one of the world's most famous law professors, had borrowed too freely from the work of the University of Virginia's Henry Abraham in the course of his 1985 history of the U.S. Supreme Court, *God Save This Honorable Court*. Tribe had acknowledged Abraham's work in passing, to be sure, but not in such a way as to justify a whole lot of very close paraphrasing of the older scholar's work, with one nineteen-word passage reproduced verbatim.

Both Ogletree and Tribe weathered the brief storm with ease. The most revealing thing about the two episodes was the explanation faculty colleagues offered in their defense: no one imagined they'd written the books themselves. Both had relied on unpaid or underpaid students or assistants to compile content destined to go out under their names. The *Weekly Standard* talked with friends of a (then) first-year law student who "[said] that he wrote large sections of the [Tribe] book." Ogletree told the *Harvard Crimson* "that he had not read the passage of Balkin's book that appears in his own work." Under the well-worn liability theory of *respondeat superior*, as widely cheered by the likes of Prosser and, well, much of the Harvard law faculty, courts often make business owners pay dearly for the missteps of underlings, whether or not they knew or approved. But it would hardly be fair—would it?—to punish a Harvard professor for borrowings by assistants of which he had probably not been aware. "There was no deliberate wrongdoing at all," agreed the former Harvard president Derek Bok, soothingly.

Far from Cambridge, Mass., some innocent buyers might still think that when you shell out $25.95 for a book "by" a Harvard law professor you can assume he has actually written it. But Tribe and Ogletree were hardly alone in resorting to what has been termed the "atelier" method of book and article production, which sounds much more high-toned than "lining up ghostwriters." Apparently we can no more expect academic stars to write all of the published work that goes out in their names than we can expect Hollywood stars to personally write their autobiographies.

—∿∿—

If some big-name law professors are too busy to write their own books, what are they doing instead?

Some are litigating. So long as their major affiliation remains that of the academy, it's long been accepted for faculty to moonlight in real-life legal practice. Professor Tribe famously has argued dozens of cases before the U.S. Supreme Court and has turned down million-dollar offers to take cases. One law firm somewhat grandly billing itself as "National Legal Scholars" has offered the services of a whole roster of big names including those of Erwin Chemerinsky, Richard Lazarus, and Stephen Saltzburg. (Civil defendants that might want to engage its services are out of luck, incidentally; it only takes plaintiff's work.)

High-profile law professors are also in demand for ongoing affiliations with major conventional law firms, to whom they bring skills, access to high-profile causes, and of course prestige. Thus Tribe has a regular relationship with the large firm of Akin Gump, and other big names have comparable arrangements. A partner at one big West Coast firm said that by signing up one well regarded legal academic, the whole firm benefited from a "halo effect."

What could be wrong with that? After all, we encourage medical school professors to set aside time to treat actual patients, so they can retain a feel for the world of practice, test out cutting-edge ideas in real applications, and not least do some good for the individuals they help. And earlier, lower-cost models of legal education had leaned heavily on the figure of the teacher-practitioner whose practice came first.

But the dangers are real as well. Among them are distraction: many faculty lounges whisper about one or another colleague known as absent, noncollegial, or unavailable to students because of the demands of outside practice. ABA accreditation standards in this particular instance tend toward the vague and toothless, merely indicating that outside work should not interfere with teaching. A standard policy is to limit consulting to one day a week, but that is obviously hard to enforce. While for many professors outside consulting may formally occupy but one day in the week, as Charles Sykes has written, it is a "very important day among [their] days."

Top schools occasionally say—with a nod to the need to remain competitive for the best minds in the field—that they let star professors earn as much on the outside as if they were a partner at a big-name law firm, a euphemism for the $1 to $3 million range. How is that to be accomplished in just one day a week? After all, the class of persons who make that kind of money at big law firms includes many exceptionally bright people, who nonetheless put in sixty- and seventy-hour weeks to handle the workload. What seems likely is that the professors are being compensated in part for the intangibles they bring to the table, such as authority and recognition. And at such rarefied levels of academic law—if not among the rank and file professoriate—it can be the outside consultancy that delivers the major source of income, while the actual teaching side is left as the economic equivalent of moonlighting, just as in the old days.

Many legal academics see no reason to make any particular public disclosure of their consulting relationships, which means, as in the Daynard case, that they may come to light only in the occasional instances in which a relationship publicly breaks down. The tobacco-fee wars resulted in another revelation of this sort, when one of Harvard's best-known law professors, Alan Dershowitz, found himself in court battling a team of lawyers who had bagged a stupendous $3.4 billion for representing the state of Florida in the affair. Dershowitz, it seems, had been assisting them behind the scenes, though unlike Daynard he hadn't assumed a highly visible role as a go-to expert for reporters covering the story. Dershowitz said the lawyers had promised him 1 percent of the fees—which would amount to $34 million—for work that according to the lawyers amounted to 118 hours, though in their telling he hadn't actually submitted time sheets to back up that claim. If that 118-hour figure were accepted as accurate, Dershowitz's fee would work out to $288,000 an hour. An attorney for the lawyers called the Harvard celebrity's numbers "preposterous" and said the professor "has an ego the size of a mountain." Dershowitz countered with a promise of an open airing of matters the lawyers might prefer to keep confidential: "Now the public can finally see the inside of the cigarette lawyers industry." Alas, that was not to be: the dispute, like Daynard's, was later quietly settled on confidential terms.

—⁂—

Academics often carry on scholarly research and writing on the same issues that have arisen in their paid outside work. Even when they do not write specifically about those projects, the ideas, theories, facts, and statistics that cross their desks in the course of consulting relationships often influence their choice of topics and treatments when wearing their scholarly hats.

Aside from confusion as to which hat is being worn at any given moment, there can be acute tension between academic and advocacy roles. Under accepted lawyerly norms of zealous advocacy, nothing whatsoever is to be conceded to the opponent's cause unless the concession happens to offer some tactical advantage. Spontaneity, intellectual give and take, curiosity as a value in itself? The advocate should ask no public questions whose answers might prove damaging, and must stifle any impulsive observations about the world that might inhibit the target decisionmaker from closing the sale with a favorable ruling or verdict. As an academic, one is expected to assess ideas dispassionately, call attention to gaps or defects in one's own hypotheses, candidly concede when a critic makes a good point, and so forth. Such generosity of argumentative spirit, carried on by a team member in litigation, entails virtual professional malpractice.

—❦—

It has long been common for professors in other parts of the university to accept outside consulting assignments. In the hard sciences, the trend picked up pace after a 1980 federal law encouraged universities and their researchers to secure patent protection for their inventions and discoveries. More academics, especially in fields like pharmaceutical research, launched their own outside firms or accepted a stake in startups. Whole university departments in areas like biotechnology began forging partnerships and research collaborations with corporate giants.

There was great promise in these new developments, but there were also troublesome ethical aspects. Medical school professors who published journal articles evaluating the efficacy of new drugs sometimes had a direct or indirect stake in the drugs' success. Studies found that when academics had a pecuniary interest of this sort their papers were a good bit more likely to reflect favorably on drugs than when they had none. Moreover, medical journal editors had not been overly strict about enforcing disclosure of such connections. In some cases pharmaceutical companies had even drafted text for journal articles and sent it over to academic scientists for them to submit over their own names. When these practices were brought to light, a furor resulted in the press, followed by Congressional investigations.

The possible corruption of research findings is only one concern. Many companies that sponsor research, after all, pick scientists of solid integrity, avoid trying to influence their findings, and publish research results even when they are discouraging. Yet the worries can remain. Sponsorship availabilities might, in Derek Bok's words, "cause a massive shift of research activity from basic science to applied problems of immediate economic interest." Within that sphere, they might steer the course of research toward patentable products or processes and away from approaches more promising in advancing human welfare but less readily captured as intellectual property. And while the tradition of academic research is to make data freely available to one's peers, outside businesses have a keen interest in keeping findings secret from potential competitors.

In the past decade, and led in part by voices from the law schools, there has emerged a reaction to all this, summed up in the title of Bok's 2003 book: *Universities in the Marketplace: The Commercialization of Higher Education*. A whole mini-literature advances the critique: *Universities, Inc.*, "Bartering Brains for Bread," "The Kept University," and so forth. According to the critics, both universities and scholars are losing their independence from the interested parties outside the gates. Much fun has been had with the proliferation of buildings and professorships named after donors, as with Washington State's naming of a Taco Bell Distinguished Professor in Hospitality Business Management. But how well do the law schools themselves do in avoiding such entanglements?

"ADVOCACY RESEARCH" AND ITS CRITICS

Every so often concern is expressed about funder influence in academic legal inquiry, but it is a concern that itself tends to be shaped by partisan commitments. Consider, for example, the brouhaha that broke out over a large-scale research project on juries and punitive damages led by scholars at the University of Chicago and elsewhere.

The studies, which went on for more than a decade and resulted in a 2002 University of Chicago Press volume, were based on simulations in which 8,000 persons agreed to serve on mock juries attempting to resolve demands for punitive damages in sample cases. The resulting punitive damage mock-awards were "erratic and unpredictable" in amount, the study found, even though juries "tended to agree in their moral judgments about the defendant's conduct." Interestingly, the deliberation process did not move juries toward middling positions, as had been commonly assumed, but often pushed them instead to extreme punitive awards not originally favored by most members of the panel. To quote the publisher:

> Jurors also tended to ignore instructions from the judges; were influenced by whatever amount the plaintiff happened to request; showed "hindsight bias," believing that what happened should have been foreseen; and penalized corporations that had based their decisions on careful cost-benefit analyses. While judges made many of the same errors, they performed better in some areas, suggesting that judges (or other specialists) may be better equipped than juries to decide punitive damages.

Why were these results controversial? Well, practically anything touching upon juries and punitive damages has implications for the ever-heated arena of tort politics, in which plaintiffs' interests generally favor untrammeled jury discretion while defense interests favor closer review by judges. Moreover, the results were a challenge to earlier, far less elaborate research which had hypothesized that punitives were generally reasonable, closely related to underlying evidence, and not excessive. Lawyers had cited that earlier research hundreds of times in court in defense of punitive damages. And, not to put too fine a point on it, the new Chicago studies blew the old ones out of the water. They were not only giant in scale but also carefully designed by prominent scholars in law, psychology, and economics, including a soon-to-be-Nobelist in the last-named field. The lead writer on the project was the liberal icon and later Obama administration official Cass Sunstein, hailed by the Harvard law dean and later Supreme Court justice Elena Kagan as "the pre-eminent legal scholar of our time."

Prominent in the counterattack was organized trial lawyerdom in the form of the American Association for Justice (AAJ). Its argument was simple. The study, it said, had been funded in part with an estimated $1 million-plus from ExxonMobil, the nation's biggest oil company, which was as interested a party as you could find. It was the target of a jury's $5 billion punitive award, still on appeal, arising from the catastrophic Valdez spill in Alaska. As a giant company, Exxon regularly faced punitive damage demands before other juries as well. The scholars, in short, had allowed themselves to be used in what an AAJ spokesman called business's "furtive attempts to manipulate science for their own ends." The *Los Angeles Times* ran a condemnatory article raising the prospect that "academic researchers are becoming hired guns for industry." It quoted a Tufts environmental professor named Sheldon Krimsky who denounced the Sunstein *et al.* jury studies as mere "advocacy research."

—⚍—

So what had happened? The scholars—to the extent anyone was listening to them—tried to explain their side. Yes, they said, to meet the formidable cost of assembling the experimental panels, they had sought and received funding from multiple sources, including Exxon as well as National Science Foundation and university money. They had fully disclosed that support during the peer review process as well as in the eventually published papers. They had, they said, demanded and received entire freedom from interference in both the design of the studies and later stages of the process. To make his independence clear, Sunstein had refused to accept compensation on the project beyond travel expenses.

Many of those details got downplayed or entirely lost in the press furor, but in any case they were unlikely to put the worries to rest. Even if you accepted the idea that the researchers had tenaciously defended their independence in this particular instance, others might not be so scrupulous in the future.

The main question that didn't get asked in the furor, though, was: Is this anything new? And the answer was: no. In fact it has long been common for law professors' research and scholarship to be underwritten in part or whole by donors financially interested in the areas of law under scrutiny. Research on labor law gets underwritten by pro-union or pro-management groups; on intellectual property, by holders, leasers, and challengers of intangible rights of that sort;

on tort law, by insurance companies and plaintiff's lawyers; and so forth.

It was awfully rich, for example, for the anti-Exxon outcry to be amplified by the contingency-fee bar, organized as the American Association for Justice (known before 2006 as the Association of Trial Lawyers of America). For decades AAJ has quietly maintained the Roscoe Pound Institute, a project that funnels money to legal academics whose work it considers agreeable. That is not its only entry in the field: thus a symposium at Rhode Island's Roger Williams University at which law professors traded ideas on expanding chances to sue credited a "generous grant" from a more recent AAJ project, the Robert L. Habush Endowment, named after a wealthy plaintiff's attorney and former president of the association. Even as AAJ's chief railed in the *National Law Journal* against "furtive attempts to manipulate science," none of the coverage mentioned that the earlier research on punitive damages toppled by the newer Chicago findings—that is, the research that had so often been cited for the proposition that punitive damages are reasonable and nonexcessive—happened to have originated in a Pound Institute grant.

And what of Professor Krimsky, who was so exercised about the dangers of "advocacy research"? It turned out he was closely associated with something called the Project on Scientific Knowledge and Public Policy, housed at George Washington University, which campaigns against business interests on issues relating to science, law, and regulation. SKAPP, it turns out, was founded with a large grant from a fund controlled by plaintiff's lawyers in the gigantic (and, as a scientific matter, profoundly discredited) litigation alleging autoimmune disease from silicone breast implants.

It may be that the harder task is to find legal research that *isn't* connected in one way or another with an interested party.

ETHICS FOR HIRE

Another involvement of legal academics with real-world law is in the giving of expert testimony on behalf of lawyers and litigants. Such testimony can make the difference in whether judges approve fee requests from class action lawyers following the settlement of the case. Law firms also seek out academics who specialize in legal ethics to provide affidavits or so-called comfort letters which can make the difference in whether they avoid sanctions or bar discipline after some fragrant conduct is exposed.

The result is an obscure circuit in which a small community of highly credentialed and well remunerated experts make the rounds to aver that a certain requested fee is indeed reasonable and not excessive or that certain actions by a law firm did not transgress the bounds of accepted ethical practice. Big-name professors are sought after precisely for their big names. "A lot of judges just wilt" when faced with one of these eminences, says Lawrence Schonbrun, a Berkeley, California solo lawyer and frequent class action objector.

Perhaps the dean of the class action fee testifiers is Arthur R. Miller, a longtime Harvard faculty fixture who more recently moved to NYU (and formally affiliated himself with the large Milberg class action firm, after years of less formal association). In a giant 2000 settlement of stock-fraud charges against the Cendant Corp., Miller went to bat in defense of $262 million in class action fees. The request was so exorbitant that even the then-NYC comptroller Alan Hevesi, considered no foe to the class action bar, proceeded to contest it; the Third Circuit overturned a trial court's approval of the fees, Miller's efforts notwithstanding. The law firms wound up settling for $55 million, a remarkable 80 percent climb-down from their original demand.

Professor John ("Jack") Coffee of Columbia, a top specialist in corporate law, is in steady demand as well. In 2008 he testified for various law firms seeking nearly $700 million in fees in the litigation that followed the collapse of the Enron Corporation. Courts had dismissed many of the lawyers' claims against third party defendants as overreaching, but Coffee argued that the failed claims should actually be grounds for increasing the lawyers' fees, since it demonstrated their willingness to be creative and take risks.

If Miller and Coffee are in demand singly, why not hire both? In 1998 the two testified in favor of a then-record award of $174 million for lawyers who had sued the stock exchange NASDAQ. The lawyers won big when Coffee successfully argued against the oft-adopted "sliding scale" approach, under which lawyers' fees decline as a percentage as the size of a settlement goes up.

—⟵—

Then there is the branch of the expertise business concerned with the comforting of lawyers who wish to certify their actions as consistent with legal ethics. Lester Brickman of New York's Yeshiva University/Cardozo School of Law, who has himself put in time on what he calls the expert circuit, has in recent years emerged as an acerbic critic of his colleagues. Someone assigned to do a truly independent "audit" of a law firm's ethics, he points out, would presumably want to get a broad, integrated look at the legal situation that gave rise to a request for an ethics opinion. Instead, he says, many sought-after ethics witnesses agree to "put on blinders" and develop an opinion under highly artificial constraints. These may include being provided only with facts about the situation narrowly selected by their lawyer clients, while refraining from asking questions that might expose as false the favorable assumptions that are implied. In short, Brickman says, they adopt a "see no evil" approach with the goal of delivering the opinion that is sought: "It's worse than sneaky."

What about being exposed on the witness stand by lawyers for a well-prepared opponent? Well, part of the trick to a successful testimony practice is to select cases in which there is not likely to be a well-prepared opponent. In most of the class action fee cases, the opponent in the original litigation has already agreed not to contest the fee request, which means the opposition, if any, is likely to come from class action objectors working on a shoestring. Even in the case of ethics testimony, it is fairly exceptional for a hired expert to have to defend his methods of analysis against hostile scrutiny in open court. And according to Brickman, that is another key to making the system go 'round: since most of the proceedings never draw much public attention, the experts are free to take positions they would never take in their published writings.

—⟵—

The skunk well and truly arrived at the garden party in 2007 when the prominent Columbia legal ethicist William Simon published an article excoriating leading colleagues by name for (he charged) trimming ethical opinions to please clients. The dubious premise underlying the system, Simon wrote, is "that the expert is disinterested and testifying to what she genuinely believes to be the best answer to the question." And yet the "conception of the expert witness's role that prevails among litigators" is quite different and in fact "virtually erases the distinction between expert and advocate." The expert is seen as a team player who needs to be as committed to victory as the others. "I have heard more than one academic expert justify large retainers on the ground that the mere announcement that he has agreed to testify substantially increases the settlement value of the client's claim."

Current expert practice, Simon contends, is also at variance with academic "norms of openness." "It instructs the witness to develop her opinions in private, consulting only the party who retained her and the party's partisan advisors. And it tells her to avoid making records of her preliminary thoughts. It forbids outside consultation and casual writing in order to prevent later disclosures that might reduce strategically advantageous surprise at trial or create opportunities for impeachment with what turn out to be prior inconsistent statements."

The resultant ethics opinion, Simon writes, is released under circumstances "tightly controlled" by the hiring lawyers, who release it only if and as convenient. Indeed, they may "distribute a written statement by the expert vetted by the client or perhaps prepared by the client's lawyers and approved by the expert." In the latter we have a reasonably exact analogue of the much-reviled drug company practice of drafting a self-serving research report and then sending it to an academic medical researcher for submission to a medical journal. And you might think it would raise a similar furor—though in fact Simon's charges about his colleagues, unlike the drug research revelations, never became a front-page story or the subject of Congressional investigations.

Nor was it just an individual ethical challenge, Simon pointed out; universities as institutions had failed to provide needed oversight. Experts' academic affiliation is crucial to the whole system:

the law firm client in disseminating the views "invariably invokes the expert's University affiliation" and the effect of the views on judges or other decision-makers "depends, often heavily, on the University's reputation for impartiality and reliability." Respected universities couldn't just sit by and let their good names be traded on opportunistically. Could they?

1-800-B-E-N-E-F-A-C-T-O-R

In 2001 Michigan State announced a major new addition to its law school, made possible by a $4 million donation from the state's most famous lawyer, to be called the Geoffrey Fieger Trial Practice Institute. It would be the nation's first law school program "designed specifically to train law students as successful trial lawyers."

For anyone familiar with the Michigan legal scene, the name Geoffrey Fieger needed no introduction. Known nationally for representing the suicide doctor Jack Kevorkian, Fieger cut a much bigger figure locally as the winner of many million-dollar jury awards, a flamboyant candidate for office, and a political kingmaker. Just as famous were his many run-ins with disciplinary authorities. One state probe commenced after he used his radio show to unleash "an obscenity-laced tirade" against three state appeals judges who had ruled against him in a case. Another came over his having "[called] two men who served on the jury 'Nazis' and 'creeps'" after he lost a murder case for a client in Florida. In a third episode Fieger escaped a feared indictment for extortion over tactics used against a political adversary, but he did not escape a tongue-lashing from the prosecutor for suburban Oakland County, who upbraided him for "severe and reprehensible ethical violations."

No one really expected that the press release MSU sent out announcing the new institute would dwell on such matters. What did raise eyebrows was the way Dean Terence Blackburn went out of his way in the press release to hold up the school's wayward benefactor as a role model for attorneys, yea, a prince among men. "Mr. Fieger is arguably the most preeminent [sic] trial lawyer in the country, and he is an inspiration to our students," Blackburn declared in the release. "It is Mr. Fieger's dedication to his clients, his thorough preparation for each case and his skill in the courtroom that serve as a model for this institute." That wasn't enough; in fact, Dean Blackburn was barely getting started. In language raising perhaps a faint suspicion that he might have had help in the drafting, he went on about how this "champion of the people" had "a deep commitment to equality and fairness." It quoted the great man himself: "I am motivated by compassion for individuals—men, women and children—whose constitutional freedoms are threatened." On a rather more workaday level—and again, in language seldom met with outside client recruitment brochures—it specified that the litigator's "practice areas include litigation, medical and professional malpractice, negligence law, personal injury, products liability and class actions. He has won more multimillion dollar verdicts for his clients than any other U.S. attorney." Practically the only thing missing was the 1-800 number with operators standing by to field your call.

Had for some reason the college decided to dwell on Fieger's setbacks rather than triumphs in its press release, it might have mentioned the phenomenally high rate at which his jury wins were later overturned by judges. Indeed, it was often Fieger's dubious conduct in and out of the courtroom that led to the later reversals, as when a unanimous court of appeals chastised him for misconduct it called "truly egregious—far exceeding permissible bounds" in a suit against a suburban Detroit hospital; along with other misdemeanors, it found that he had "insinuated, outrageously, and with no supporting evidence that [a certain doctor] 'abandoned' [the patient] to engage in a sexual tryst with a nurse."

The *Detroit Free Press*, in one of the many profiles Fieger has received over his career, found him unapologetic about charges that he bullied and badgered witnesses on the stand. "Trials are battles," he said. Intimidating witnesses "is what trial attorneys do." In a neat interdisciplinary twist, the aspiring trial lawyers at the new Fieger Institute would be required to take drama courses from the university's theater department, the better to master courtroom demeanor. The school's press release did not specify whether the skills taught would include tips on how best to bully, badger, and intimidate witnesses.

—⁓—

There is nothing really new, of course, about the sale of naming rights at schools. Yale and Harvard were named after early benefactors, and innumerable donors over the years have gotten their names on buildings, although some prudent administrators used to prefer waiting until the person being honored was safely dead. Truth to tell, the endowed William Nelson Cromwell chair at Yale probably does not bring all that much ongoing visibility to the still-eminent firm of Sullivan & Cromwell, let alone serve to advertise its current line-up of legal services.

Before 1989, only a handful of law schools had renamed themselves for donors. Since then nine more have done so, according to an article on the subject in the *Journal of Legal Education*. Temple, for instance, turned its century-old school into the James E. Beasley School of Law in tribute to the dean of the Philadelphia personal injury bar. But only about half the benefactors were lawyers; many other namers made their fortunes in business, often endowing multiple departments at their favored universities. The going rate, according to that article, averages around $25 million, more expensive than business schools but cheaper than medical schools. "As it happens, this [$25 million] is the exact figure the University of Pittsburgh pegged its law school at when it announced a lengthy list of naming opportunities." Arizona got $115 million in 1999, but that was a fluke.

Unfortunately, a law school may not always be doing its students a service by giving up a familiar institutional or geographic name in favor of a donor's. After the University of Florida's law school renamed itself in 1999 to honor the prominent Pensacola asbestos-tobacco lawyer Frederic Levin—he got it on the cheap, at only $10 million—grads were heard to grumble that out-of-state employers who would instantly have accorded credibility to the University of Florida College of Law were left instead to puzzle over references to Levin College of Law.

—⁂—

The University of Houston in 1996 chose to associate itself with the fabulously successful if ethically challenged litigator John

O'Quinn (breast implants, asbestos), naming its law library after him notwithstanding murmurings about his long record of disputes with bar authorities over infractions that included the illegal use of "runners" to acquire clients. By yielding a multi-billion-dollar fee haul, Texas's stake in the tobacco-Medicaid litigation set off a veritable binge of naming activity at the state's other law schools. Baylor acquired a new Sheila and Walter Umphrey Law Center following a $20 million donation. Then Wayne Reaud, like Umphrey a tobacco- and asbestos-suit magnate from Beaumont, was reported to be in talks with his alma mater, Texas Tech, to rename its law school after him for $12.5 million. After soliciting the donation, it turned out, the school's dean, Frank Newton, had agreed to serve on a fee arbitration panel that awarded Reaud and other lawyers an eventual $3.3 billion. The whispers subsided when Tech, setting a high price on its virtue, put out word that it wasn't going to rename its law school unless someone offered twice as high a figure as had been mentioned.

It was said of the old Chicago slaughterhouses that they sold every part of the pig except the squeal. Something of the same spirit may have entered into the expansion design of the University of Mississippi School of Law. The plans lay out a sort of warren of more than thirty-five endowed fiefdoms, including the D. McCormick Moot Court Staff Workroom, T. Avent Law Journal Articles Editors' Office, the B. Smith Family Career Services Interview Room, and so forth, each claimed by a particular law firm or family that has prospered by way of the Magnolia State's legal system, or hopes to. By far the grandest and most impressive item on the list is, or was, the Richard F. Scruggs Classroom Wing.

Oops! Scratch that last one. Even as the Scruggs Classroom Wing awaited construction, its namesake was caught trying to bribe a judge in one of the highest-profile legal scandals in memory, resulting in his imprisonment. And that brought up one of the risks in accepting money from benefactors whose careers are still very much in progress: that their names will become bywords for embarrassment. No institutions want to follow in the paths of either the University of Missouri, which created a Kenneth L. Lay Chair in Economics before the Enron chief become the most reviled businessman in America, or Seton Hall, which had to remove Dennis

Kozlowski's name from a building after scandal brought down the Tyco chieftain.

—ⱱⱱ—

Given all this, there might be a logical next step. In the ideas they nurture, the careers they make possible, and the rationalizations they spin, law schools already facilitate billions of dollars' worth of highly profitable litigation. Isn't it time (someone is bound to propose) to cut them in on its benefits more directly, much as universities can now capture streams of royalties from the inventions and discoveries of their science departments?

There are stirrings already. In class action settlements, when members of a plaintiff class cannot be identified or given refunds, judges sometimes dispose of settlement funds under a principle known as "*cy près*"—old French for "as close as possible"—to groups nominated as worthy by the lawyers in the case. The practice has mushroomed in recent years, and law schools have begun to emerge as frequent and munificent *cy près* beneficiaries. Antitrust lawyers sent $2.9 million to Vanderbilt—a professor explained "that the case started in Nashville and the law school trains students to negotiate similar settlements." Consumer class action lawyers dropped $8 million on West Virginia University's College of Law; the judge suggested that one. More than $1 million from another case went to endow a chair at the University of New Mexico School of Law.

The next logical step? In 2007, following the settlement of an antitrust suit against various chemical companies, it was announced that at the request of the prominent class action lawyer Michael Hausfeld and his colleagues, $5.1 million would go to the George Washington University (GWU) School of Law, Hausfeld's alma mater. In return, GWU would do something nice for them, launching a new Center for Competition Law. According to the college's press release, the center's mission would be to promote research on antitrust law and related topics, and to hold seminars on the subject aimed at judges, high government officials and other influentials, a job to which the GWU campus's location, blocks from the White House, would be well suited.

In particular, the new center would focus on the "private enforcement" of antitrust law, that being lawyers' way of referring to the filing of private antitrust lawsuits, mostly by class action law firms. The new center would also serve "as a resource for those seeking to promote private enforcement in competition law in the United States and abroad," or, again to translate from law-speak, as a resource for those who wished to promote lawsuits of this kind. In other words, it would—or at least so some of its backers hoped—serve as a Washington advocacy center to furnish policy ammunition for the plaintiffs' bar on antitrust issues.

The idea of an academic law center with such a mission was in fact not new. For years already a group called the Institute for Consumer Antitrust Studies, at Loyola-Chicago's law school, had been turning out regular work favorably disposed toward expanding the scope of antitrust litigation. And the Loyola center, too, found its fundraising prayers answered not long after GWU's, when lawyers arranged to divert to it its very own *cy près* windfall: $1.5 million from the settlement of a class action against makers of rubber products.

It was all a magically circular, gratifyingly mutual, and wonderfully back-scratching new way of doing things. The law schools would promote litigation, and the proceeds from the litigation would in turn serve to support law schools. Was there any doubt that this was the wave of the future?

chapter SIX

the classroom of advocacy

OVER THE YEARS A LONG SUCCESSION OF GOVERNORS, presidents, and mayors of both parties have sought to reform the welfare system to curb expenditures, reduce dependency, and move recipients to paying work. While generally popular with voters, these efforts are undertaken at political peril, because the body of advocates who work to defend and expand welfare benefits is seasoned and effective. Their main line of defense is litigation: any change in benefits to which they object is apt to be tied up in court challenges for years. But courtroom action is only one front in the battle. The welfare lobby makes its voice heard in legislatures both behind the scenes and in public hearings; it develops advocacy-oriented research and statistics, passes tips to friendly reporters, and agitates in other ways, sometimes playing hardball to trip up politicians who cross its wishes.

A notable thing about all this lobbying is how much of it originates on university campuses, at law schools in particular. When Ronald Reagan was governor of California, his longstanding nemesis on welfare issues was a group called the Western Center on Law and Poverty, based at the University of Southern

California and run as a consortium with nearby Loyola/Los Angeles and (state university system component) UCLA. In New York City, a group called the Economic Justice Project at CUNY/Queens College School of Law was launched in 1997, according to its website, "in response to the social justice crisis triggered by regressive welfare reform legislation"—that is to say, in response to the historic reforms signed by Democratic President Bill Clinton in 1996. According to its site, EJP acts as "legal arm and counsel" to a private group calling itself Welfare Rights Initiative, with which it has engaged "in a broad array of advocacy, educational and social change activity [including] legislative advocacy that recently yielded progressive reforms to state and local welfare laws," making itself a constant irritant to welfare-skeptical New York officials like those in the administration of the Republican mayor Rudolph Giuliani. Nor do CUNY faculty or students maintain the project as some extracurricular pursuit; as part of the school's clinical law apparatus, it's a fully official function of the university, and thus itself a unit of the same New York City government it regularly sues on welfare issues.

Of course law school clinics don't confine their advocacy to welfare subjects. Participants in Seton Hall's Impact Litigation Clinic file many sorts of "cutting-edge cases that further social justice." A Yale clinic helped win the 2010 case in which the Connecticut Supreme Court decreed equalization of school finance. "Students Fight for Social Justice at Columbia's Sexuality and Gender Law Clinic," declares a headline about one of many clinics that devote themselves to similar issues. Rutgers says at its Constitutional Litigation Clinic "students not only learn the law, they make the law."

Environmental law clinics vie in boasting of their project-stopping prowess. Columbia's clinic is proud of having stopped the construction of a shopping mall in New Jersey, perhaps laying down a subtle turf challenge to Rutgers' Environmental Law Clinic, which fancies itself the "public interest law firm for New Jersey's environmental community." In nearby Westchester, students at Pace can't claim to have stopped a whole mall, but they did stop a pretty big Ikea furniture store.

Occasionally a less-than-sympathetic outsider will express discontent at all this. Thus in 2006 Heather Mac Donald recounted highlights of clinics' track record:

> In the last few years alone, law school clinics have put the Berkeley, California, school system under judicial supervision for disciplining black and Hispanic students disproportionately to their population (yes, that's Berkeley, the most racially sensitive spot on earth); sued the New York Police Department for its conduct during the 2004 Republican National Convention; fought "gentrification" (read: economic revitalization) in "neighborhoods of color" in Boston, New Haven, and New York; sued the Bush administration for virtually every aspect of its conduct of the war on terror; and lobbied for more restrictive "tobacco control" laws.
>
> Over their history, clinics can claim credit for making New Jersey pay for abortions for the poor; blocking job-providing industrial facilities; setting up needle exchanges for drug addicts in residential neighborhoods; forcing Princeton's eating clubs to admit women; allowing female murderers to beat the rap by claiming "battered women's syndrome"; and preventing New Jersey libraries from ejecting foul-smelling vagrants who are disturbing library users.

Some critics even say that as parents or alumni supporting the school—or, in the case of public law schools like CUNY, as taxpayers—they'd just as soon their money not go to support ideological adventurism. Such objections are met with peals of outrage: have you no respect for academic freedom?

CLINICS' SUDDEN RISE

Curricular change is usually a slow and painful matter in legal academia, which makes it all the more remarkable how quickly clinical legal education managed to establish itself in a few years around 1970. As of 1968, notes Steven Teles, "only a dozen law schools gave credit for clinical work." Just four years later, the number had risen to 125 of 147. Today, the clinics have settled comfortably into institutional status, with more than 1,400 clinical instructors presiding over hundreds of thousands of hours of student legal work annually. While no two schools offer exactly the same line-up, most programs are divided into an array of specialized clinics devoted to representing (say) prisoners, immigrants, senior citizens, tenants, consumers, and so forth—in effect, a mini-law firm operated under law school auspices.

There is no real mystery as to how this all happened so fast: through a mighty effort of will by the Ford Foundation. In 1968 Ford launched a group called the Council on Legal Education for Professional Responsibility (CLEPR) to promote the clinical idea. It then began pouring large sums into the establishment of new clinical programs around the country (it expected individual law schools to take over their support after a while). It was emblematic of the way philanthropy in general, and Ford in particular, had begun to transform the workings of legal academia and through it American law, a topic that deserves an excursion of its own.

—⁓—

Ford had long been the biggest and the most influential of the foundations. It had pioneered the phenomenon of staff-led emancipation from the wishes of its founding family (a process confirmed and completed in 1977 when Henry Ford II threw in the towel and quit its board in frustration). It had also been a pioneer in plunging into politically controversial areas, especially after 1966 when McGeorge Bundy became its president and brought on board many other veterans of the Kennedy/Johnson administrations such as Robert McNamara, Dean Rusk, and Chester Bowles. For a while, indeed, it got in trouble by too openly promoting outright politicking and election activity, pulling back only after serious rumblings from tax authorities.

Few sectors of society were bit harder by the Sixties bug than the philanthropy establishment, and Ford again led the way. When the period began, most foundations in line with the wishes of their original benefactors tended to pursue a "service" ethic of direct assistance to human needs: scholarships for deserving students, services to the disabled, home visits for the elderly, medical research, recreation for city kids, and so forth.

But now charitable administrators were urged to move in a new direction. Effective philanthropy (it was argued) required changing the unjust social conditions that permitted poverty, ill health, and deprivation to arise in the first place. That required politically aware giving to organizers and activists who could best challenge old institutions. The old programmatic service ethic of direct help to the needy was passé—"merely ameliorative," in the telling phrase of one new-style grantmaker. The services it provided might be all very well in their way, but if so, they should be provided as a responsibility of government, and it would hasten the recognition of that fact if foundations stopped being so willing to step into the gap. In short, direct relief of need was out; the financing of adversarial politics and insurgent organizing was in.

Where Bundy was ahead of his time was in recognizing that traditional electoral politics—or even the rowdy street politics of marches and building occupations—was no longer where the real action was. That distinction fell to the courts, led by Earl Warren's Supreme Court. Already, creative lawyering had been the catalyst for bold judicial action in such areas as racial desegregation, criminal procedure reform, and legislative redistricting. What if this new lawyering style were set loose at America's other intractable social problems—at pollution, poverty, unequal schooling, the problems of women, and so forth? Litigation—lots and lots of it—was needed.

What seemed to work best was a strategic and anticipatory approach, in which lawyers identified key cases offering an opportunity to make new law, lined up sympathetic clients with which to bring such actions, and worked closely with the media to build public support. It was all given a new and flattering title: *public interest law.*

—⚬—

Within a few years between 1966 and 1969 there were launched most of the institutions that have dominated the field of public interest law ever since: in civil rights law, the Lawyers Committee for Civil Rights Under Law, Mexican American Legal Defense and

Education Fund (MALDEF), Puerto Rican Legal Defense Fund, and Native American Rights Fund; in women's rights law, the ACLU Women's Rights Project and National Women's Law Center; in environmental law, the Environmental Defense Fund, Sierra Club Legal Defense Fund (later EarthJustice), and Natural Resources Defense Council; and many others, including groups devoted to welfare rights and school finance equalization. Bundy and his Ford colleagues made themselves truly the Johnny Appleseeds of litigation liberalism, staking start-up money and sometimes ongoing funding for all the groups named above.

For a while things were touch and go because it was far from clear that the new kind of law would be granted the highly preferential tax status its proponents sought. Looking for opportunities to sue people did not in itself sound like a particularly charitable endeavor, and if you accepted the idea that the ultimate point of the exercise was to get the laws changed, you made it sound sort of like lobbying, which was not entitled to charitable tax treatment either. Some in the Nixon administration strongly opposed the bid for charitable status, but following a big Establishment blitz, including a statement by former presidents of the ABA, the Treasury Department caved and ruled in its favor in 1970.

Other foundations followed Ford's lead. Thus the Carnegie endowment threw itself into the support of courtroom efforts to require public schools to instruct immigrant children in their first language, while the Edna McConnell Clark Foundation, based on the Avon fortune, did much to assist lawsuits that forced mass deinstitutionalization of mental patients. Soon grantmaking aimed at changing the world through lawsuits came to seem normal and even uncontroversial. In his 1975 president's report, Bundy conceded that many still viewed the promotion of large-scale litigation as "an inappropriate choosing up of sides" for a philanthropic institution. But his colleagues had rejected that view: "we decided that there was only one right side to the question of equal opportunity." Only one right side? That certainly simplified things.

—⁕—

Some of the new legal strike forces were based on campus, among them Columbia's Center for Social Welfare Policy and Law, which took the lead in an elaborate, Ford-directed welfare rights campaign, and Georgetown's Institute for Public Interest Representation. Particularly influential were so-called backup centers, such as Berkeley's National Housing Law Project, which lent strategic and appellate help to lawyers around the country seeking to liberalize particular areas of the law; later some of these groups obtained large infusions of tax money by way of the federal legal services program. Even when the new litigation groups had no university affiliation, they were often founded with vital assistance from law faculty. Thus Yale's Charles Reich and Boris Bittker served as go-betweens in the founding of the Natural Resources Defense Council, linking eager students with lawyers at big firms interested in blocking a Con Ed power plant in New York.

A distinctive strength of the new legal network was its success at getting favorable notice in the press for its cases. Public interest litigation tends to be complicated, and reporters depend on a relatively few sources who are in a position to analyze its detail. To assist in this process, foundation grants enabled the formation of many law school projects and centers that might not themselves sue but served as allies, researchers, and public explainers for the groups filing the suits. In New Jersey, after the freestanding Education Law Center (founded by the Rutgers law prof Paul Tractenberg with Ford funding) launched a series of school finance suits that convulsed the state's politics for the next thirty years, reporters covering the suits often turned for commentary and analysis to the Institute on Education Law and Policy (also founded by the Rutgers law prof Paul Tractenberg with Ford funding but housed, unlike the Education Law Center, within the law school itself.) The *New York Times* so routinely accorded favorable ink to cases filed by Ford grantees that you might have assumed some underground system of pneumatic tubes linked the paper's headquarters on W. 43rd with the Foundation's on E. 43rd.

POVERTY LAW FOR THE NON-POOR

Ford's adopted pedagogical innovation, the law school clinic, was very much part of the overall plan. Many subsidiary changes were necessary to make the new idea happen. Local court rules, for example, needed to be changed to allow law students to make court appearances, a privilege ordinarily reserved for licensed attorneys. To train leadership for the new programs, Ford furnished Harvard with money to launch a graduate center that was soon turning out five clinical professors a year.

Backers of the new clinical movement embraced a series of objectives that were seen as interconnected. First and more obvious was the pedagogical: clinics would take students beyond books and lectures to impart skills by entrusting them with actual legal work. A second goal was to marshal a pool of resources with which to provide *pro bono* legal representation to the poor, a traditional responsibility of the established bar that had often gone ill-served. Third, and growing out of the work for poorer clients, the new clinics would get involved in test cases and other law reform litigation. Finally, the very experience of being thrown in with poor and oppressed clients would raise law students' consciousness and accelerate the schools' engagement with movements for "social change."

Whatever else might be said of these four objectives, it soon became clear that they were to varying extents at cross purposes with each other. What worked well pedagogically did not always serve the needs of law reform, the best ways of addressing the pro bono gap did not always raise students' political consciousness in the hoped-for ways, and so forth.

Almost inevitably, to open a clinic offering free help for those who cannot afford a lawyer is to be inundated by demand. But most of the legal services that poorer people want have little to do with changing society. Many want a divorce, or an alteration to custody or visitation. Or they have a small collections matter, traffic dispute, or misdemeanor case that does not call for any particular change in the law. It can all seem discouragingly "ameliorative." Proposals were soon heard for guidelines authorizing clinics to turn away more walk-in cases so as to allow more time for class actions, institutional reform suits, constitutional challenges, and other high-profile cases—the rationale being that thereby lawyers could "save thousands instead of a few."

There was also pressure from a second direction to restrict client intake. An initially suspicious old-line bar leadership had been placated by reassurances that the new clinics would be set up so as not to siphon potential paying clients away from the existing bar. So work that existing lawyers would be glad to take—accident cases they would accept on contingency fee, for instance—was out of bounds more or less from the start.

At the same time many of the contemplated law-reform and social-change campaigns would not readily fit into a scheme of representing poorer individuals. Advocates had the answer to that one: they were defending *interests* that otherwise might go un- or underrepresented. That covered the environmental cases where (once you got past the fictions of standing) there was often no real client at all, or where neighbors harmed by noise, congestion, or loss of scenic views were by no means impoverished.

—⟋⟍—

Just as a free clinic will attract too many walk-in clients to serve them all, so there is an endless surfeit of causes going underrepresented, and one's selection among these reflects one's political preferences. Would the feminist-run family law clinic take the case of a father floundering under unsustainable child support obligations? Would the urban law clinic represent the much-robbed bodega owner getting the runaround from City Hall on permission to carry a firearm? Would the rural-poor law clinic represent the backwoods family in trouble for burning trash or hunting without a license? It might depend on the clinic director's politics.

Many clinics were willing, in the name of the poor, to consider challenging a decision by City Hall to hike bus fares. But what if the decision was instead to hike bridge tolls for drivers? These days more poor people drive than take buses, and drivers, like bus riders, are politically and legally ill-organized. In practice, not many clinics would challenge the bridge toll hike, which may have more to do with a political sense that buses are good and cars bad than with any consistent commitment either to the poor or to the representation of underrepresented interests.

Then again, poor people's legal interests often clash with each other, and which you pick reflects your politics. Law school clinics often act to protect unruly students from school discipline and to stave off disruptive tenants' eviction from public housing, even though fellow students and tenants in poor neighborhoods are among the chief losers. They also work to overturn convictions of wrongdoers whose future victim base will consist mostly of persons of modest means. The website of Fordham's Community Economic Development clinic says it works to "limit gentrification," that is, the influx of high-income housing and retail activity into poorer areas. Is gentrification in fact unwelcome to poorer residents? Well, that depends: some dread rising rents and the disappearance of favorite stores, while others look forward to a drop in crime rates, better upkeep of the housing stock, and the arrival of civic-minded new neighbors.

One might extend such a list indefinitely through controversies over busing, bilingual education, remedies for police use of excessive force, and many other issues. If litigation forces fire departments to weaken strength tests so that more women can join up, has there been a step forward for employment equality or a step backward for older or feebler persons who might need rescuing from burning buildings? If lawsuits prevent states from insisting on waiting periods for granting welfare to persons who arrive from elsewhere, will they be willing to maintain as high a level of benefits in the first place? If the law makes it harder for landlords to evict tenants for unpaid rent, will they start demanding higher security deposits? To Ford, there may have been "only one right side" to these questions, but others would wonder whether all lawyering for the poor really leaves the poor better off.

The early proposals to limit the volume of actual clients so as to free up time for law reform drew a caustic rebuttal from, of all people, William Pincus, the CLEPR director and a Ford alumnus. "We are speaking," Pincus wrote, "of turning away clients from legal aid so that lawyers may save their time to reform the system." In other words, the plan was to provide less service to actual poor people because many lawyers "find law reform and the restructuring of the society providing for their psyches a much more satisfying outlet." It symbolized a wider phenomenon: "the common man as an individual tends to get lost. They're for him as a cause, but they don't want to cope with him in person," except insofar as he can furnish "apparent endorsement of plans which have already been contrived by those who are leading a movement." Pincus deserves due credit on the point: in part because of his efforts, law reform goals were not always permitted to override the goals of service and pedagogy.

DASHED HOPES

Decades later, it is clear that the clinics have lived up to some but not others of the goals envisioned for them.

When it comes to ideologically charged litigation, they get enough done to appall many on the Right but not enough to satisfy many on the Left. Georgetown's David Luban concludes that while it "seems likely" that "the overwhelming majority of clinical teachers would identify themselves as political progressives," most clinical work fails to rise to the level of "cause" lawyering at all. At some schools, especially in big cities, a majority of clinics have a recognizably leftist or identity-politics mission, but it is more typical for an equilibrium to be reached in which there are one or two such entries in a school's lineup, outnumbered by others with less politicized-sounding descriptions.

Why the dashed hopes? For one thing, new ways were found in the outside world to finance law reform litigation that did not depend on free student labor. For another, the all-law-reform-all-the-time model proved to have limited appeal to law students themselves.

Even as clinics were getting off the ground, other models for public interest litigation were establishing themselves. Legal services programs, for example, could provide clients with fully licensed attorneys with no worries about fitting cases into an academic calendar. From the late 1960s on they began drawing large allocations from government budgets, not only for the service of conventional legal needs but also (and more controversially) for the pursuit of ambitious law reform agendas.

More important was the rise of fee-shifting, specifically "one-way" fee shfting. Through a combination of legislative victories and some fancy footwork in interpreting statutory language, it was established around this period that prevailing plaintiffs across many areas of litigation could collect legal fees from losing defendants, but not usually vice versa. The fees are generously calculated, both as to the quantum awarded and as to the definition of "prevailing" (winning on even one of the points in dispute can be enough to trigger a full fee shift.)

The availability of one-way fees made for a favorable economic climate for the public interest law firms. Indeed, if they exercised a modicum of care in case selection, they might even emerge as highly lucrative enterprises. The same developments also ensured that a copious amount of reformist lawyering would be forthcoming from elite law firms on what was couched as a *pro bono* basis—the term often being somewhat misleading, since when the firms prevail on such a basis they often demand and are awarded enormous fees at the expense of hapless opponents. With courts willing to order defendants to pony up fee shifts of $800 an hour and more, plus expenses, to seasoned attorneys, why give up a good thing by steering a promising case to a student clinic? Thus the clinical movement found itself somewhat obsolete almost from its start when it came to providing front-rank talent for law reform litigation. With pros happy to take over the field, was there still a role for amateurs?

—ⅢⅢ—

Complicating matters further for the directors of clinical programs were the students' own preferences. To compete with other schools, a range of clinical options has to be offered that most students will find attractive, and the offerings within a school in effect also wind up competing against each other for student enrollments.

Most students want programs that confer skills in demand from future employers while providing a satisfying experience, including a feeling of having accomplished something solid for others. With the possible exception of Death Row cases, messy or guilty clients are not usually a first choice, nor are vicious-minded areas of litigation.

Many will gravitate toward a chance to help a kid in the foster care system, a widow coping with Social Security paperwork, or a family trying to set the affairs of an incompetent elder in order—exactly the sort of legal services a grantmaker might dismiss as "ameliorative." Also popular are environmental law, animal welfare, and lawyering for the arts, all middle-class favorites at some remove from a "lawyering for the poor" schema.

No less frustrating from the radical standpoint, many students are keen to pick up skills in areas like transaction planning and business counseling. Making the best of things, some schools have started up clinics in which students can advise progressive-minded nonprofits, or fledgling entrepreneurs who intend to serve poor communities, on business and transactional matters. But the sense of defeat can still hang in the air: Wasn't one of the whole points of the exercise to steer students *away* from a future in business law?

—⟡—

Clinical work can indeed raise students' consciousness about clients and legal practice, but not always in the expected ways. From an early CLEPR newsletter:

> I had believed my client when she first came in, young, distraught, trapped in an unhappy marriage. Her little girl, the victim of parental abuse, had been taken from her. She determined to divorce her violent husband, get her daughter back, and build a life for herself. I agreed to help.
>
> Several months later, after an endless series of court appearances, conversations with social workers, hassles with state's attorneys, I discovered that my own client had, in fact, been the abusive parent.
>
> What to do. It was a problem never considered in my legal ethics course with its emphasis on keeping other professions from infringing upon the business of the lawyer.

One of the real contributions of clinical law training is that it can usefully help sort out such emotional allegiances before too many commitments to practice are made. ("I didn't realize they'd be *that* guilty!" as the classic line of the idealistic public defender has it.) Your eviction work might keep the poor tenant going for a few more months rent-free, but eventually he'll still probably wind up having to move, and he'll still be poor. "My first victory was getting someone out," recalled one clinician who specialized in representing mental patients. "Within a month, he died in a rooming house fire."

Clinical work can indeed yield much insight into human nature, but the result may or may not be to increase students' engagement with the "movement." One project ("Reclamation of Southern Assets") used law students and other volunteers to interview black Chicago families who believed they had been wrongfully done out of land ownership back in the South. Rep. Bobby Rush (D-Ill.), explaining his interest in the project, cited "the treacherous theft of African American-owned land during the Jim Crow era." To the organizers' chagrin, however, it turned out that while black families signed up in impressive numbers for the service, they mostly wanted to pursue grudges against their own family members rather than thieving whites.

—⟋⟋⟍—

Clinical law advocates sometimes strike a stance of beleaguerment, as if they were beset by powerful opponents bent on denying their academic freedom to sue whoever and whenever they want. The truth is that even when they do controversial-sounding things like suing high officials in their own states, they seldom run into much real controversy. It is true that environmental clinics at Tulane and Maryland provoked a legislative backlash when they picked fights with dominant industries in their states (chemical manufacturers in Louisiana and chicken producers in Maryland). Tulane's clinic had successfully blocked construction of a plastics plant, arguing that its siting in an impoverished community north of New Orleans constituted "environmental racism"—even though many local black residents, with help from the NAACP, had worked hard to attract the plant. The Maryland clinic had set itself up as a virtual litigation alter ego of the well-funded Waterkeeper group, known for its strident national spokesman Robert F. Kennedy, Jr., and had proceeded to launch legal action against a family chicken farm on the Eastern Shore, a part of the state whose economy is dependent on that line of business. After defenders argued that it would violate the clinic's academic freedom even to ask it to furnish state lawmakers with the names of its clients, the Maryland critics fell back in disarray.

THE ESTABLISHED BAR'S STAKE

Part of the reason for the clinical movement's success is that it did address a very real gap in the curriculum: when the old apprentice/mentor model gave way to the twentieth century's classroom model, much was lost. And hands-on learning works well at engaging some students, just as others are best engaged by book study or classroom give-and-take. Clinics can help with an array of vital practice skills often neglected in the standard curriculum, including fact gathering, client counseling, witness preparation, negotiating, and so forth.

So the clinics serve the interests of practicing lawyers in multiple ways. They train newcomers. Their pro bono aspects help relieve some of the old professional burden of assistance to the poor. And far from cutting into the business of "regular" lawyers, the clinics actually promote their continued prosperity. After all, if nonpaying tenants who would once quietly have moved out manage to postpone eviction with help from a law school volunteer, there will be more work for the landlord's lawyer too. More "access to legal services" for the Waterkeeper people means the chicken-farming family will have to hire lawyers too. Once again everything had worked out for the best for the legal profession in a happy cycle of mutual self-interest.

—m—

Whatever it may have done in the outside world, the rise of clinical law has surely exerted a leftward influence within the law school itself, as to both general atmosphere and faculty governance. Many if not most clinical professors strongly identify with public interest law as a movement, and it is common for them to keep a foot in both camps, actively advising outside litigation groups as well as their own clinics. Indeed, a revolving door of hiring is common in which talent moves back and forth between on- and off-campus litigation groups.

Where law schools remain insufficiently gung-ho for clinicism, steady pressure is kept up. Accreditation committees play a key role; clinical advocates have pushed through rules that require law schools to give directors of clinical programs tenure-like rights and a voice in faculty hiring. One of the last holdouts sticking to the pre-1966 model of legal education was Louisiana State University, but in recent years the ABA has threatened to yank its accreditation unless it too set up a clinical program. Of course no one saw the least menace to academic freedom in *that*.

—⁂—

Alarmed, perhaps, at signs of flagging enthusiasm, advocates have sought to organize a revival. In 1989 the Ford Foundation established something called the Interuniversity Consortium on Poverty Law, whose stated purposes include promoting "the mobilization of law schools for poverty law advocacy." George Soros's Open Society Institute staked impressive sums to enable the American Association of Law Schools to launch an Equal Justice Project, which staged nineteen colloquia attracting more than 2,000 faculty and activists; its final report posited hopefully that the "pendulum of activism among students" was overdue for a favorable swing. Carnegie, Mott, and MacArthur have supported work in an emergent movement that calls itself "Law and Organizing," which proposes that street-level activism is just as valid an application of legal skills as any other.

Virtually every school has a substantial apparatus encouraging students to pursue "public interest" careers after graduation. Except in periods of dire recession, relatively few students from elite schools choose that route; when they do, it is typically to enter government lawyering jobs from which they will jump after a decent number of years into better-paying work on the opposite side of the aisle in such fields as white-collar crime defense and regulatory compliance. Redoubling their efforts, schools have offered tuition-forgiveness programs—Harvard made waves in 2008 with a plan to forgive a year's tuition for students entering public interest work. Other schools have proposed to hold aside a certain share of entering seats for applicants who pledge to practice public-interest, legal-aid, or other favored forms of law after graduation, though how students would be held to such a pledge is far from clear. And some schools, including the tirelessly activist-friendly CUNY and Tulane, have even adopted public interest minimum practice requirements for students generally.

The most politicized examples of the clinic genre are regularly held up as models for emulation. Recall the CUNY "economic justice" program founded to combat welfare reform, the extent of whose politicization can be inferred from its rhetorical boilerplate ("We encourage the students to examine and struggle with the professional and social-justice implications of lawyering for the disempowered and lawyering within an unjust system."). It won prizes from both the Clinical Legal Education Association and the New York State Bar Association.

Then there are the official units increasingly set up within the law school for purposes of "advancing the cause of social justice" (to quote the self-description of the Social Justice Institute at New Hampshire's Franklin Pierce Law School). Sometimes the units are given authority over the school's clinics, as at Seton Hall, whose clinics are now overseen by its Center for Social Justice. Santa Clara's Center for Social Justice and Public Service offers a busy calendar of events including "at least two major lectures each year featuring Critical Race theorists." Vanderbilt's Social Justice Program includes as part of its mission to "ensure that Vanderbilt Law Students receive an education that instills a commitment to social justice." It also

> promotes a wide variety of educational and scholarly activities aimed at exploring the role of law in creating, perpetuating and eradicating hierarchies of power and privilege in our society. The program seeks to address inequalities based on race, ethnicity, gender, sexual orientation and social and economic status, as well as the responsibility of the legal profession to

protect the interests of marginalized, subordinated, and under-represented clients and causes.

—〽—

Are students being indoctrinated? (Sorry, "ensured" of having a "commitment to social justice" fully "instilled" in them, as Vanderbilt puts it, or, as at CUNY, encouraged to "struggle with" the implications of "lawyering within an unjust system.") Well, the subject of indoctrination in the modern law school turns out to have generated a bit of an academic literature itself. Unfortunately, the theme of the literature is that schools are falling down on their duty to indoctrinate and need to be doing a much better job of it. The overall law school experience, complains one report, tends "to undermine student activism." For one thing, the work demands on students are so extreme that little time is left for marches and rallies. But the problems go further. You're "taught to see that there are two equal sides of any issue," as a student complains in one widely cited volume. "Two equal sides" is assuredly a misstatement; no law professor ever would or has presented both sides of all issues as truly equal. But it captures a kernel of truth about standard law training, which is that it conveys the skill of looking for ways in which the other guy—even a polluter, harasser, or bigot—might have something of a case. In being forced to rationalize positions directly opposed to their own, one book laments, "most altruistic-oriented students are confronted with a perspective that seriously upsets their view of justice."

What happens to professors and students who don't find it useful to talk about hierarchies of power and subordinated causes? What if they don't regard economic inequality as presumptively unjust? What if they see Critical Theory as a misguided dead end for the outsiders whose voice it purports to rescue? What if they don't think the legal profession should play favorites on behalf of marginalized as against non-marginalized clients? Maybe the subtext is that those who resist the "instilling" of the requisite "commitment" would be happier at a different school or in a different profession.

But at least no one's academic freedom has been put at risk.

—ᴜᴜ—

The successful launch of public interest law was to have far-reaching effects in the decades that followed. The private litigation groups that soon flourished began to develop for themselves a position of enormous if often hidden discretion and power, first by initiating and managing the suits, thus providing courts with their agenda, and even more so by their later decisions in negotiating with targets of the suits during and after settlement. As a result, the whole nature of the progressive project changed. Down through Lasswell's day it was assumed that many of the brightest progressive-minded law grads would plan on careers in government. After 1970 or so, it was more likely that they would plan on careers in *suing* government. The next few chapters look at how this came to be.

poor *pitiful gulliver*

SOME YEARS AGO, TOWARD THE END OF THE CLINTON
Administration, the Associated Press reported that
officials of the Interior Department were frustrated: they were so swamped by suits demanding
that they enforce the Endangered Species Act that
they were having trouble protecting endangered
species. Under the terms of the law, any private
citizen or group can file an action demanding that
the Department's Fish and Wildlife Service designate some parcel of land as critical habitat for one
of the thousand-plus species on the threatened or
endangered list. Not many of these critical-habitat
petitions originate with biologists concerned about
extinction; most are meant as tactical objections to
one or another prospective land development that
is being opposed for other reasons. Some of these
habitat-protection petitions prove meritorious and
others not, but either way they are quite effective
in stalling development and raising its cost. It was
not that the Clinton Interior Department necessarily frowned on the habitat demands—in general,
it enjoyed reasonably good relations with environ-
mentalist groups. The problem was that responding
to the lawsuits was so close to a full-time job that

the Service could not spare the staff and budget for the arguably more vital task of adding new species to the protected list. In fact its resources had been so thoroughly tied up by the suits that it had failed to add any species at all in the preceding year.

Nor could it escape its plight simply by yielding to litigants' demands. Five years later, another AP item reported on how the Service was being sued by the Agua Caliente Indian tribe for having designated a swath of desert in Southern California as critical habitat for the Peninsular bighorn sheep, thus impairing the tribe's ability to develop 14,000 acres of land. A spokeswoman for the Service said it had designated the land in response to an earlier lawsuit brought by environmentalists. "We get sued to designate critical habitat. Then when the habitat is designated, we get sued again," she said. "Our budget is being used to comply with court-ordered deadlines, leaving us with almost no ability to set our own listing priorities."

—❦—

Somewhere, Franklin Delano Roosevelt's ghost would have understood. In the year 1940, late in his second term, Congress passed and sent to FDR's desk a measure hailed by its supporters as an overdue step in restoring citizen control over government. The Walter-Logan Bill, as it was known after its Democratic sponsors Rep. Francis Walter (Penn.) and Sen. William Logan (Ky.), aimed at improving the public accountability of federal bureaus and agencies—in itself, a universally shared goal. Its most important provision proclaimed a new right of persons affected by government actions to challenge those actions in court. Under the bill, a private complainant could sue on the claim that the agency had acted in a way harmful to his interests *unlawfully*—by overstepping the statutory or Constitutional limits to its powers—or *arbitrarily*—without being able to offer substantial evidence and reasoning to back up its decision. It hardly seemed out of line, after all, to grant every American his day in court. And it was not as if the government was claiming some right to behave unlawfully or arbitrarily. So why should it feel threatened by being made answerable in this way? What could go wrong?

The Roosevelt administration had not concealed its displeasure at the progress of the bill. It conceded that its various departments and agencies had sometimes committed missteps in dealing with the citizenry, and it had tried to establish internal procedures by which mistakes might be appealed and corrected. But agencies were already spending much time in court doing battle with those whose interests were protected under existing common law, such as regulated businesses claiming that federal action had interfered with the use of their land or goods. The Walter-Logan Bill would have conferred standing to sue on a far wider class than that, in fact on anyone "aggrieved" by a given government action, which (as a later author put it) might amount to "practically everybody affected" by such action. Moreover, in requiring that agencies be prepared to show "substantial evidence" to back up their decisions, the bill seemed to invite judges to substitute their own judgment for that of agency officials. Most judges were generalists, lacking expertise in the far-flung and complex subjects of concern to specialized federal agencies. And yet here they were being invited to second-guess decisions that had been based on informed advice from the government's own corps of geologists, bank examiners, pharmaceutical chemists, and so forth.

The bill's fate was a foreordained conclusion: it was sent back without the president's signature. FDR's veto statement was unsparing of the measure's deficiencies. To "subject all administrative acts and processes to the control of the judiciary," he declared, would be to "place the entire functioning of the Government at the mercy of never-ending lawsuits." That would be inconsistent, to say the least, with the kind of purposeful and vigorous decision-making that public managers, just like those in private business, often needed to exercise. In practice, Roosevelt concluded, the bill would usher in "the utmost chaos and paralysis" in public administration.

Beyond that, the President thrashed the motivations of the bill's proponents. Among the most vocal supporters of Walter-Logan had been highly placed members of the organized bar, or as Roosevelt's veto statement described them with some acerbity, "lawyers who desire to have all processes of Government conducted through lawsuits." The nation, however, could ill afford to indulge this group in its parochial if not self-serving taste for "the luxury of litigation." High expense and delay were only the start of the problems with civil litigation as a check on official decisionmaking. "Its technical rules of procedure are often traps for the unwary, and technical rules of evidence often prevent common-sense determinations on information which would be regarded as adequate for any business decision."

Along with lawyers, the measure had also drawn support from political forces and interest groups that had been opposed to his administration, including industries chafing under Roosevelt's tough New Deal regulations. These antagonists might talk about the importance of due process and the right to a day in court all they liked, but the fact was that, for many of them, tying the agencies up in knots was not some sort of unintended effect of the bill: it was exactly what they hoped it would do. Though dressed up in the raiment of procedural fairness, their bill was in fact a disguised bid to gain ground on substance. Through an apparent oversight—one had to assume it was that—the bill's drafters had even forgotten fully to exclude from its coverage the government's most essential task of all, its national defense function, which presumably no one would wish to conduct through lawsuits. The House of Representatives sustained FDR's veto, and the bill failed. Not until six years later did proponents manage to enact the general idea into law, in the form of the 1946 Administrative Procedure Act, which President Harry Truman chose to sign rather than vetoing. And by that time, thanks to the stout resistance of New Deal loyalists, the original ambitions of the Walter-Logan Act had been much trimmed, with the new APA providing a far narrower definition of who could sue as well as less latitude to the courts in second-guessing administrative decisions.

LAOCOÖN ON THE POTOMAC

Today, for managers of many government agencies, litigation and its threat is a time-consuming priority, sometimes the top priority. Although the litigation is usually couched in the form of complaints that an agency is "breaking the law," it often arises from fundamentally political disagreements regarding the direction of government policy. How should scarce funds be allocated? Where should enforcement priorities lie? Should a major new project be built, and if so where? Alexander Hamilton in *Federalist* #70 famously observed that "energy in the executive" can be essential to the "steady administration of the laws." That hope is but a distant one for many executive agencies that today find themselves tangled Laocoön-like in legal coils.

Ironically or otherwise, the sorts of programs for which FDR and the New Deal were so famous—in areas like education, poor relief, and regulation—have been particularly hobbled by litigation. So have the grand-scale public works programs in which the Thirties and Forties abounded—dams, land reclamation, levee-building, power transmission, and so forth. Whole categories of projects and activities requiring extensive government permits and licenses were brought virtually to a halt, including the construction of new nuclear power plants and oil refineries, both of which had once been regarded as key contributors to defense as well as civilian security. And speaking of defense, there is no longer considered to be anything strange about lawsuits that second-guess basic military operations, such as gunnery practice in scenic areas. For years environmental groups have challenged the U.S. Navy's regular Pacific Ocean testing of submarine-detecting sonar, arguing that the resulting sound waves are bothersome to marine mammals. Despite elaborate steps by the Navy to minimize the impact on whales— and repeated efforts by the President and Department of Defense to invoke exemptions to the law on grounds of critical national security concerns—the Ninth Circuit U.S. Court of Appeals has repeatedly ordered a halt to the testing. Opinion in the law schools has generally applauded these developments: the Pentagon, it is explained, must not be "above the law."

Modern legal academia has been instrumental in cheering on, rationalizing, and often helping invent the new developments in administrative law. That includes the liberalization of *standing* (What sort of injury is needed to sue?). And the rise of the so-called *hard look doctrine* (How much deference should courts afford to an agency and its expertise?). And impatience with older rules mandating *exhaustion of remedies* (Should courts avoid interfering until an agency's internal grievance processes have definitely rejected a complaint?). And a greater reluctance to throw out lawsuits on the grounds that they raise *political questions* (Should other branches of government be resolving them?) or lack *justiciability* (Do they call for remedies that courts are simply incapable of providing?).

Proponents of greater judicial supervision of government decisionmaking promised that their new approach would improve the rationality and transparency of agency action, allow greater public participation by previously excluded groups, and substitute judges' impartiality and fairness for improper political considerations. How well they succeeded at these objectives may be judged in the pages ahead.

REICH AND "THE NEW PROPERTY"

If there was such a thing as a peak moment in the media build-up of the Sixties as a phenomenon, it came with the wall-to-wall publicity accorded the Yale professor Charles Reich's bestselling 1970 daydream of liberation, *The Greening of America*. The book briefly made Reich a national celebrity, but his fame in law schools, based on scholarly output not greatly known to the wider public, was to be much longer-lasting. Back in 1964 Reich had published what was destined to become the most-cited article in the history of the *Yale Law Journal*, "The New Property."

The law in general had long drawn a sharp line between rights and privileges. When it came to the right to use and enjoy money and other economic goods, this line tended to track the distinction between acknowledged *property* and what you might call *largesse*. Government could not confiscate property without elaborate procedures and sometimes compensation, but it was free to withhold largesse, or attach unpleasant or unwelcome conditions to its receipt. As one court had pithily explained: "In accepting charity, the appellant has consented to the provision of the law under which the charity is bestowed."

Reich's argument runs roughly as follows. Because of the enormous growth of government, public largesse has come to support whole sectors of society. Countless families and individuals depend on public welfare and social insurance funds. Millions work as government employees or in private employment sustained by government contracts. Still others practice in licensed occupations—not only as doctors and lawyers but as plumbers and opticians, airline pilots and funeral directors—and will be out of work if the government revokes the permissions they need to practice their trades.

It is hard to deny that left to their own devices, governments are sometimes arbitrary or paternalistic in how they dispense these various forms of largesse. Businesses and their employees can lose their livelihood when government contracts are redirected to others through favoritism. Occupational licensure boards have been known to turn down newcomers or strip incumbents of their right to practice for bad reasons, including sometimes the wish to protect members of the incumbent "club" from competition. Even pension and social-insurance checks, which might be expected to arrive on a more or less automatic basis, have sometimes been meddled with, as in a case arising from the security scare of the 1950s in which an alleged subversive was stripped of the veteran's pension otherwise due him. Single mothers as a condition of receiving welfare were (at the time Reich was writing) made to submit to moralizing, or demoralizing, home visits by social workers intended to make sure there was not a live-in boyfriend lurking about who should be supporting them.

Deprivations of this sort might be felt as just as devastating as deprivations of ordinary property, yet there were at the time few rights to sue over most of them. This left government with too much arbitrary power, while leaving the populace with too much uncertainty, too little independence, and too great a fear of the penalties for nonconformity. What was needed was a new sense of property: "The presumption should be that the professional man will keep his license, and the welfare recipient his pension." On exactly how this would be implemented Reich gave few details, but he called for courts to exercise more procedural scrutiny of government decisions to withdraw benefits once granted, and perhaps also its decisions not to grant them in the first place.

Sober in tone and seemingly cautious in its policy proposals, "The New Property" does not on its surface much look like the kind of article capable of kicking off a "rights revolution" in the courtroom, launching on its course the concept of welfare as an entitlement, or doing the other things it has been credited with doing. Part of its durable appeal is that its ideological coloration seems at first hard to make out; observers of many different predilections can read into it their own views. Many of the social problems Reich discussed were in the air, so to speak, in the early 1960s. In applauding "individualism," in raising doubts about the "magnification of government power" and the "dependence" it might instill in recipients, Reich might even have been seen as working in a vein similar to that of Milton Friedman, who had just two years earlier (in 1962) been in the public eye with his book *Capitalism and Freedom*. In one of the most celebrated chapters of that book, Friedman had detailed at length the abuses of occupational licensure and proposed its abolition. And as part of his longtime interest in "negative income tax" proposals, Friedman too criticized some paternalistic and intrusive social-welfare rules that were aimed in part at monitoring and uplifting recipients' way of life.

Reich's idea of making it easier to sue over license denial might come across as a less drastic alternative to Friedman's idea of doing away with professional and occupational boards. And you might argue that by advancing the concept of a right to welfare, Reich was echoing Friedman's critique of welfare bureaucracy. In short, so long as you didn't examine matters too closely, Reich and Friedman might almost come off as co-thinkers in seeking to constrain the size and power of government.

There is much circumstantial evidence (including his foundation-supported contemporaneous work) that establishing welfare as a right was much on Reich's mind when he wrote "The New Property." Yet the article devotes surprisingly little space to examples from that field, spending much more time on examples perhaps more resonant with his audience of highly educated professionals, such as one in which an entirely competent doctor had been menaced with loss of his medical license. What would it mean on a practical level to throw over the old distinctions between rights and privileges, property and largesse, in such areas as government employment? If (say) teachers and principals were to be accorded new quasi-property rights in their jobs, what would the implications be for students, parents, and taxpayers? Although relentless in deconstructing the old distinctions, Reich was determinedly vague about exactly what he expected to happen after they were gone.

—⁓—

The Supreme Court's speedy adoption of the "new property" idea in the years that followed became the stuff of law-school legend. In *Goldberg v. Kelly* (1970), a majority led by Justice Brennan discerned an entirely new Constitutional right not to be cut off from welfare payments without notice and a more than perfunctory hearing. Justice Black, on behalf of the three dissenters, pointed out in vain that of nine million Americans on the welfare rolls, some were certainly collecting benefits to which they were not entitled in either law or fact:

> In other words, although some recipients might be on the lists for payment wholly because of deliberate fraud on their part, the Court holds that the government is helpless, and must continue, until after an evidentiary hearing, to pay money that it does not owe, never has owed, and never could owe. I do not believe there is any provision in our Constitution that should thus paralyze the government's efforts to protect itself against making payments to people who are not entitled to them.

Public interest lawyers were soon gearing up systematic challenges to terms and rules that stood in the way of welfare as an entitlement— work requirements, "man in the house" rules, minimum residency provisions, and so forth. While they did not win every case, they racked up a long series of victories (some later overturned) extending welfare to college students, excluding income from stepparents and others from eligibility calculations, forcing counties to participate in the federal food stamp program, and generally compelling local governments to make the rules of that program more generous, more uniform, and more centrally coordinated. Multiple causes were at work, to be sure, and the assignment of cause and effect can never be exact, but within just a few years participation in welfare programs proceeded to double—the fateful Sixties "welfare revolution."

And the welfare revolution was but emblematic of a wider "due process revolution" of which federal contractors, doctors threatened with loss of their licenses, and government employees were all beneficiaries. The Supreme Court and lower courts also discerned similar due process rights in such areas as school suspensions, juvenile justice, and parole credits owed to prison inmates. To a generation of law professors who assigned Reich's article to incoming students, it all made perfect sense. As time went on, the article came to stand for an even broader proposition: due process aside, courts should start enforcing more positive rights to have government do things on one's behalf, as distinct from negative rights to be left alone by it.

OF SAINTLINESS AND CITIZEN STANDING

A second, equally momentous development was also afoot. *Goldberg* v. *Kelly* and the other early cases involved benefits that inured to complainants personally—the right to receive a monthly check, or to go on attending a certain school, or to be awarded good-time credits toward parole. Under the then-accepted rules of standing and capacity to sue, as commentator Thomas O'Brien has noted, "it took a genuinely aggrieved single person, who could demonstrate an injury to his legal interests, to get into court. Mere ideological interest in challenging state policy was not enough."

The more daring proposition that now began to be heard regularly was that persons (in practice lawyers) should be able to sue over government action in which they had *no* special personal stake—over, say, a decision to permit the tearing down of an admired local building, or to allow some dangerous product to be sold to willing buyers, or to permit some other occurrence detrimental to the public welfare. The answer was to adopt as a concept what went by the name of the "citizen suit," available to anyone at all as a way of getting into court. In practice, the right to file a "citizen suit" usually meant the right to sue the government for not taking action adversarial toward someone *else*.

The key case was almost too perfectly contrived as a morality play pitting saintly complainant against villainous respondent. The Jackson, Mississippi television station WLBT had blatantly supported the segregationist side during the civil rights struggle; in doing so it had probably violated various obligations of licensed broadcasters under the regulations of the Federal Communications Commission. Some on the FCC staff believed the violations were serious enough that the agency should revoke the station's broadcast license when its renewal came up, but the full commission refrained from that step as too drastic. Opponents of the station proceeded to file a court action demanding that the station's license be denied. (Formally, the petition was filed by a group called the Office of Communications of the United Church of Christ, a unit of the historic Congregationalist denomination; notwithstanding its ecclesiastical vestments, the OC-UCC was in fact a loyal Ford grantee that worked closely alongside other civil rights litigators, who perhaps reckoned that the sensitive work of going after people's broadcast licenses was best assigned to a member of the team relatively insulated from political attack.)

The groundbreaking aspect of the resulting court battle was not just that WLBT lost its license, which it did. It was that the church, which had not itself suffered any particular injury, could sue. Indeed, federal courts recognized a momentous new right for anyone at all to file a challenge against any broadcaster's license. In almost no time scores of groups sprang up that used license challenges, or the threat thereof, to arm-twist stations into altering their programming and employment practices. Most of these groups were ideologically tinged, funded by the liberal foundations with the aim of getting (e.g.) more of a minority and female presence in the newsrooms and on the air. But many challengers also arose that were willing to settle for more tangible benefits, ginning up a license challenge and then accepting hundreds of thousands, even millions, of dollars from the broadcaster to go away.

Between similar court decisions and helpful action by Congress, the idea of "citizen standing" had become commonplace as the 1970s got under way. To get into court against the granting of a permit to a power plant, you didn't have to be a landowner with a directly blighted view; it was enough to be someone three states away who was pained at the thought of the blight. Various federal agencies could now be sued by anyone who felt they had not been tough enough in discharging their regulatory duties. For example, anyone off the street could sue the Food and Drug Administration for not taking steps to ban a drug, whether or not they had ever been in any position to consider using that drug (and whether or not other patients passionately wanted that drug to remain on the market).

Meanwhile the courts were starting to ramp up the skepticism with which they evaluated agency action. It was generally acknowledged that the 1946 Administrative Procedure Act signed by President Truman was less legally onerous to agencies than the Walter-Logan Act vetoed by FDR six years earlier. Not only did the APA greatly narrow the liberal standing rules of the earlier bill, but in most cases it instructed courts to strike down government action only if they found it to be "arbitrary and capricious," a standard more lenient toward agencies than that of the unsuccessful bill, which had demanded that they produce "substantial evidence" to back up their decisions. For years thereafter the new Administrative Procedure Act had operated with relatively little controversy as the basic legal framework for government regulation, and it was unusual, though not wholly unheard of, for courts to find agency action arbitrary or capricious.

As the atmosphere changed, however, the trend was toward tougher scrutiny. In a 1971 decision, *Citizens to Preserve Overton Park v. Volpe*, the Supreme Court ruled that despite the seeming lenience of the "arbitrary and capricious" standard, judges should undertake a "thorough, probing, in-depth" inquiry into the agency's decision—the so-called "hard look" doctrine. Complainants were soon winning more cases, just as advocates of the new standard intended.

ONE ADVOCATE'S CANDOR

Few areas were transformed as profoundly as that of environmental litigation, in which many of the new doctrines made an early and strong appearance. And that many of the paralytic effects were recognized at an earlier point—and not just by critics of the new doctrines but by some staunch supporters—can be seen in the 1971 book *Defending the Environment* by the law professor Joseph Sax.

Sax, a prominent figure in environmental law first at Michigan and later at Berkeley/Boalt Hall, was an ardent advocate of the new methods of litigation, lionized over the years by conservation groups; the Ford Foundation itself underwrote his book as part of its push to legitimize the new field. Even so, he is reasonably frank in conveying the yawning gulf between the way idealists might have hoped the new kind of litigation would work and the way it actually did work.

Much of *Defending the Environment* consists of case histories of trailblazing environmental disputes, the centerpiece being the successful effort to halt the construction of a large apartment complex on the banks of the Potomac in Alexandria, Va., just south of Washington, D.C. Sax, who sides wholeheartedly with the objectors, leaves a distinct impression that their triumph owed much to the sowing of destructive legal uncertainty:

No one knows exactly what the lawsuit achieved. Those who initiated it firmly believe that it stopped the project from going forward, if for no other reason because it now put what lawyers call a "cloud on the title" of the developers to the submerged land, and that it served to prevent the obtaining of needed title insurance and financing without which the building could not progress.

Notwithstanding the implications of handing out this sort of weapon to all comers, Sax dismisses as unfounded fears that the new body of law "engenders interminable delay," "acts as an invitation to cranks," or might "impede rational planning" of land use. Instead, he predicts, public decision-makers who are constantly aware of the prospect of being sued will be more likely to "operate rationally, thoughtfully, and with a sense of responsiveness to the entire range of government concerns." Naysayers might talk of paralysis, but Sax blithely sees the likelier result as a "far more limber governmental process"—*limber* being an adjective not often used to describe heavily lawyered-up and adversarial processes, except perhaps in the sense that a person being shot at is said to dance.

Naturally, Sax was strongly in favor of "hard look"-style scrutiny, and one of his constant themes is that courts should cease paying excessive deference to agencies and their claims of superior expertise. The agencies are often political in their thinking, to say nothing of being too close to those they regulate. Judges' deficit in expertise, he announces in what he concedes is a paradox, is in fact their "greatest strength." Unlike administrators they "do not have an agency's program or budget to balance against the merits of a particular case," nor do they maintain ongoing relations with interested constituent groups. Lawmakers or governors trying to help out one side cannot with propriety approach them by way of phone calls. They need not trim or compromise in hopes of making themselves popular or keeping everyone happy. Although perhaps insiders in society by a conventional measure, judges in this context were "outsiders," Sax argued. And outsider status was good, while insider status was—obviously—something to be deplored.

Of course, even if all this made judges the perfect candidates to govern the rest of us, it could not but be observed that their methods of governance might at times be peculiar. In a second case history, Sax tells the story of how a proposed expressway along the Hudson River in New York City was forced by objectors onto an alternate route, not because the court ever got around to addressing the basic environmental objections, but on "utterly fortuitous" and peripheral grounds arising from what he portrays as pettifogging disputes over word definitions and the like. Moreover, and strikingly, he makes clear that this type of resolution is closer to the norm than the exception in these disputes: most judges tenaciously resist reaching and weighing the ultimate merits in this sort of dispute, perhaps recognizing that to do so would require them to step into the agency administrators' shoes and assume the responsibility of evaluating huge amounts of technical information.

Instead, Sax notes, the "great bulk" of environmental litigation was fought on the terrain of process and procedure. Has an agency followed its own rules to the letter? Has it commissioned the right sorts of studies on each relevant issue? According to Sax, with courts avoiding the second-guessing of ultimate destination and instead fly-specking the road map that agencies use to get there, "the result is haphazard instances in which delay of questionable projects can be obtained . . . without the true merits of the controversy ever being considered—while cases are sent back again and again for more administrative fiddling, consuming years of time and scarce resources of money and manpower to make gigantic, and usually pointless, amplified records before some bureaucratic tribunal."

Remember that these are the words of a leading *advocate* of what was happening.

There would always be ample fuel for objectors to get the process started: "in the ever expanding and elaborate procedures that the legislatures impose upon administrative agencies it is usually rather easy to find some procedural blunder or failing that can be called to the attention of a court." Adequate studies? "There is probably not a development plan anywhere in the United States that could not be attacked—as objectors attacked the expressway plans—for failure to study thoroughly some issue." The paradox was that environmental litigation was much better at slowing down construction efforts and running up their cost than at actually providing any firm "no" to bad projects. If the agency were determined enough, it might correct all the paperwork errors it had made in earlier rounds and play-act its way through the mummery of studying each angle and balancing each consideration—and then build the bad project after all.

—⁂—

Proponents described the new rights to sue as a form of "public participation," as if dragging a federal agency to court were the modern-day equivalent of an old-fashioned New England town meeting. And yet the whole topic seemed to attract little durable attention beyond the ingrown community of public interest lawyers and activists. As Jeremy Rabkin recounts, one of the most momentous expansions of the law came when citizen standing was slipped into the Clean Air Act with little discussion or public attention. That was fairly typical: Congress saw such provisions as a relatively cheap sop to environmentalists, consumerists, and other advocates.

For all the talk of public participation, it was evident from the start that some sectors of the public were far more adept than others at using the new methods. In siting an unwanted new disamenity such as a power substation or service truck barn, for example, the localities where the decision is most apt to be sued over are very apt to be those where many well-to-do lawyers (or those who can afford such lawyers) happen to live. Putting the best face on this, Sax portrayed affluent complainants as front-line troops leading a battle that would benefit the rest of society: they might be heading to court for self-regarding reasons, to keep smokestacks out of their back yards, but the rest of us would breathe easier as well when the smoke was done away with. No doubt that analysis holds for some types of environmental disamenity, and yet Sax's own case histories suggest its incompleteness. In two of them, environmental objections led not to the abandonment of proposed highway projects, but to their re-routing through other towns. Was it that the alternate routes were truly less environmentally damaging? Or did they pass through communities with less access to trained legal talent? And how reliably can we distinguish between the two possibilities?

Citizen suits and liberal standing were often defended by way of an appeal to naïve legality—unless we let someone sue to stop them, won't government officials get away with breaking the law? And yet here, too, hardly anyone chose to apply the maxims in any sort of thoroughgoing or across-the-board way. Consider the reception of the concept of "taxpayer standing." Just as government agencies break the law in other ways, so they sometimes behave unlawfully or unconstitutionally in how they spend money. Liberal principles of standing might therefore call for giving any taxpayer, or any citizen whatsoever, the right to sue to block a public expenditure. But (despite interesting experiments in California) the notion of taxpayer standing has generally not caught on, certainly not among legal academics. The reason, no doubt, is all sides' understanding that a proliferation of taxpayer suits would tend to complicate and impede the expansion of government spending, and that spending (at least when not related to the building of dams, roads, and so forth) is seen as predominantly a Good Thing.

But it doesn't stop there. In 1968 a Supreme Court majority decided to poke a hole in the general rule against taxpayer standing by inventing a new right to sue against expenditures that might infringe on the First Amendment by improperly advancing religion. Did this signal a shift in which taxpayer standing would be entertained as a way to vindicate important Constitutional rights? Not at all. It soon emerged that the Court would not allow taxpayer suits challenging *other* potentially unconstitutional expenditures, just the religious kind. It is hard to escape the conclusion that the new standing doctrines have a high tactical or instrumental component, raised and lowered like a drawbridge to admit friends and exclude foes.

—Ɱ—

Sax's book also faithfully reflects and records a steady animosity, typical of its era, toward the conventional workings of representative government. At one point he quotes an activist trying to halt a ski tramway project in the Berkshires who approaches the state legislature in Boston and is shocked to find it in the grip of politics:

> We had tried hard to kill the Authority in the Legislature in 1965 [prior to the successful court action] but failed. This was such an exhausting and frustrating experience that I hate to think about it. It was, as they say, a lesson in "political reality". The reality is that in the Massachusetts legislature (in 1965, anyway), appeals to reason generally don't work; one must play the politicians at their own game, on their own terms, which means he who has the most votes wins.

Legislatures in which he who has the most votes wins—what a disappointment that must have been. At another point, discussing the Hudson River Expressway episode, Sax declares that decision-making in such matters is still afflicted by a "disease," the name of that disease being "politics." With judges as the exception, he damns government officials of almost every sort as mere "insiders" with "insider perspectives" and therefore not to be trusted. (As it happens, several of the political appointees Sax depicts as overly cautious and compromising, such as the LBJ-era interior secretary Stewart Udall, have gone down in history as conservationist icons.) Without the new citizen-suit-driven environmental law, he concludes, the only alternative would be to "leave the public interest to hired hands"— the "hired hands" in question being of course people placed in their positions by the machinery of ordinary representative government. But what of the new class of activist lawyers filing the suits? Weren't they also hired hands—perhaps more accurately, self-hired hands?

Except that you as a voter couldn't fire them.

chapter EIGHT

the permanent government

BEGINNING IN THE 1980S THE CITY OF NEW YORK EMBARKED
on one of the most ambitious social welfare programs ever pursued by an American local government. It set out to house all the city's homeless
inhabitants, not just in the grim cots-in-armories
type of shelter commonly used in other cities, but
in safe and agreeable apartment-style housing.
Toward that end it began renovating for permanent
use by homeless clients a large stock of apartments
in buildings seized for back taxes. Within a decade,
at a construction cost exceeding $1 billion, it had
completed 26,000 living units, enough to house
roughly the population of Cheyenne, Wyoming, or
Olympia, Washington. As one commentator later
noted, New York furnished "more housing for the
homeless than all other large cities combined, [and]
more housing than the federal government provided for the entire country."

The billion dollars spent on construction was
just the start. Clients moving into the units were
provided with new furniture at city expense. And
while waiting for a permanent abode, they were put
up in what the city called transitional housing, often
once-grand hotels in tourist areas of Manhattan.

Keeping a homeless family in such lodgings cost $35,000 a year on average, with side benefits such as restaurant vouchers that might run to hundreds of dollars a week. City outlays on homeless services far outdistanced what other big cities spent.

But it was a funny thing: the harder New York worked to bail out the pool of homelessness need, the faster it seemed to keep filling up again. Most of the new clients showing up, agency staffers noticed, were dressed and groomed in ways that suggested they hadn't been sleeping in the open air. And the applicants were getting to be downright picky about what sorts of placements they would accept. If told the only options that evening were an armory cot or a motel in a remote neighborhood of Queens, some would turn on their heels and depart, their need for shelter seemingly not so desperate after all. Many would come back night after night until offered a desirable Manhattan hotel placement.

Soon it was an open secret: most of the clients showing up were not by any normal definition homeless at all. Many were among the estimated 200,000 to 300,000 city residents living "doubled up" with parents or friends. Declaring themselves to be homeless gave them a shot at getting their own place, which was well worth the discomfort of spending hours or even days slumped on chairs at an intake center. Of course the city did have a very active program of conventional public housing, in fact the nation's largest by far, but it was subject to a six- to eight- year waiting list. As one of the nation's most desirable, expensive, and crowded cities, New York provided a more or less boundless supply of potential clients interested in free housing. Aside from the locals, persons recently living in states as distant as Florida had been known to show up too, and since the courts were quite hostile toward anything that smacked of residency waiting periods for social welfare benefits, the city turned them away at its legal peril. The total client count soared from 7,600 in 1982 to 12,500 in 1983 and 24,900 in 1986, leveled off for a decade and a half, then leaped again to 38,300 in 2003.

No doubt a variety of factors contributed to the debacle of the New York homeless program, including onerous state regulations and the city's own unrealistic early views of what it could achieve. By far the most important factor, though, was litigation. For nearly thirty years, advocacy groups suing the city in pursuit of a judicially created "right to shelter" had won court orders tying the city's hands on a long series of eligibility and policy issues.

In particular, the Legal Aid Society's Homeless Families Rights Project had prevailed on a judge to penalize the city if it did not provide all families with placements within twenty-four hours, even though state regulations on their face seemed to provide it with forty-eight hours in which to do so. The judge likewise struck down city regulations allowing administrators to kick families out of the program for misconduct, requiring clients to discuss with social workers their use of the program, and permitting shelter staff to raise with beneficiaries the touchy subject of workfare jobs. The judge had ordered many other changes as well, requiring, for example, that all hotel rooms for families be fitted out with cooking facilities.

A succession of City Hall administrations of otherwise disparate views—Koch, Dinkins, Giuliani, Bloomberg—joined in pleading in vain for more leeway to run the program. By 2007 the city was spending the better part of a billion dollars a year on "homeless services" and had also been drawn into spending a further $200 million annually on additional social services labeled "homelessness prevention"—bestowing money on poorer city tenants in private housing, or paying for free lawyers with which to fight their landlords' eviction efforts, in hopes of keeping them from becoming eventual shelter clients. Twenty-seven years after the court orders began, no end was in sight.

And the court orders that tied up the homeless program were but a few of the legal ropes binding the municipal Gulliver that was the New York City government. Judges had assumed control of Gotham's foster care system, the special ed division within its schools, its jails and Rikers Island prison, and so on. Each of these branches of city government was governed by a set of dauntingly complex court orders, and city managers interacted regularly with adverse litigants in hopes of getting permission for one or another minor change in policy, forming a sort of mini-government with its own internal political dynamic, quite separate from the official power chart that assigns power within city government. As Ross Sandler and David Schoenbrod of New York Law School note, almost every city effort to change practices at Rikers Island came to require "expensive and time-consuming litigation," down to such matters as city proposals to ban gang jewelry or "change the court-ordered protocol for providing hot food for inmates." Sol Stern describes the everyday workings of the quarter-century-long lawsuit that took control of the city's special-ed program for disabled students, driving its spending along the way to $2.7 billion a year:

> [Michael] Rebell and several other plaintiff lawyers became de facto chancellors of a separate education system—some observers even unofficially called them the Board of Special Ed. They could hire consultants, say how many social workers and special-ed evaluators were needed, and ask for more money for the program. At meetings, the "master," an official appointed by [federal judge Eugene] Nickerson to oversee city compliance with the decree, often asked Rebell: "What should we do now?"

If some Gotham-watchers had by the 1980s come to write the city off as "ungovernable," the court orders were a major reason why. And New York was and is in no way unique: similar court orders on corrections, education, and social services also bind Chicago, Los Angeles, and other cities and states across the country.

"GOVERNMENT BY INJUNCTION"

The most visible branch of judicial power in civil cases is the power to levy damages. The other main branch is the power to order parties either to refrain from or to take some action, called the injunction power. It descends from the Chancery courts, with their system of "equity," administered under looser rules of procedure and evidence than were followed by the common-law courts. As one source puts it, the injunction "seeks to prevent a meditated wrong more than to redress an injury already done." Enforcement of decrees rests ultimately on judges' power to declare parties in contempt of court and, should they remain obdurate or "contumelious," to imprison them. And equity cases, unlike those at common law, proceed without juries, removing one major check on the power of the judge. While injunctions are subject to appeal to higher courts, they are reviewed under a relatively lenient standard ("abuse of discretion") and the judge will have done much to shape the factual record.

Even before they were scathingly immortalized in the pages of Dickens' *Bleak House*, the Chancery courts and their equity jurisprudence had been the target of long and pointed criticism. Being oriented more toward the development of a paper record and less toward public trial, they were bureaucratic, impenetrable, and above all slow. It was hard to get cases over with because the sprawling, untidy nature of equity often reached out to draw in multiple parties and claims. And equity confided so much discretion to the judge in charge that case outcomes could be hard to predict, varying wildly depending on which judge happened to be hearing the case. The justice meted out in Chancery, according to a famous old saying, was measured by the length of the Chancellor's foot, and each Chancellor's foot was of a different size.

Long ago, partly as a response to such concerns, the courts' equity power had been hedged about with many limiting doctrines and maxims that served to narrow judges' discretion and discourage unnecessary use of the process. Thus injunctions were deemed an "extraordinary remedy" reserved for situations when "irreparable injury" was imminent and ordinary after-the-fact legal relief would fail. Decrees were supposed to be closely "tailored" to the injuries to be prevented and the earlier violations proved, and were to operate only against named persons or entities, not against the world at large.

—⚬—

It is a truism of politics that rival factions periodically swap stances with each other on questions of process, so that those who staunchly defend the Senate filibuster or the president's recess appointment power during one era switch to the opposite position after the political landscape undergoes a reversal. In American legal debates, the shifts of opinion on the judicial injunction power have been of the most neck-wrenchingly hairpin nature. During the first

half of the twentieth century the progressive wing of American politics ardently deplored "government by injunction," while conservatives countered by proclaiming that without broad powers of this
sort the courts could not protect individual rights. In the century's
second half—as on a sports field where the home team and visitors
trade sides at half-time—it was the conservatives who chafed at governance by court order and the progressives who were well pleased
with it.

The injunction had long been closely associated with the rights
of property owners and in particular those of the employers of labor.
Businesses often sought and obtained injunctions against coercive
tactics used by unionists during strikes, such as intimidation of visitors at factory gates. In one of the archetypal texts of proto-New
Deal legal scholarship, *The Labor Injunction* (1930), Felix Frankfurter
and Nathan Greene presented an exhaustive critique of this litigation and its results. While not defending blockades or violence,
Frankfurter and Greene made clear that the remedies intended to
restrain those evils brought many evils of their own. Injunctions
often displayed *overbreadth*, for example, laying bans on actions not
in themselves unlawful (such as approaching nearly to a business's
door in groups) and using the misconduct of some strikers to justify
restraints on all. Thus a plaintiff employer might seize on scattered
reports of violence to obtain a broad injunction curtailing protests at
plants where nothing improper had gone on.

Moreover, business owners with lawyers on ready retainer had
deployed the injunction as a *tactical* weapon, a way to take the legal
offensive and inflict cost, difficulty, distraction, and reputational
damage on the opponent. The burdens of courtroom defense itself
did much to wear down strikers' morale and momentum ("even if
we win, we lose," one labor leader lamented) to the point that just
being rid of the litigation was a reason to accept a bad deal to end a
strike. Litigation also worked well at sowing divisions in the union
camp, causing friction between more and less risk-averse factions.
It even happened on occasion that the suits were collusive, with the
nominal defendant consenting to go through a mock show of dispute
to obtain an order whose real purpose was to bind others not present
in the courtroom.

Finally, given the unchecked discretion afforded judges, the injunction mechanism was not reliable *as law*. Judge A. would rule one way and Judge B. the other, depending on biases and presuppositions arising from the circles in which they moved. "The heart of the problem," wrote Frankfurter and Greene, "is the power, for all practical purposes, of a single judge to issue orders, to interpret them, to declare disobedience and to sentence."

The landmark Norris-LaGuardia Anti-Injunction Act of 1932, among the century's most significant labor enactments, was grounded to a significant extent on Frankfurter and Greene's arguments. And the injunction's use in labor disputes was not the only reason for its unpopularity among progressives. Courts had often used the power to block the enforcement of newly enacted statutes on constitutional or other grounds. In response, liberals and progressives successfully steered through Congress a series of measures stripping away or otherwise restraining the jurisdiction of federal courts to issue injunctions against governments. In the Tax Injunction Act of 1937, Congress forbade federal judges from enjoining the collection of state taxes which could have been challenged in state court instead. Much later, it would be liberal opinion leaders who would deplore what they termed "court-stripping" measures. But at this point they enthusiastically cheered them on.

Then everything changed, with the 1954 decision in *Brown* v. *Board of Education*.

—⟋⟍—

In the series of cases that followed *Brown*, the federal courts aggressively used the injunction power to compel desegregation by recalcitrant school districts and southern governments, often in the teeth of blatant defiance, a circumstance that had long provoked even mild-mannered judges into using the injunction power. Some who approved of these injunctions viewed the case of Jim Crow and segregation as *sui generis*, but that was not the view that came to predominate on law school campuses. There, the sweeping injunctions that followed *Brown* were seen as not only right in themselves, but as *the* model that should henceforth be applied in other areas of law.

Yale's Owen Fiss, the best-known academic theorist and admirer of the new institutional litigation, observed: "Indeed, by the late 1960s, *Brown* was viewed as so legitimate that it commonly functioned as an *axiom* [his emphasis]—a decision of unquestioned correctness, a starting point for normative reasoning in domains far removed from schools and race. It was the foundation for arguments of the form, 'If this use of the injunction is denied, *Brown* is being denied, and therefore, this use cannot be denied."

Among the first effects was to advance a movement, backed by strong support from law schools, to apply the new injunction techniques for the assistance of inmates of custodial institutions such as prisons, mental asylums, and juvenile justice systems. Many had suffered from neglect and deplorable conditions which (it was argued) should be recognized as systematic constitutional violations. The remedy was clear: federal judges should not just order a change in particular individuals' treatment, but should take these institutions by the collar the same way southern counties had been taken after *Brown*, with plenary orders accompanied by timetables and specifics. Conveniently, the new and wider availability of the class action format made it easier to put suits in motion representing entire groups of program clients. A 1964 Supreme Court case soon threw open the procedural gates for class lawsuits on behalf of prisoners.

COURTS AS LEGISLATORS

The resulting phenomenon, known variously as *institutional reform litigation* or *public law litigation*, was unlike anything seen before the Warren era. School districts' practices on race, of course, fell under widespread judicial decree in both South and North. But courts also took over control of child welfare departments in thirty-five states, prisons in more than forty, and jails in all fifty. Other courts grabbed the management reins of police forces, public housing authorities, foster care programs, state education agencies, and many other operating units of the modern state. The process thrust courts deeply into management, with reform orders often going on for hundreds of pages specifying such details as the required square footage of prison cells, the wattage of light bulbs, the temperature at which food had to be served, and so forth. Following the landmark *Serrano* decision in California, courts in more than half the states took control of school financing systems, ordering the redistribution of hundreds of billions of dollars through various combinations of "Robin Hood" equalization schemes, mandated tax increases, and payments to underachieving districts.

Prominent legal academics greeted these developments with great if not rhapsodic enthusiasm. Fiss, of Yale, hailed it as a "Second Reconstruction" recognizing the "new social reality" of our era, in which courts replayed the *Brown* script for many other social institutions: a "total transformational process in which the judge undertook the reconstitution of an ongoing social institution," in so doing (to quote Fiss's not un-grandiose formulation) "giving meaning to our public values."

The Harvard law professor Abram Chayes's 1976 law review article "The Role of the Judge in Public Law Adjudication" was to become the standard account of the newly emergent litigation format, and one of the most cited law review articles of its day, perfectly encapsulating as it did the emergent wisdom. Chayes observed that in the new injunction many of the defining features of traditional litigation had seemingly vanished, including a finite array of parties in clear opposition to each other, a conception of the judge as passive umpire between the two, and a goal of remedying a specific past injury or preventing a specific future one. A much-observed drawback of the old system of equity—that instead of reaching definite and final resolutions, cases instead meandered over a longer course in inchwise phases through ambiguous postures—had been heightened to the point that it was no longer clear whether or when the litigation process would sputter to an end at all.

At the same time many of the tasks judges were beginning to take on at the agencies they ran—budgeting, personnel decisions, priority-setting, ordering statistics collection, and so forth—had long been considered peculiar to the executive and legislative branches of government. Some critics had begun decrying this as entrenchment on the rightful prerogatives of other branches and suggesting that if it continued, judges might bring on themselves the mantle of legislators, with the risk that the judicial process itself might come to be politicized. To which Chayes's answer was essentially: What's so scary about that? Cheerfully acknowledging that the "whole process begins to look like the traditional description of legislation," he dismissed the separation-of-powers concerns and called for welcoming a new age in which "litigation inevitably becomes an explicitly political forum and the court a visible arm of the political process." Judges, he argued, are both more independent-minded and more public-spirited than legislators; they even (contrary to what had been thought about them over the centuries) can draw on wider and more reliable sources of information in weighing and balancing policy. They would do a better job of setting fiscal priorities. Or, put differently: stop worrying about judges starting to act as legislators; they'll do a better job at it than the ones you elect.

—∿∿—

Until the 1960s, Duke's Donald Horowitz has written, court orders directed to governments were typically not only rare but terse and easily understood, along the lines of "issue this permit" or "release this person from custody" or "don't bulldoze this house." The new-style injunctions, by contrast, often mapped out grand compliance plans stretching years into the future, with murky and subject-to-revision goals, day-to-day court involvement in picayune details, and commands that defendants raise and spend more than incidental sums of money.

A chief complaint against the old labor injunction, it will be recalled, was overbreadth. By letting the named strikers stand in for potential disrupters in general, courts would sometimes be persuaded to issue orders imposing onerous rules on the previously blameless. It works that way in modern institutional reform litigation too: evidence of misconduct at certain station houses or special education failures at certain schools can call forth stringent court orders binding the entire police force or school system. Scattered allegations of hiring bias can result in broad restrictions on promotions of whites or males, most of whom never benefited from earlier favoritism.

Since judges have many other cases to tend to, they began routinely installing "special masters" or monitors to oversee day-to-day implementation of their orders. Federal rules had long discouraged the use of such masters in any but "exceptional" situations and for any but limited purposes such as fact-finding. Now, however, masters began doing almost everything a judge could do, maybe more: ruling on motions, auditing compliance, determining contempt, and presiding over negotiations between parties. In a big case the special master might work as a full-timer, opening an office at the prison system or school district headquarters while reporting to the judge. The defendant would have the privilege of shouldering the master's often-substantial fees, along with those of other pricey experts and consultants, and of course the plaintiff's lawyers themselves, payable under "one-way" fee-shifting rules.

Because suits are couched as class actions, lawyers are usually the parties in real control. They can select as figureheads clients whose stories reflect the desired public profile of the suit, but who will not engage in backseat driving on how to run it. If they talk back too much, they might even find themselves replaced with other representative clients. Most members of the represented class, of course, never find their opinions consulted at all.

An old, deceptively simple-sounding maxim of equity had been: "Equity will not issue a decree it cannot enforce." One way to read that maxim is as a caution against embarking on what might prove the juridical equivalent of a land war in Asia, issuing orders that are either impractical or of a vagueness or complexity such that determining compliance will require a second round of litigation as elaborate as the first. Now, as compliance efforts fell short, judges and their agents began inevitably to be drawn into a messy process of threats and ultimatums, negotiations and jawboning, wheedling and logrolling, directed not only at defendants but at obdurate third parties, such as state lawmakers reluctant to vote the contemplated funding. Although supervision was initially assumed to be temporary, judges can and do keep control of institutions for twenty, thirty years, or more, yielding up control only if they're persuaded that noncompliance is no longer at serious risk of recurring, in many cases an exercise in intrinsically subjective guesswork.

POLITICS BY OTHER MEANS

Perhaps the oldest complaint about equity was that what kind of justice you got depended on which judge you happened to draw. Nothing had changed in that department either. Consider the New York City homeless program litigation. While many New York judges would no doubt have thrown out that litigation at an early stage, the plaintiffs had been lucky enough to draw the Manhattan state judge Helen Freedman, who had very close ties to the public-interest-law establishment (her husband directed Columbia's Center for Social Welfare Policy and Law, the nation's best-known welfare-rights legal advocacy group). Judge Freedman proceeded to rule over the homeless program for twenty-five years, routinely siding with the plaintiffs. The very liberal Dinkins administration, for example, chose to fight Judge Freedman's order that the city place all families within twenty-four hours of their arrival at the intake office, which it said was not always possible given its available physical housing stock. Judge Freedman responded—in the "we're the boss around here" spirit for which equity courts had long been held in dread—by ordering four city officials to spend the night personally in the emergency shelter. (A higher court agreed that order went too far, in one of the city's infrequent successes on appeal.)

On another occasion Freedman decreed that if the city took too long to place applicants it would have to pay them cash penalties; signs announcing the entitlement to fines were encouragingly mounted on the walls of intake offices. Before long the city had paid out millions of dollars, including several thousand apiece to a number of families each of whom had showed up dozens of times. Higher courts deferentially upheld most of the judge's rulings, and even occasional successes on appeal for the city would typically just send matters back to Judge Freedman for further litigation. In 2005 an independent panel appointed by the judge herself recommended that the city be released from court oversight; she ignored its findings. In the round of litigation that followed, the Legal Aid team forced the city to assemble and turn over another 300,000 pages of documents; paperwork on the case had long since filled an entire room at the city's legal offices.

—⟶ɯ⟶—

Institutional reform litigation was at first praised as a superior alternative to the workings of interest-group politics in public governance. It soon emerged as a way for shrewd interest groups to pursue politics by other means. The Campaign for Fiscal Equity, which runs the school finance suit currently ongoing in New York, does not bother to conceal its close working ties to the New York City teacher's union and to various school districts that would benefit from the billions in additional spending it sues for. Indeed, school finance litigation itself has changed substantially over the years as it was shaped by the self-interest of various key players in the educational provider establishment who came to throw their support behind the suits. Thus early *Serrano*-style fiscal equalization theories fell by the wayside because they could too easily result in budget cuts within a state's highest-spending districts. They were instead replaced by suits on new "educational adequacy" theories which directed judicial pressure toward spending increases alone, a happier outcome for the provider groups.

While not all public-interest-law groups filing such suits were radical or intransigent in their stands, the whole process seemed to attract and reward those who were; it held out few inducements to be moderate. As has often been recounted in histories of the era, much of the 1960s welfare litigation pursued a calculated strategy mapped out around 1966 by the circle of sociologists, political scientists, and lawyers around Columbia's Center for Social Welfare Policy and Law, of whom the best known were the husband-and-wife team Richard Cloward and Frances Fox Piven. As Steven Teles and other historians have related, the Cloward-Piven circle aimed at precipitating a crisis by encouraging the filing of so many legal actions that the cost of existing programs would overwhelm state and local budgets. Once that collapse had been brought on, political pressure would force the federal government to step in with a uniform generous nationwide program.

Crisis strategies—in which impractical court demands and chaotic results are conceived not as a bug but as a feature—seem to recur often in institutional reform litigation. Thus the Washington University professor Margo Schlanger, a strong supporter of prison overcrowding litigation, has acknowledged that much of it is in practice meant to "further a decarceration strategy" by "mak[ing] incarceration both difficult and expensive." An advocate writing in the *California Law Review* early on frankly described the crisis strategy of some prison litigation proponents: "They are convinced that implementing prisoner's rights will upset the balance of power within the institutions, making prisons as we know them inoperable."

Frequently, many members of the ostensible beneficiary class neither want nor welcome the changes ushered in by court order. Overcrowding suits often result in inmates' transfer from a cramped and rundown in-town facility to a more modern but remote facility that is harder for friends and family to visit. Many Texas inmates who held jobs as clerks and nurses under the old trusty system were angered when the court ordered their jobs abolished, to be replaced by newly hired public employees on the taxpayer's dime. In one consent decree, New York City agreed to elaborate new rules restricting its ability to evict disruptive families from its housing projects. But most residents in fact feared the crime spawned by such households, with the result that leaders of the projects' tenant councils wound up hiring lawyers to intervene in the proceedings against their "own" side.

DEFENDANTS WHO WANT TO LOSE

Many institutional reform lawsuits are in fact not nearly as adversarial as they might appear on the surface. The lawsuit may demand that the agency modernize its facilities, hire more staff, and even (no! anything but that!) lobby for higher annual budgets from lawmakers. The resulting court order can lock the agency into policies it was glad to adopt anyway while tying the hands of voters, budgeters or later administrations who might take a different view. As one jail official explained:

> we used "court orders" and "consent decrees" for leverage. We ranted and raved for decades about getting federal judges "out of our business"; but we secretly smiled as we requested greater and greater budgets to build facilities, hire staff, and upgrade equipment. We "cussed" the federal courts all the way to the bank.

In one case, outside lawyers sued a federal agency to force the expenditure of $18 million in unspent funds, and the result was a cozy deal in which, to quote the magazine *Regulation*, the agency pledged "to divvy up the funds by giving roughly half to various advocacy and legal services groups and half to a number of grant programs which the agency had been unable to interest Congress in funding. . . . Later, in a dramatic turnabout, the Chicago judge who had approved the decree vacated it. He explained that he had been 'lulled by the appearance of an adversarial situation' into approving 'an unjustified substitution of judicial fiat for legislative action.'" Duke's Horowitz, getting at the same point, refers to the phenomenon of "defendants who would like to lose."

In school finance litigation it became a regular part of plaintiffs' strategy to approach staffers or high-level administrators at the defendant state education department to point out how much new money might flow to its operations should a judge be prevailed on to rule in the suit's favor. The result is that the departments have often wound up feeding information to their nominal opponents, advising them on strategy, and even taking the stand as openly friendly witnesses, notwithstanding the contrary interests of their putative taxpayer bosses. Thomas O'Brien notes that in New York forty-two of the fifty-eight friendly witnesses called by the plaintiffs worked for one or another branch of the state government, including the head of the state education department and seven employees.

Plaintiffs in the Alabama school finance litigation having "forged an early and important alliance" (as one lawyer recalls) with the state department of education, a court eventually acknowledged the department's true posture by allowing it to switch in mid-suit from a role as defendant to one as plaintiff. Similarly, in a celebrated school finance case that reached the U.S. Supreme Court, the San Antonio, Texas district was originally named as a defendant in the suit, then dismissed, and eventually allowed back in as an intervenor on the plaintiff's side in a case that still bore its name as defendant. It was as if both sides of the litigation were conspiring together against the voters and taxpayers.

WHEN "CRISIS STRATEGY" WORKS

Has institutional reform litigation been a success? It's true that it has shaken up some badly run institutions and helped put an end to some widely detested abuses. At the same time, the public backlash it provoked set many liberal causes back by a generation. School desegregation itself, after its grand initial victories, soon blundered into the comprehensive disaster of the busing wars. Mental hospital reform, while closing down some very bad and some less-bad institutions, led to the dumping of hundreds of thousands of patients into community settings that often degenerated into unmedicated madness on the streets. Prison-reform orders helped clean up some of the nation's worst penitentiaries but also demoralized staff and destabilized complicated balances of power, with the result that inmate violence and gang activity skyrocketed in some systems. When a judge ordered a cap on the number of arrestees Philadelphia could hold in jail, word soon spread on the street that the city was letting perpetrators go after their bookings, and thousands of additional crimes were committed during the resulting lawbreaking spree. In case after case the public reacted with revulsion to endless sagas of runaway expense, unintended consequences, disruptive showdowns and brinksmanship, strategic behavior by litigants, and inability to achieve finality.

While results have varied widely from state to state, school finance litigation has had more calamitous failures than arguable successes. In New Jersey, where thirty-five years of continuous litigation has resulted in voter anger that toppled both a governor and a legislative majority perceived as too friendly to the court orders, an investigation by the *New York Times*—not exactly a source hostile toward suits of this sort—found the results of the "ambitious court-ordered social experiment" to be dismal, with millions wasted by scandal-wracked school managements and the highest-spending poor districts "making the fewest gains." In California, voters reacted to a stringent equalization plan by passing Proposition 13, the tax-limit measure which unexpectedly cut a huge chunk of the former property tax base out from under the state's public schools, with highly disruptive effects.

Did the court orders at least improve fairness? Richard Arun's 2003 book *Judging School Discipline* found that where courts had been active in second-guessing school punishments, students perceived the discipline at their schools to be not only less strict but also less fair. Part of the reason why may be conveyed by one teacher's comment: "It all depends on who you grab. Grab the dumb ones—they don't know what the hell to do. Don't grab a lawyer's kid." Another court took control for decades of the federal government's civil rights enforcement efforts in the field of education. One effect of the takeover, found Jeremy Rabkin, was to skew enforcement toward the priorities of complainants who were relatively sophisticated about using the legal system, such as middle-class parents in search of special-education services and feminists seeking to influence universities' hiring practices.

Even relatively successful litigation often fails to secure its ultimate goals, stated or otherwise. The "crisis strategy" in welfare litigation, for example, did work, but only up to a point: outlays soared as intended, putting local finances under much pressure for a while. But at the same time public opinion—which as late as the early 1960s had been strongly supportive of the welfare program and backed steps to make it more generous—turned sharply hostile, quite possibly dooming the legislative prospects for a generous national program. As Congress swung behind the new mood, many of the early courtroom gains were reversed by legislative action. The Supreme Court, for its part, had stopped short of announcing the sort of constitutional entitlement that would have lifted the welfare program (forever?) above legislative challenge, which meant the continuing political pressure for cutbacks and work requirements, while subject to much delay through rear-guard legal efforts, could not be stalled indefinitely. Welfare advocates found their cause a perennial drag on liberal election prospects until reforms were at last adopted into law under the Clinton administration.

In the prison-crowding area, likewise, crisis strategy worked as to some of its secondary objectives while failing spectacularly in an ultimate sense. As intended, the litigation drove up the cost of imprisonment tremendously in many states, and also sometimes achieved the goal of rendering prisons ungovernable, at least for a time. What hardly anyone anticipated was that the public and its elected officials would prove willing to spend vast amounts to build new prisons that could withstand the litigation siege. The ensuing prison-building boom was certainly not what the litigators had had in mind. And following outcries over such episodes as the Philadelphia court-order-enabled crime spree, Congress enacted a bill restricting prisoner litigation more sharply than would have been dreamed possible even a few years earlier.

To cries of dismay from academia, the Supreme Court has backtracked from much of its earlier enthusiasm for institutional litigation, even beyond its early and prudent retreat on busing. In one widely noted case it ruled that a court order prescribing complaint procedures for police brutality had gone too far in infringing the "latitude" local authorities needed to run city affairs. In another it declined to rule that the "double bunking" of pretrial detainees (two in a cell) was a due process violation. It has suggested that court decrees ought not to be so tightly drawn that defendant institutions cannot adapt to changes in conditions, and has accorded more leeway for defendants to ask for the decrees to be lifted, disengaging from earlier principles that had encouraged the orders to stretch on more or less indefinitely.

—ᴍ—

Occasionally one hears talk that these developments have spelled an end to the era of heroic, sweeping institutional reform litigation. But as New York's homeless-program saga makes clear, lawsuits continue to tie local hands in ways that pre-1960s lawyers would have considered faintly incredible. A sampling of recent news stories furnishes examples:

- Six years after a federal judge appointed a monitor to watch over the Cincinnati police following charges of racial bias in policing, city officials were still locked in a bitter dispute over the $1 million annual bill for the monitor's services, which when itemized turned out to include billing for talking to newspaper reporters, attending an NAACP banquet, and preparing for travel to Ohio from the monitor's base in Berkeley, California.
- As the state of California careened toward fiscal crisis, a monitor threatened to seize $8 billion from its treasury to pay for court-ordered improvements in its prison health system. The monitor had been negotiating for months with the administration of Governor Arnold Schwarzenegger, but said his patience was running out. Sacramento lawmakers had dragged their heels on a plan to float bonds to pay for the plan, some saying they thought the ongoing lack of health insurance coverage for many non-inmate Californians should be given higher priority.
- Plaintiffs fared less well in another widely publicized lawsuit which asked a federal court to order the federal Veterans Administration to broaden the mental health services made available to returning Middle East veterans. Judge Samuel Conti politely declined the request, writing that whatever the grievances' merits, they should have been addressed to the VA itself or to Congress.

Fading away? If anything, this litigation has been normalized as an everyday part of public governance. At any given moment, the press pays attention to at most a few of the hundreds of active suits and decrees. And precisely because its workings have fallen into a shadow of obscurity, institutional reform litigation is a remarkably effective way for litigators and their academic allies to exercise a power in American public life that is hidden, unaccountable, and irresponsible.

THE "CONTROLLING GROUP"

The standard rap against institutional reform litigation is that it gives too much power to the judge. But in their thorough and devastating book *Democracy by Decree*, Ross Sandler and David Schoenbrod say the larger problem is the power it gives the advocacy groups that control the suits. The public might rail at the judge who signs the decree, but in most cases it will have been private lawyers who drafted most of the decree's language.

Settlement, of course, is the rule: most institutional reform cases are resolved by negotiated consent decrees rather than unilateral judicial decision, just as most criminal cases result in plea bargains rather than trials, and most successful damage claims in insurance settlements rather than jury awards. A distinctive feature of the injunctive device, though, is that the terms lawyers include in consent decrees are often quite different from anything the judge would or even could have ordered. Sandler and Schoenbrod: "In the horse trading that produces the plan, some rights are let slide and commitments unessential to vindicating any rights are included in the plan because they seem like good ideas to the controlling group. [. . . Administration of the decree] typically results in the decree broadening. One reason for this broadening is that some of the hopeful ideas in the original decree prove unworkable, so defendants must ask plaintiff's attorneys to consent to modifications. As the price of consent, plaintiffs usually demand adding new requirements to the decree." Thus does a decree originally fifty pages long grow to hundreds, expanding into entirely new areas of agency policy at the will of the "control group"—itself a term pregnant with meaning.

It would be hard to find a process less transparent or accountable. Sunshine, open-records, and public-meetings laws commonly require agencies to make important decisions following advance notice, with the public invited to be present, to publish a detailed record of what has been done with supporting reasons, to grant any citizen's request later for minutes and documents, and so forth. Some agencies are even forbidden to hold informal meetings with interested groups behind closed doors, lest it appear those groups are getting special access.

These sunshine and openness rules are entirely forgotten when policy decisions are hammered out behind closed doors by litigation insiders. Both initial settlement negotiations and later rounds of decree management and renegotiation commonly take place in private sessions from which the press and curious public are excluded. Even scholarly researchers who show up asking for case documents may be sent packing as intermeddlers, although both parties in the litigation claim to be representing broad public constituencies. It is even common for the text of the decree itself to be withheld from the public: thus as one account notes, at a time when the long-running *Jose P.* consent decrees over the New York City special education program had grown to 515 pages in length and were directing the allocation of hundreds of millions of dollars a year, they had never been actually published anywhere for outsiders to look at, not even in periodicals devoted to special education litigation.

—ᴍ—

At the time these suits were becoming popular, a catch-phrase was popular in vaguely radical circles: the "permanent government." The idea is that some interests in society wield such durable power that whatever illusion of choice voters may be given, whichever nominal officeholders may come and go, the real power remains in the same hands. And yet something of the sort happens every time we allow institutional litigation and consent decrees to privatize policy-making, delegating it to a control group of zealous organizations and attorneys unanswerable to the public. As Sandler and Schoenbrod note, the upshot of forty years of litigation is that private advocacy groups (and even in some cases individual private attorneys) in effect "own" entire fields of public policy "by virtue of their command of the court orders. The Eastern Paralyzed Veterans Association owns the issue of accessibility in many jurisdictions . . . the Children's

Defense Fund and Children's Rights, Inc., own foster care, and so on."

New Property, indeed. And meanwhile the legal status of the old property was changing in disturbing ways as well.

chapter NINE

"responsibilities flow eternal"

THROUGH MOST OF THE CENTURY AND A HALF SINCE 1865, when the Thirteenth Amendment abolished slavery, the idea of legal action demanding reparations for slave descendants was widely dismissed as a fringe cause, outside the political mainstream and with no practical hope of success. Then suddenly in the late 1990s a concerted campaign for reparations began winning respectful notice in the mainstream press, support from big-city lawmakers, and scattered endorsements from liberal publications and organizations.

Excitement built quickly, and late in the year 2000 a task force of prominent lawyers announced they were preparing the first of a series of giant lawsuits to recover ill-gotten wealth attributable to slavery and its aftermath. The venture had drawn as participants big-name attorneys like Richard (Dickie) Scruggs, Johnnie Cochran, and Willie Gary, some of whom had recovered billions of dollars for clients in class actions and mass tort cases, as well as nonlawyers like Randall Robinson, the author of the bestselling book *The Debt: What America Owes Blacks*. "This will be the most important case in the history of our country," one of the lawyers said.

The public spokesman for the reparations working group was none other than the Harvard law professor Charles Ogletree, Jr., the director of the school's clinical programs and a longtime activist who had edited a Black Panther newspaper in his youth. While Ogletree "declined to discuss specifics," the Associated Press reported, he said the group planned to sue "both public and private parties" and "had already held a series of planning meetings" toward that end. "We will be seeking more than just monetary compensation" Ogletree said. "We want a change in America." The United States, he charged, "has never dealt with slavery." The AP coverage also nodded in passing to the views of unnamed opponents who "say it isn't fair for taxpayers and corporations who never owned slaves to be burdened with possible multibillion dollar settlements."

Many onlookers were taken aback by the sudden emergence of the reparations issue on the national scene, but those who followed the state of opinion at America's law schools had less cause for surprise. There, the subject had been vigorously agitated for a decade, with activism on every major campus and scholarly contributions from a wide array of faculty, most of whom made clear their sympathy for the cause. As a legal matter, the campaign has fared poorly—for now at least. Courts have rejected reparations suits, and the cause proved particularly badly suited to the mood of the nation. Why had it proved so well suited to the mood of the law schools?

" . . . HE'S DEAD AND NOBODY OWES ME ANYTHING"

In his conquering march through Georgia, General William T. Sherman issued orders providing that each newly freed slave family be provided with forty acres of confiscated land and a mule. Some hoped the U.S. government would adopt and formalize such a policy after the Civil War ended, but that was not to be, and over the decades that followed the idea eventually subsided into a historical footnote. Interest in reparations momentarily flared anew in 1915 when one Cornelius J. Jones sued the U.S. Department of the Treasury demanding $68 million in compensation for former slaves, to be financed by a tax on raw cotton. But a federal appeals panel upheld the dismissal of that action as barred by the government's sovereign immunity.

Half a century later, at more or less the height of Sixties giddiness, it once again returned to the headlines. Grantmaking by liberal church groups had resulted in the founding of a group calling itself the National Black Economic Development Conference. In 1969 this outfit issued a curious manifesto announcing a series of demands it was making in the collective name of American blacks as reparations for slavery and its aftermath. The first of the demands, in the nature of a down payment, was for the sum of $500 million, to be paid by "the Christian white churches and the Jewish synagogues" (that is to say, more or less its own benefactors). It intended to take charge of this sum itself, applying it to various separatist and propaganda enterprises.

Helping propel the message onto the front pages was the manner in which it was delivered. The manifesto's guiding spirit, the black radical James Forman, publicly declaimed the demands by interrupting Sunday services at the nation's best-known citadel of liberal Protestantism, New York's Riverside Church. Soon Forman's followers were disrupting services in other cities. Indeed, the manifesto itself threatened to back up its demands with a campaign of "total disruption" of target church institutions. Along with sit-ins at worship services, it vowed to "seize the offices" of church agencies and hold them "in trusteeship until our demands are met. . . . The principle of self-defense should be applied if attacked." The capitalist system, it announced, needed to be brought to an end "by whatever means necessary, including armed struggle. . . . ALL ROADS MUST LEAD TO REVOLUTION."

This being the height of the Sixties, there was much earnest discussion of whether the justice of the demands should be acknowledged at once and apologies made for having driven Forman and his followers to such exasperation. The era's bulletin board of fashionable radicalism, the *New York Review of Books*, reprinted the manifesto in its pages, and the affair became a full-blown *cause célèbre*, drawing fifteen *New York Times* mentions in 1969 alone. Within the liberal churches themselves, some hailed the manifesto as "prophetic," while others were put off by its tone and thought it regrettable that (as it was briefly speculated, at least) congregations might henceforth need to line up police protection. As it happened, the NBEDC itself disappeared from the scene almost as swiftly as it had stormed on; charges soon circulated that its leadership was spending donations for personal benefit rather than the advertised revolution-making purposes, at which point even the Episcopalians gave up on them.

Before playing itself out, the affair stimulated a good bit of talk about the pros and cons of reparations. The maverick civil rights activist Bayard Rustin, writing in *Harper's*, dismissed with some asperity the idea's pretensions to justice: "If my grandfather picked cotton for fifty years, then he may deserve some money, but he's dead and nobody owes me anything." Rustin furthermore predicted that demands of this sort would tend to cut blacks off from hopes of a political alliance with working-class whites. And an editorial in the *New York Times*, of all places, urged caution: "There is neither wealth nor wisdom enough in the world to compensate in money for all the wrongs in history."

BITTKER ON BLACK REPARATIONS

The hullabaloo over the Forman manifesto had at least one other longer-term consequence. It inspired a liberal Yale law professor named Boris Bittker to write a book published by Random House in 1973 entitled *The Case for Black Reparations*.

Bittker, whose specialty was tax law, was sympathetic to the reparations idea—according to Laura Kalman's history of the Sixties at Yale Law, he "had been involved with the Old Left as a student in the 1930s." But he explored the issue in the sort of calm, systematic tones one might bring to a more conventional policy question, and even with occasional dry humor. One of his goals, he announced, was to "reduce the emotional temperature" surrounding the issue. In short, his style could hardly have been more different from Forman's.

Bittker's principal aim in *The Case for Black Reparations* was to ascertain what sorts of payout scheme might plausibly 1) win acceptance within the existing structure of American law and politics and 2) be capable of practical implementation without impossible strain on race relations or the workings of society generally. Along the way, he took the opportunity to lay out an analysis worth reading today of such questions as whether reparations would be better structured as cash payments to individuals (in which case much of it would inevitably be spent in pursuit of immediate personal goals, contributing little to long-term racial uplift) or instead channeled to groups deemed to represent black interests generally (in which case leaders and institutions defined by whites' willingness to select them as negotiating partners "would be transformed overnight . . . into major social and political institutions," perhaps with little answerability to their nominal constituents).

More fundamental yet, how should the quest for reparations be pursued? By seeking legislative relief from lawmakers? Or by seeking civil relief from judges? Much of the book was devoted to this question. And Bittker's conclusion was that legislation was far more likely to prove a viable route than lawsuits. Given the state of the law in the early 1970s, it was a conclusion that was hard to escape.

However horrendous the actions people might want to sue over, it was highly relevant from a legal point of view that most of those actions had been fully sanctioned by law at the time they were taken. While courts do not flatly rule out all retroactive applications of civil liability, age-old traditions of jurisprudence still militated against holding defendants liable for actions approved by the law of their day.

Moreover, most plantation owners and the slaveholding power generally had been ruined by the Civil War and its aftermath. To the extent some Southern fortunes had been spared, it was as part of a comprehensive, fundamentally political settlement following the war, in which the U.S. Congress and other authorities spelled out who would and would not be subject to confiscation or other legal penalties. As a result, defendants would probably succeed in invoking the *political question* doctrine.

What about the morality of it all? The idea that the entire nation had been tainted by the evil of slavery was of course not new; it had been a favorite theme of the abolitionists. But—contrary to Ogletree's claim that the nation had "never dealt with" the issue—it was a deeply held premise of America's civic culture that the nation had gone to extraordinary lengths to expiate its foundational guilt, by way of the vast slaughter of its sons on both sides of the Civil War. In the image of Lincoln's Second Inaugural, each drop of blood drawn by the lash had been paid by another drawn by the sword.

All of which served as reason enough why ordinary reparations suits would have failed even in the near aftermath of the Civil War. But the further passage of more than a hundred years had added a powerful further reason, in the form of the principles that underlie the statute of limitation. At some point—or so most legal systems have long held—the correction of old injustice must give way to the need for finality and security of property: as time goes on, witnesses scatter, evidence decays, and it becomes unreasonable to expect persons to keep on hand the information needed to defend themselves (or their great-great-great-grandparents) from new accusations. The moral edges get blunted as well: if the long-penitent seventy year old is brought to account for misdeeds he committed at twenty, should we even think of him as more than nominally the same moral entity he had been in his youth? In the century and a half since Emancipation, generations of immigrants had arrived on these shores who (one might think) bore little guilt for what happened then. For that matter, what about the descendants of Lincoln-era American families who never owned slaves and supported Abolition? In what sense were they guilty?

—⟋⟍⟍—

Shrewdly, Bittker concluded that the reparations idea would be more likely to gain ground if keyed not to antebellum slavery but to the oppression wrought by Jim Crow in the twentieth-century South. In the first place, while no one was still alive in 1973 who could remember the state of bondage, Jim Crow was very much fresh in memory, many of its key elements having lasted well into the 1960s. Moreover, the sin of Jim Crow had been expiated by no great calamity or tribulation.

Even as regarded the relatively recent harms of Jim Crow, however, Bittker concluded that litigation would mostly fail as a remedy. Many injustices would be unreachable because defendants' actions had been sanctioned by law, or because the wrongs arose from the behavior of the white community generally, rather than from the relatively particularized misdeeds of individual culprits, as the law requires. Most claims that survived these hurdles would fall to the statute of limitations.

One other possibility was to sue governments, as opposed to private actors. Morally, governments certainly looked like prime candidates for suit, since it was they that had adopted and maintained the oppressive laws. Yet they were further insulated from damage suits by the doctrines of *sovereign immunity*; indeed, the federal courts had dismissed the Cotton Tax case in 1915 on exactly that ground. It was unlikely that they would voluntarily consent to waive that immunity, making the fight an uphill one at best.

The logical conclusion, Bittker saw, was to pursue reparations not through courtroom action but through legislation, by way of the government's power to tax and spend. That way benefits could be disbursed according to deliberate and considered formulas establishing who would be entitled to what, and they could be paid for by drawing on a relatively broad tax base.

As a tax-law specialist, Bittker must have been well acquainted with the maxim attributed to Colbert that the art of public finance lies in obtaining from the goose the most feathers with the least squawking. Case-by-case, chancy, hard-fought litigation against current asset holders—even if somehow it could surmount the many legal hurdles—would result in a maximum of squawking for the weight of feathers obtained.

Like many others who have considered the issue, Bittker also expressed considerable unease about making race as such a trigger for compensation. (What to do about persons of multiracial parentage, recent immigrants from the Caribbean, and so forth?) As an alternative, he suggested as one possibility a program to compensate persons who as children had been obliged to attend black-only schools before the desegregration set in motion by the Supreme Court's 1954 *Brown* decision. That would have the advantage of directing payments to individuals who could plausibly claim to have suffered specific, targeted legal disadvantage. Consistent with this approach, Bittker chose to stress the guilt of governments during the Jim Crow period as opposed to that of private actors. This too

carried a plausible appeal to moderate sentiment: blaming government kept the recrimination to manageable levels, and even many
who would resist the idea that their own family's actions were tainted
might well accept the idea that victims of government misconduct
should have a claim against tax funds.

The idea that benefit programs are better targeted toward the
disadvantaged than toward blacks-as-blacks was of course hardly
original to Bittker. Martin Luther King, Jr. had himself taken this
position, and the very first modern law review article to advance the
reparations idea, by Graham Hughes in the *N.Y.U. Law Review* in
1968, had proposed as a suitable gesture toward reparations generous new federal programs in such areas as housing, job training,
and education. In the years that followed the federal Congress had
enacted exactly such programs, conceiving of them in large measure
as a way of relieving then-epidemic rates of black poverty. At the
same time, the federal and many local governments proceeded to
adopt a variety of racially conscious policies including preferences
in employment, higher education, and government contracting.
In short, by one plausible definition of the term, reparations were
indeed adopted as national policy, and on a mass scale.

—ɷ—

Despite its skillful execution, Bittker's effort drew little attention
outside the legal academy. Even there, when enthusiasm for reparations was to break out more than a decade later, it was to take a
decidedly different form.

One reason is that the landscape of the law was changing even
as Bittker wrote. As of 1973 broad-scale reparations suits seemed
certain to fail absent truly revolutionary changes to old legal rules.
But just such revolutionary changes—urged on of course by the law
schools—would soon be afoot. As the persistence of Prosser and
others began to pay off, courts relaxed centuries-old constraints on
liability, and field after field of mass tort and class action litigation
began to open up.

Many of the new developments were directly helpful to the reparations cause. Group as distinct from individualized justice? Heeding

Kalven and others, courts were increasingly willing to sweep together grievances of millions of people whether or not their situations truly appeared identical. In the past, courts had been hesitant to tag current businesses with the sins of defunct predecessors through liberal rules of "successor" and related-entity liability. Now, to loud cheers from Prosser followers, they were more inclined to trace out remote and vicarious chains of responsibility in search of deep pockets.

The success of institutional reform litigation was beginning seriously to erode the various doctrines grounded in deference to other branches of government, such as the political question doctrine, standing, and justiciability. True, the doctrine of sovereign immunity remained a major stumbling block to cash suits against governments. But that doctrine was deeply unpopular among academic commentators who could be relied on to applaud every time a court decision chipped another bit of it away.

Equally important was the ongoing erosion of the statute of limitations as a defense. Where courts did not consent to work-arounds, lawmakers (after lobbying by victims' and lawyers' groups) were increasingly willing to consider legislation extending statutes of limitation for old injuries or even reopening lapsed ones. Defendants continued to argue—but now often in vain—that it was unfair for the courts to develop new legal standards and then reach back to apply them to actions taken years or decades earlier. In the great tobacco affair, remarkably, the legislatures of Maryland and Florida enacted new and boldly retroactive laws designed to knock out manufacturers' defenses in *pending litigation* filed by the two states. "We changed centuries of precedent to ensure a win in this case," said the president of the Maryland state senate. There was no particular outcry; cigarette manufacturers were very rich and very unpopular, so who cared about defending their legal rights? Besides, some academic commentators regarded talk of repose and finality as a mere holdover from the days of formalism and an impediment to the doing of full justice.

A RALLYING POINT FOR CRITICAL RACE THEORY

Meanwhile, intellectual fashion in law schools was taking some new turns. For a while the popular thing was Critical Legal Studies

(CLS), with its promise to deconstruct the law's con game of pur-ported logic and neutrality and unmask the exploitative power rela-tions beneath. CLS won considerable attention in the national press with its swashbuckling style, but by the late 1980s it had begun to yield ground rapidly to newer approaches like Critical Race Theory in whose eyes it was—that's right—not radical *enough*.

In its own terms, actually, this critique made a certain amount of sense. CLS was very much an intellectuals' game, and while effec-tively showcasing its adherents' cleverness, it advanced few positive ideas for what people in law should *do* (other than not be suckered by the mystifications). It lacked, that is to say, programmatic content. In addition, with the passage of time, CLS's intellectual stars seemed to be turning into a generation of bookish, tenured, furry middle-aged white males not altogether unlike the generation of bow-tied, pipe-smoking New Frontier liberals they had replaced. "When they find out what we're doing, they're going to come after us with guns," Mark Tushnet had once predicted. But no such exciting thing had happened.

The movements that bid to replace CLS at law school center-stage—Critical Race Theory (CRT), FemCrit, and their many iden-tity-based analogues—promised to be different. To begin with, they rejoiced in diversity, and would never be confused with a gathering of middle-aged straight Anglo white males. While equally or more radical than the CLS crowd, they intended to spend more time lis-tening to the stories of those affected by law at street level and less time on arid doctrine-chopping. Above all, they would aspire to act and not just develop critiques.

One of CRT's key manifestos appeared in 1987 in the *Harvard Civil Rights-Civil Liberties Law Review*, a flagship of Left scholar-ship. Its author was a star of the emerging school of thought, Mari Matsuda, then of Stanford (later Georgetown). Matsuda was to win fame as one of the authors of *Words that Wound*, the book that made the case for legal suppression of racist and otherwise hurtful speech, and thus helped prepare the way for university speech codes—CRT's first and still most notable real-world accomplishment. In her Harvard article, Matsuda laid out a version of one of the theories for which CRT and Critical Studies would soon become best known—sometimes called *standpoint epistemology*—and then proposed a new practical objective toward which like-minded colleagues could work.

While many hundreds of thousands of words would eventually be spilled on the topic, the idea behind standpoint epistemology was simple. Law, like other scholarly and professional subjects, had up to now been carried on in a "voice" that was white, male, Anglo, and so forth. While female or minority scholars might be allowed into the club, it was at the cost of having to adopt this expected tone and surrender their own distinctive voices. This was to be deplored: outsider voices in fact supply insights others cannot duplicate. More broadly, scholars should listen more carefully for ideas and observations generated "from the bottom," from the downtrodden themselves. The direct personal experience of oppression is uniquely valuable: "those who have experienced discrimination speak with a special voice to which we should listen."

The objections to this line of thinking were also obvious from the start. If a middle-aged white male can never achieve certain sorts of insight on his own, whatever his cleverness, diligence, or empathy, how is one to fend off the symmetrical claim that there are insights young, female, or nonwhite scholars simply cannot come up with? And it is odd to speak of "the" voice or standpoint of women generally, or Latinos, or gays, or other aggregations of persons who hold highly disparate views on every topic under the sun. What to do about minority persons who speak in other than the expected minority voice? Write them off as inauthentic or suffering from false consciousness?

Standpoint epistemology, however, was a huge hit, not so much in the outside world as in academia itself (which provided the main audience and constituency for Critical Race Theory, just as it had for CLS before that). Whatever else the talk of voices, standpoints, and unique views meant, it meant one thing clearly: your conferences, publications, and faculty roster are missing something unless you include *our* voices. This did not just amount to a demand that female or minority faculty members be hired; that had already happened to a large extent. But often the scholarship of the new hires was indistinguishable in content or "voice" from that of the white males who had come before. The real need was for faculty who would make identity a central theme in their scholarly output.

With CRT and its analogues, a big wave of young recruits proposed to enter the legal academy specifically to pursue identity-law topics. Many administrators were more than willing to heed the call. For one thing, identity law was a highly fundable area. Even before the resulting influx of new hires, legal academia had been pretty much unanimous on topics of race, gender, and so on; now the conformity pressure would ratchet up. And, not to put too fine a point on it, all those new hires were going to need something to do.

—◊◊◊—

The other half of Matsuda's article supplied the answer to that. The new critical scholars, she argued, should distinguish themselves from CLS by throwing themselves into a real-world law campaign, and the right subject for such a campaign would be the achievement of minority reparations. Reparations was, after all, a classic cause "from the bottom": even as it had faded from discussion elsewhere, it had never lost its popularity among the nation's poorest blacks. Many law professors even on the Left had tended to dismiss reparations as an impractical idea, but that just showed how out of touch they were. And she quoted none other than William Prosser to the effect that the ever-evolving frontiers of legally imposed responsibility should align with "policy—with our more or less inadequately expressed ideas of what justice demands, or of what is administratively possible and convenient." Once the will was summoned, the old doctrinal impediments could be made to yield.

When it came to details, the difference between Bittker's approach and Matsuda's was the difference between wily caution and sweeping, want-it-all insistence. He spent pages threading the complications raised by differing individual levels of deservingness; she forthrightly raised a standard of "group rights rather than individual rights." He suggested that a reparations program last a "decade or two;" she proposed that an obligation to pay be made permanent and ongoing, pending the eradication of any underlying inequalities that might lead the majority group to feel superior to the minority—in practice, you might say, pending the abolition of human nature. He proposed going back to the relatively recent Jim Crow era to find a basis for reparations; she saw no reason to stop with the antebellum South in setting the backward controls on the time machine. The trigger for reparations-worthiness, she wrote, should be "the ability to identify a victim class that continues to suffer a stigmatized position enhanced or promoted by the wrongful act in question." Under such a standard, the wrongful acts of Christopher Columbus's crew might quite possibly be cognizable.

Reparations became a signature cause of Critical Race Theory, and since there were rather a lot of CRT-ers in the legal academy entering upon their prime writing and conference-going years, there ensued a veritable boomlet of interest in the subject. As the 1990s proceeded, respectful (and usually much more than respectful) hearings of the idea appeared in the Virginia, Penn, Harvard, Columbia, Tulane, Georgetown, and Texas law reviews, among many others. Randall Robinson's *The Debt*, the ardently pro-reparations book that hit bestseller lists in 2000, drew heavily upon and in turn helped popularize the work of law-school reparations advocates.

What about the old questions of fairness to immigrants, descendants of abolitionists, and the like? The standard CRT position was that these persons were bearers of "white privilege" and could have no fair objection if some of it were taken away. Significantly, there came a shift in focus on how reparations should be pursued and from whom. The new reparationists were not opposed, exactly, to the Bittker prescription of legislatively devised programs rationalized as atonement for past official guilt. To the extent that could be arranged politically, they would not object. But their greater passion was for tracing guilt to private parties through litigation.

TRACING LINKS AND TIES

Perhaps the most distinctive contribution of the new reparations movement was its zealous tracing of links, ties, and connections between the institution of slavery and private institutions of today—

the more respectable, liberal, and Northern those institutions, the better. Thus some prominent Northern newspapers (it emerged) had published classified ads announcing slave auctions and seeking the recapture of runaways. New England insurance companies had collected premiums from slaveholders for policies written on slaves' lives. Slaveholders and -traders had been important early benefactors of universities like Harvard and Brown, while one antebellum president of Princeton was recorded as owning two slaves at the time of his death.

Finding ties and links to present-day big businesses was easy enough because so many of today's banks, railroads, and industrial concerns have been built up from hundreds of smaller predecessors around the country; to score a hit, you just needed to tag one of those earlier companies. Thus the big Wachovia banking concern was not founded until 1879, seventeen years after the Emancipation Proclamation. But over the years it had agglomerated into itself through merger and acquisition the remains of about 400 earlier institutions, among them (bingo!) the Bank of Charleston and the Georgia Railroad and Banking Co. If that didn't work, it could be argued that a business had profited by its commerce in or use of slave-produced products, such as the tobacco, rice, sugar, and turpentine that Southern merchants sent around the world. Or perhaps it had ties to the "shipbuilders, sailors, ropemakers, caulkers, and countless other northern businesses that serviced and benefited from the cotton trade," as Robinson put it. As one researcher explained, almost every business could be pulled in through one means or another. "There's never going to be a solid number because the idea of how you connect a company to slavery is more a political one than a historical one." For that matter, why stop with Americans? People in almost any country around the globe could be tagged with guilt too, down to the nineteenth-century Irish housewife with her frock made of cotton imported through Liverpool.

For advocates, the benefits were manifold. Psychologically, it helped in fighting the irritating complacency of many whites who felt themselves above the issue because *their* ancestors had never owned slaves. Beyond that, the quest for links and ties was a way to make the issue come alive for potential allies in the North such as university students, and to raise the general ruckus level surrounding the issue.

It all touched off a temporary (at least) boom among business archivists and economic historians. In California, reparations advocates steered through the state legislature a bill directing the University of California to conduct research linking the state's modern economy to the efforts of slaves, the better to pave the way for later legal efforts. Several large companies, hoping to improve their relations with organized minorities, examined their own histories and regretfully reported links and ties to the slave economy. But these revelations were to come at a price: the businesses that made them were numbered among the first targets of reparations suits. The result was predictable: if opening the history of one's business to historical inquiry was a ticket to unknowable liability, then more companies would lock up their archives or quietly send them to the shredder. The historian John Steele Gordon quotes one historical society officer to the effect that since the rise of reparations suits, "corporations have reconsidered or requested the return of donated archives."

With voluntary corporate revelations coming to an abrupt halt, the next step was to employ government clout to pry the archives open. Reparations-friendly city councils in Chicago, Los Angeles, Detroit, Philadelphia, and Milwaukee enacted ordinances requiring companies wishing to do business with the city to make public their records of the sorts of links-and-ties that might serve as a basis for future legal action. In California, state Senator Tom Hayden sponsored a similar law imposing such requirements on insurers that did business in the state.

Not that it was about the money, of course. "It's never about money," said the lawyer Alexander Pires of the Reparations Coordinating Committee, who had made his name as plaintiff's attorney in a successful billion-dollar class action on behalf of black farmers against the U.S. Department of Agriculture. "To me it's not fundamentally about the money," said the radical Columbia scholar Manning Marable, among the many academics active in the reparations effort. As the movement allied itself with private trial lawyers, however, it developed that many of the lawyers had no intention of working for free: indeed, some were planning to charge contingency fees consisting of a percentage of the sums collected. They did not disclose the percentages they had in mind, but in other mass injury cases, it was not uncommon for lawyers to capture 20, 30 percent or more as their share. One reason this was significant was that the sums talked of were so large, tending to start in the trillions and go up from there. A famous, if dated, estimate published in *Harper's* magazine set the figure at $97 trillion, the financing of which would require extracting approximately $300,000 from every American of non-slave descent.

—ⱳ—

Statutes of limitations were obviously an enormous obstacle to the suits, and reparations advocates were glad to grab and run with the liberal precedents forged recently in tort law. Product liability courts had been willing to go back sixty or eighty years to pin guilt on manufacturers. Why not another sixty or eighty years further than that? "Just because slavery ended over a hundred years ago doesn't excuse them," said one reparations lawyer. Randall Robinson agreed: "Social rights, wrongs, obligations and responsibilities flow eternal."

Recall some of the situations in which courts had "tolled" the statute: when, for example, a defendant had concealed its wrong-doing, or a child's interests were at stake, or the full extent of a plaintiff's injury had not been apparent at first. Well, weren't the ill effects of slavery something that whites had tried to cover up, that blighted the prospects of many children, and that regularly burst out in surprising new manners? The prolific reparations scholar Alfred Brophy of the University of Alabama has proposed that the statute should be tolled when relief "should have been available through the courts at the time" but wasn't. As Brophy notes, governments might prove unwilling to extend statutes by way of legislation if they expect to be themselves the targets of a suit. But, he adds helpfully, "state legislatures may be willing to impose the liability on companies, particularly if they do most of their business outside the state."

—ɯɯ—

Once loosed, there was no particular reason why the logic of reparations should be confined to American race relations. Lawyers launched actions in American courts arising from past atrocities committed around the world, including those carried on by Germany and Japan during World War II. One lawsuit demanded damages from Japan on behalf of all Americans killed or injured during the Pacific hostilities. A treaty between the Allies and Japan explicitly waived all such claims; indeed, postwar legal undertakings between nations plainly barred most of the international reparations suits. But why should the political question doctrine deserve any more respect internationally than it was getting domestically? And the deviser of the suit over Japanese wartime treatment of Americans, the Northwestern law professor Anthony D'Amato, believed at any rate he'd found a loophole in the treaty language. "I think we're being conservative," he said of the $1 trillion demanded.

California's legislature, more inclined than any other state's to put itself at the disposal of reparationists, proceeded to enact a series of bills reopening lapsed statutes of limitations over many European wartime insurance claims as well as claims dating from the Ottoman Empire's 1915–18 slaughter of Armenians (Armenian-Americans constituting an ethnic lobby of some importance in California). Given such developments, advocates of slavery reparations not altogether unreasonably hoped their time might soon come as well.

Through 2000 and early 2001, the movement built force. All the major black organizations signed on to support the idea, including the Southern Christian Leadership Conference, National Urban League, and NAACP. It did not escape ironic notice that large American businesses, including some of those targeted by the reparations demands, were among the biggest financial benefactors of many of these groups. This didn't faze the NAACP's interim president, Dennis C. Hayes: "We will take your money today," he explained, "and sue you tomorrow."

Confident of success, advocates were rounding up more grievances to fold into the format and forecasting the sorts of use to which court-ordered payouts could be put. Robinson believed that in addition to facilitating such benefits as free college tuition for blacks, a reparations program should include a trust fund that would "generously" support "broad civil rights advocacy" as well as "the political work of black organizations." A George Washington University law professor liked the idea of awarding plaintiffs part ownership of the corporations they were suing. One of the reparations committee lawyers was reported to be planning to "sue history book publishers that give blacks short shrift," First Amendment or no.

By the summer of 2001 the *New York Times* could report that the reparations movement was "gaining steam," having "taken on substantial force this year." Black radio and the black press couldn't get enough of the issue; rallies were taking place regularly on campus; even the white-owned *Philadelphia Inquirer* had editorially lent its support, as had the Congregationalists and one or two other historically white Protestant denominations.

SEPTEMBER 11 AND RACIAL RECONCILIATION

In the spring of 2002, the activists Deadria Farmer-Paellmann and Richard Barber filed what was billed as the biggest slavery-reparations action yet, demanding $1.4 trillion from eight major corporations including Aetna, FleetBoston (later Bank of America), and the railroad concern CSX. The suit was soon consolidated with other similar actions in an Illinois federal courtroom. But Farmer-Paellmann and Barber were acting essentially as freelancers; the much-ballyhooed Reparations Committee with its big-name lawyers had not yet managed to file any of its long-promised national lawsuits, though it had been conferring for more than a year.

Perhaps this is because the big-name lawyers had a better feel for the state of public opinion. The fact is that the movement's momentum, considerable as it had been as of earlier that year, had been broken with an abrupt jolt by the events of September 11, 2001. It was not just that the terrorist attacks on New York and Washington focused the attention of the American public and press for months afterward on issues unrelated to reparations; it was also that some of the persistent themes that ran through those days, such as national unity, mutual dependence, individual heroism, and the implications of mortality, ran at somewhat cross purposes to the reparations narrative.

The plan had been to unite black opinion while gradually making progress among whites, but it soon became clear that wasn't happening. Newspaper editorialists and liberal churchmen aside, an almost vanishingly small share of whites supported the idea—5 percent in one poll, 4 percent in another—while those opposed routinely topped 90 percent. Indeed, it became clear that a substantial sector of black opinion was quietly opposed to the proposal, and sometimes not so quietly, as when the prominent journalist Juan Williams slammed it as "a dangerous, evil idea [that could] take American race relations on a crash course." By 2004 the Democratic presidential candidate John Kerry, then challenging the incumbent George W. Bush and overwhelmingly favored by African-Americans, drew "marked applause" before students at the historically black Howard University when he flatly opposed the reparations idea as one that would divide the nation.

It came as something of an anticlimax in 2005 when a federal judge briskly tossed out the main cluster of reparations suits, in a decision largely upheld by the Seventh Circuit the next year. The claims failed on account of the political question doctrine (decisions on how best to clean up after the Civil War were entrusted to the other branches, not the judiciary); standing (the ones injured were the plaintiffs' ancestors, not themselves); and the statute of limitations.

And what of the suits promised by Professor Ogletree's much-trumpeted reparations working group? Well, even though years had gone by, none had actually been filed. The high-rolling private lawyers whose names had prominently adorned the enterprise were hardly complaining; they had reaped a bounty of favorable publicity in the black press, which would no doubt come in handy in pulling in other, unrelated client business. But once they got a close look at the actual legalities, there had apparently not been enough there to stake their reputations on any follow-through.

The reparation claims arising from atrocities in wartime Europe, which had been accorded wide and uncritical coverage in the press, likewise mostly fared poorly when it came to rulings by actual judges. Thus a federal judge threw out four class actions over slave labor in Nazi Germany, pointing out that a postwar treaty had already addressed and resolved the claims. To reopen the question by judicial fiat, the judge wrote in a 78-page opinion, "would be to express the ultimate lack of respect" for the work of Truman-era U.S. policymakers.

—⁓—

Before some audiences, reparations movement leaders were willing to characterize their cause—trillion-dollar demands and all—as a soothing, tension-lowering aid to racial amity. Ogletree described the lawsuits as part of a "national project of racial reconciliation," while Harvard's law-alumni magazine, profiling him, cooed that the reparations movement "rides on hopes of racial healing."

For all the talk of reconciliation and healing, few topics could more thoroughly inflame American public sentiment. On the pro-reparations side, Robinson could write of "the staggering breadth of America's crime against us," the "great still-unfolding massive crime," specifying at another point that "the black holocaust is far and away the most heinous human rights crime visited upon any group of people in the world over the last five hundred years." As for the effects of entering into a courtroom struggle, he grew downright lyrical: the pursuit of reparations "will be a learning experience in self-discovery" in the course of which "we will discover, if nothing else, ourselves."

Feelings ran high on the other side as well. A political science professor who helped administer one survey, in Alabama, said it had been the most racially polarizing issue the pollsters had ever asked, and "added that the mere mention of reparations and an official U.S. government apology for slavery—another issue addressed in the poll—caused many white respondents to get so angry that they had trouble completing the interview."

The fact is that mass litigation worked better at laying bare psychological wounds and stoking feelings of righteousness than at advancing racial amity or for that matter black economic betterment.

It was a kind of gestural politics. One might almost think the objective was to provoke as much squawking from the goose as possible, whether or not any great yield in feathers resulted.

chapter TEN

forever unsettled: the return of indian claims

IN 1970 RESIDENTS OF A STRETCH OF UPSTATE NEW YORK between Utica and Syracuse learned that the title to their homes and farms had come under legal challenge. The Oneida tribe, part of the historic Iroquois confederacy, had filed suit to demand the return of the core of its ancestral territory; the state of New York had purchased its lands in the early years of the American Republic, but the tribe claimed that these transactions, dating back to the 1790s, were never authorized by federal law and should be held void. Subsequent additions would bring the size of the disputed area to 250,000 acres.

The Oneida claim was just one of many. Within a few years similar challenges sprang up in a half-dozen other states around the Northeast, including other large claims in upstate New York filed by the Cayuga and Onondaga tribes. Residents of some claim zones began encountering trouble obtaining the title insurance without which lenders won't finance a property. A writer for *The New Yorker* explained what happened in the Cape Cod town of Mashpee, Massachusetts: "After the Indians filed suit, banks refused to grant mortgages and loans, land development halted, construction came to a standstill, and people found it difficult, if not impossible, to sell their homes."

Some of the early disputes were resolved relatively quickly—at least by the standards of litigation, in which relatively quickly can mean within a few years. Not so those in New York, which continued to drag on in court for four decades or more. To be sure, real estate markets in the claim zones eventually stabilized, with title insurance and mortgages becoming generally available once more. But many owners are convinced that the ongoing complications, delays, and uncertainties served to depress property prices in what is already one of the least prosperous sections of the Northeast.

As the controversy ground on, tribes raised the pressure by declaring their legal intent to oust their opponents physically from the land. Thus officials of the Cayuga tribe announced that they had lost patience with and would seek to evict as "trespassers" the 7,000 landowners in their claim zone, some of whom had participated in rallies and protests in defense of their own (as it were) ancestral landholdings. The geographic sweep of the claims expanded as well, coming to include not only rural and small-town landscapes but also the land under sizable cities: "It's in total violation," said the Onondaga tribe's chief, referring to the city of Syracuse, the fifth-largest city in New York state, with a population of 160,000.

Naturally such striking goings-on did not pass unnoticed in the legal academy, and that academy has emphatically weighed in on the controversy—on the side of the tribes. Indeed, it was a widely noted 1971 article in the *Maine Law Review* that laid out the blueprint for the most successful Indian land claims. Professors Wenona Singel and Matthew Fletcher, who direct the Indigenous Law Program at Michigan State, argue in a more recent law review article that the courts should accord no particular deference to the "so-called 'innocent' landowners," given that they hold "void title." In case of doubt as to the meaning of the quotation marks wrapped around the word *innocent*, they approvingly quote a tribal attorney writing in another law review, who explains that the current local residents "are not 'innocent' in any sense of the word. They are trespassers. They have been sued because they are sitting on, taking advantage of, and enjoying the benefit of land that belongs to the Iroquois people."

The law professor Robert Odawi Porter appears to agree, writing that it "is both legal and just" to eject the current occupiers of ancestral Cayuga and Oneida land from tracts that "they have illegally been living on for over 200 years." Professor Porter founded and directs the Center for Indigenous Law, Governance and Citizenship at his home academic base, which is—almost too perfectly—Syracuse University, an institution that might have to turn its dormitory keys over to the Onondagas should the claims of that tribe prevail.

THE MYTHOLOGY OF INDIAN LAW

Indian law has long been a distinctive specialty within American jurisprudence, and these days it commands more academic firepower and interest than ever before. Schools that have launched centers and programs devoted to the subject include Arizona, Arizona State, Kansas, UCLA, Colorado, Tulsa, North Dakota, Syracuse, and the University of Washington. It is common for these centers and faculty to advise tribes on legal matters, reflecting a wider circumstance: academic Indian law specialists are generally expected to stand up for "our" side—that is, the tribes'—on controversial questions.

If you spend much time with the literature, it can seem that there is one basic Indian-law article that keeps getting recycled in slightly varying forms by different authors. More historical than contemporary in tone, it tells the same tale every time, namely that of the deep-seated ignorance and racism of the white majority and its wantonly cruel treatment of indigenous tribes and their members. If any mention is made of tribes' condition before European contact, it will include glimpses of harmony and sharing, ecological consciousness and true spirituality. Then the serpent slithers into Eden aboard the vessels of the Columbus and Jamestown expeditions. The most egregious settler atrocities—unprovoked massacres of Indian villages at daybreak, Georgia's treatment of the Cherokees, the career of Andrew Jackson—will be invoked as if typifying all times, places, and communities. Public campaigns through the nineteenth and early twentieth century by reformers, churches, and editorialists back East to defend and promote Indian welfare will be exposed as patronizing at best and at worst mere masks for greed and privilege.

Almost without fail, the One Typical Indian Law Article will decry at length the series of decisions by which the U.S. Supreme Court has confirmed that tribes in this country have not retained the legal footing of independent nations, but have only such sovereignty (and such aboriginal land title) as Congress concedes them. In their unwillingness to let go of this sense of tragic defeat, the Indian law chorus might even be seen to resemble those Southern scholars who used to spend careers raising monuments to their own romantic Lost Cause of sovereignty.

Of course the One Indian Law Article is not really the only one. Much Indian-law scholarship does address practical legal concerns of the moment. But it is easy for a stance of reflexive hostility to "settler" works and ways to pass unquestioned. Perhaps the most notorious of academic writers on Indian questions is the former University of Colorado ethnic-studies professor Ward Churchill, the subject of a furor when, in a rant after the September 11 attacks, he referred to office workers slaughtered at their World Trade Center desks as "little Eichmanns." Though he was eventually to fall out of favor even with some former admirers—especially after his claims of Indian ancestry turned out to be hard to document—and was also eventually ousted from his university position, Churchill's screeds denouncing the American majority had for years won routine and polite citations in the Indian-law literature; he had also published a book promoting the land-claims cause.

Others find more palatable formulas with which to dish out accusatory rhetoric. Perhaps the most widely feted of younger Indian-law specialists is Arizona's Robert A. Williams, Jr., whose résumé boasts awards from the Ford and MacArthur Foundations and a visiting gig at Harvard. Williams's 2005 book *Like a Loaded Weapon: The Rehnquist Court, Indian Rights, and the Legal History of Racism in America* builds on insights from such worthies as the revolutionary-violence-glorifier Frantz Fanon to argue (its publisher's blurb proudly announces) "that racist language has been employed by the courts to legalize a uniquely American form of racial dictatorship over Indian tribes by the U.S. government." Professor Robert Odawi Porter, the Syracuse lawprof who seems ready to yank the title deed out from under his own university, raises the question of whether America "is simply an imperial nation intent upon consuming other nations and peoples for its own purposes" and seems to answer in the affirmative: for "the United States, it has always been about accumulating land, money and power."

REVISITING AN OLD LAW

You might not guess from such statements that as crafted by Congress, executive-branch officials, and judges over the past century, federal law goes to extraordinary lengths in many respects to favor Indian tribes. Thus it requires various responsible federal officials to act "in trust" on behalf of Indians' best interests, a standard unknown in the case of ordinary citizens, whose best interests can be and are disregarded daily without legal consequence. More impressive, when interpreting treaties between the U.S. government and a tribe, courts construe ambiguities against the government's interests and in favor of the tribe's—again, a boon that can only be dreamed of by many others who would like to hold the government to its undertakings and agreements. In addition, the federal government has long assumed as part of its mission in this area the responsibility of serving as a tribune of Indian interests against those of the state governments, with whom they are frequently at odds.

It is only because of these multiply favorable and mutually reinforcing aspects of the law that the tribes' land claims stood any chance of revival at all. Were a conventional litigant to come to court asking to be installed as owner of a certain estate based on 180-year-old claims of inheritance or family descent, he would speedily be shown the door under one of a number of closely related concepts that serve the purpose of attaching time limits to litigation. These include not only statutes of limitation and repose but also the similar equitable doctrine of *laches*, which works to erase rights in equity not promptly acted on. Under the well-known principle of *adverse possession*, the failure to press a claim against a current occupier of land can lead to the eventual loss of one's right in the land. A parallel doctrine of *acquiescence* provides that incorrectly drawn political boundaries (as distinct from ownership lines) may be deemed correct with the passage of time.

The federal Non-Intercourse Act of 1790 and related statutes decreed that states could acquire Indian lands only with the case-by-case approval of the national government. Everyone agreed that this law applied to the states on the western frontier, where at the time Indian tribes held a status akin to that of neighboring foreign powers. For a brief while, opinions split on whether the legislation also bound eastern states, which had long been accustomed to purchasing lands from the Indian tribes living peacefully among them. But the controversy was soon settled (or so it seemed) in the negative: the eastern states continued to buy land from willing Indian sellers without consulting federal authorities; no one stepped forward to challenge the sales (least of all the Indian tribes, which wanted the money); and the Supreme Court never ruled on the practice. As courts noted long afterward, nothing suggested that the tribes at the time had been anything other than eager to sell the land or had received less than due value for it. By the modern era all the relevant federal agencies, including the Department of Justice and the Bureau of Indian Affairs, considered the Eastern sales ratified by custom and long acceptance.

In 1971 there appeared a law review article that summarized this seemingly remote history and explained the possibilities it might furnish for Indians today. The authors were Tom Tureen, a former law student activist who had gone on to practice with a federally funded legal services program, and Francis O'Toole, the student editor of the *Maine Law Review*, where the article appeared.

Their logic ran as follows. Since Congress had never explicitly agreed to the eastern land deals, they were not lawful. That tribes may have traded willingly and received consideration they regarded as sufficient at the time was irrelevant. Indian law had as a key premise the idea that the tribes were childlike "wards" of Washington, incapable of looking after their own interests (this seemed in tension with the hopeful, oft-expressed view of tribes as thwarted sovereign nations, but never mind). The tribes were as incapable of signing away their rights as infants would have been. It was never too late to rectify an injustice, and the way to do so was through court action restoring the tribes to their ancestral heritage.

The article's impact was immediate. Its first test came when Maine's Penobscot and Passamaquoddy tribes, which like their Iroquois brethren had sold their land nearly two centuries earlier, came to court demanding it back. The tracts in question were vast: they encompassed two-thirds of the state's land area, inhabited in the modern era by an approximate 350,000 Maine residents. For good measure, the tribes demanded damages of up to $25 billion.

To almost everyone's surprise (including that of attorney Tureen, who by this point was representing them) the tribes succeeded in getting a preliminary ruling from a federal judge in early 1975 allowing the suit to go forward. The judge accepted the tribes' contentions that their anomalous legal status exempted them from the statute of limitations and from defenses based on adverse possession or their contemporaneous consent to the sales.

Word of the ruling soon began to interfere with private land transactions, and a prominent law firm said it couldn't sign off on the soundness of municipal bonds in the claim area. There then began what an official in the Maine attorney general's office called the worst crisis he'd ever seen in state government. "There were meetings going on in the Cabinet room at one in the morning, trying to find solutions for this," John Paterson told the *Portland Press-Herald*. "It was extraordinary." Finally the Carter White House stepped in to broker a deal, which became final in 1980: the tribes accepted $81.5 million in federal money to settle the claims, and were also given authority to bring 300,000 acres into reservation status. Paterson later paid Tureen grudging credit: "He invented a claim for them that nobody had ever heard of. In 200 years, nobody had ever thought of it." Tureen himself later said of his legal ploy that it was "amazing that it worked."

The Maine ruling was carefully studied as a model for what could be done elsewhere. Its principles were generally applicable to land claims by other Eastern tribes, and Tureen (who later took up with the Ford Foundation-financed Native American Rights Fund) was soon sending emissaries down the East Coast to stimulate more tribes to file actions.

—m—

The U.S. Supreme Court made its own distinctively disastrous contributions to the unfolding debacle. The most important came in 1985 by a 5–4 vote in the second of two Court rulings on the Oneida claim (*Oneida II*). Writing for the majority, Justice Lewis Powell invoked the nation's "unique obligation" toward the Indians, as well as the principle that ambiguity in treaties should be construed favorably toward the tribes. The court declined to apply any statute of limitations whatsoever, discerning instead (with little evidence) a Congressional "policy" that potential Indian claims should remain open more or less forever. And the Court went on to rule that the tribe could sue not just units of government but also private landowners.

Given the murky state of federal Indian-law precedent, the court could probably have come out pretty much anywhere it wanted. But the dissenting Justice John Paul Stevens, joined by Justices Burger, White, and Rehnquist, offered powerful policy arguments. He noted that the Oneida elders who originally struck the deals had made no attempt to back out of them or cast doubt on their legitimacy, while their successors had "waited 175 years before bringing suit to avoid a 1795 conveyance that the Tribe freely made, for a valuable consideration." Continued Stevens: "The absence of any evidence of deception, concealment, or interference with the Tribe's right to assert a claim, together with the societal interests that always underlie statutes of repose—particularly when title to real property is at stake—convince me that this claim is barred by the extraordinary passage of time."

There would be an economic price to pay, too, Stevens predicted. "This decision upsets long-settled expectations in the ownership of real property," he observed. "The Court, no doubt, believes that it is undoing a grave historical injustice, but in doing so it has caused another, which only Congress may now rectify." Stevens quoted the 1831 case *Lewis* v. *Marshall*: "Nothing so much retards the growth and prosperity of a country as insecurity of titles to real estate. Labor is paralyzed where the enjoyment of its fruits is uncertain; and litigation without limit produces ruinous consequences to individuals."

—ɷ—

The Maine claim had reached settlement only after the better part of a decade and the application of White House political muscle, and it was not to be expected that others would go much more smoothly, especially since Washington did not repeat its offer of money from federal tax coffers to smooth things over. It took fourteen years to resolve a demand by the Wampanoag tribe for most of the 3,400 acres on Aquinnah (formerly Gay Head), Martha's Vineyard, against defendants who included the late Jacqueline Onassis, before it at last settled for $4.5 million and the transfer of 238 formerly public acres. A judge threw out the Mashpees' claim on Cape Cod, on the other hand, because that tribe had not maintained registered status.

The great triumph of the early period came when Tureen successfully steered to settlement the claims of the much-intermarried and indeed very nearly nonexistent Mashantucket Pequots, which had descended to the modern era more as a set of family traditions than as a functioning tribe. Steering adeptly among clueless and sometimes covertly friendly politicians and Hartford officials, Tureen helped engineer an extraordinary coup: permission to build the world's largest casino in the woods of eastern Connecticut.

THE UNDERDOG IMAGE

Even now, press accounts often portray tribal land claimants as plucky underdogs who surely are outgunned by the opposition's legal talent. The reality is rather more complicated. In the very early days, tribes did rely on a cobbled-up assortment of legal-services and "movement" lawyers, firms working on contingency fee, and friends-of-friends with law degrees. Soon, however, their cause was attracting volunteer talent of a very high caliber, including both law professors and lawyers from top-line law firms working *pro bono* (über-Brahmin Archibald Cox was one who helped out). Once the casino possibilities became apparent, it became common for tribes to be represented by seasoned litigators from firms with high billable-hour rates.

And the defendants? The first line of defense for farmers and homeowners were attorneys provided by title-insurance companies, who might be skilled on technical points of property law but were perhaps unfamiliar with the distinctive issues raised by this unusual new kind of suit. As time went on, state governments like New York's often assigned lawyers from civil service ranks to help with the suits' defense, in part because they saw themselves as being on the hook in an eventual settlement. Private firms with large landholdings, such as utilities and forestry companies, might also provide help. But even if these lawyers had a sense of how to engage with the wider public controversy—and often they were averse to doing so in any vigorous way—homeowners had to keep in mind that the interests of the large institutions might not always be the same as their own, especially when it came to the terms of an acceptable settlement.

Along with their other high-powered representation, the tribes had another resource: the federal government. Because of Washington's long-asserted role as guarantor of tribes' legal interests as against those of state governments, the Department of Justice often weighs in with court arguments on the Indians' behalf. Following the George W. Bush administration's accession to office, Justice dropped its backing for the suits against individual landowners, but continued to be supportive of many of the tribes' claims against state and local governments, which advanced many of the same theories. Pricelessly, the Justice Department has argued to exempt certain *federal* lands, such as post office sites, from the domain of land it considers the tribes entitled to reclaim.

The tribes' underdog status can end up as a bit of a fiction. In upstate New York, the Oneida are far better heeled than their homeowner antagonists, operating a giant casino near Syracuse as well as tax-free cigarette operations. Aside from employing high-powered legal help, the tribe donates abundantly to politicians, making it a major political force in the region. (It spreads its philanthropy farther afield, too, having funded, for instance, an Oneida Indian Nation visiting professorship at Harvard Law.) Meanwhile, the principal group opposing the claims on behalf of local landowners, calling itself

Upstate Citizens for Equality, has raised funds through such methods as holding a Saturday bottle drive and bake sale in the parking lot of the Waterloo, N.Y. Wal-Mart.

—ᙢ—

Sometimes with and sometimes without help from land claim suits, Indian gaming mushroomed over these years into a multi-billion-dollar industry. After the Pequots' huge win, most tribes made clear that they would drop their suits against homeowners in exchange for a casino permit, and of course the lucrative nature of those permits helped call forth many new actions. Lawyers began beating the bushes for theories beyond the Non-Intercourse Act that might justify claims, and suits proliferated in new sections of the country, such as the Midwest. Thus the Miami Indians asserted claims to large portions of Illinois and Indiana; the federal government had bought the tracts from the Kickapoo tribe in 1815, but the Miamis argued that the area wasn't the Kickapoos' to sell. The Eastern Shawnee realized they had mislaid four million acres in Ohio and wanted them back with all due speed. The Cheyenne-Arapaho demanded twenty-seven million acres including the city of Denver. Land claims litigation was itself developing into a big business, even as—in an irony Stendhal might have appreciated—it was also transporting some of its founding attorneys along an unlikely career arc from shirtsleeved Legal Services idealists to well-compensated casino lobbyists.

Wealthy investors often quietly foot the bill for the land grabs in exchange for a share of the casino rights it is hoped will follow. (Promoting and financing other people's litigation was punishable under common law as the offense of "champerty," but such rules have long since fallen into abeyance.) When the little-known Schaghticoke tribe claimed thousands of acres in Litchfield County, Connecticut, it demurely declined to identify the suit's backer other than as a "friend of the tribe."

Among publicly identified backers of tribal lawsuits are Detroit's pizza-and-hockey magnate Marian Ilitch, who staked Long Island's Shinnecocks, and Rochester's shopping-mall tycoon Thomas C.

Wilmot Sr., who bankrolled both the Miamis and Connecticut's Golden Hill Paugussetts, a self-proclaimed Indian body of dodgy provenance. (The federal Bureau of Indian Affairs found "little or no evidence" that the putative ancestor of the group lived "in tribal relations during his lifetime" or "was descendant from the historical Golden Hill Paugussett or from any other identified historical Indian tribe.")

Most casino proposals were hotly controversial, and as litigation bogged down tribal lawyers searched for added leverage. The Golden Hill Paugussetts, who hadn't gotten much of anywhere with a decade-long claim to portions of Bridgeport and nearby towns, decided to up the stakes in 2002 by threatening to claim much wider swaths of the southern part of the state, including Westport and other affluent New York City suburbs. Tribal leaders proceeded to call a meeting with local real-estate agents at which they outlined the chaos such a step might unleash. Another way to increase the pressure was to add legal demands for the ejectment of existing occupiers. "You have to get the state to get serious about negotiation," an Oneida chief has explained. "The pain of not settling has to be greater than the pain of settling. . . . This is all about power."

Demands for cash compensation often soared to dizzying heights, "back rent" being only the start. Tribes also argued for damages based on lost chances of economic and cultural development, a theory that might enable a smallish land claim to serve as the basis for a largish reparations demand. Demands for cash as an alternative to ejectment can be based on the current value of the land in question, leaving the question whether it would be worth such a high sum had it not fallen into the hands of the purportedly wrongful occupiers.

Above all, the plaintiffs benefited from the magic of compound interest. If one assumes a (highly optimistic) rate of return of 6 percent, an investment of $1,000 200 years ago would by now have compounded to a handsome $115 million. (At a more realistic 3 percent, the sum would be $369,000; the calculations are highly sensitive to the interest rate one plugs in.) With even longer time periods one can obtain even more striking results. According to schoolbook history, Peter Minuit in 1626 traded $24 worth of cloth, axes, and other goods for the island of Manhattan. Compounded at 6 percent, that sum would today have mounted to a staggering $105 trillion—not a bad exchange for the land (as distinct from building) value of today's Manhattan. But in fact the same $105 trillion would stand as the equivalent value of anything else improperly sold for $24 in 1626, such as a remote fishing island, whether or not it happened to have developed into today's Manhattan. And yet no prosperous family that owned $24 worth of goods in 1626 ever did manage to parlay it into a fortune of $105 trillion four centuries later—one indication that the mechanical application of compound interest over long periods partakes of the nature of a legal fiction, of a punitive sort.

NO ONE TO HELP

With the judiciary bound by the unfortunate *Oneida II* holding, and the executive branch constrained by its long practice of bending over backward to take the tribes' side, help could have come from two other quarters: the U.S. Congress, or an aroused press. But the first was part of the problem, and the second was not of much help.

As the lawmaking branch, Congress could have brought the litigation to a speedy halt by (for example) enacting an explicit time limit on claims made under the Non-Intercourse Act. But it showed no interest in doing so. Sympathy for the tribes and a wish to be seen as guardians of their interests were important factors. But there was another factor as well, which came to full public light with the Abramoff scandals of the mid-2000's: Indian gambling money had become a huge source of election money on Capitol Hill, in part because the tribes' unique political status had resulted in their exemption from otherwise applicable limits on campaign spending.

As for the media, tribal leaders mostly conformed to a shrewd policy attributed originally to Tureen, who sought to avoid letting the land claims turn into too big a story in the press for fear of galvanizing opposition. Only rarely do the suits engage more than a passing look from national reporters, and that happens most often when they impinge on a summer playground of media folks such as the Hamptons, Cape Cod, or Martha's Vineyard. That was scant consolation to targets of claims in less glamorous areas: for all the

national media pays attention to them, towns like Aurelius, Spring-
port, and Chittenango, N.Y. might as well be in Manitoba.

—⟋⟍—

Even given their sympathy with the tribes, you'd think legal
academics, with their oft-scathing critiques of the money-making
world, might take a somewhat jaundiced view of the workings of a
billion-dollar new industry with remarkably little tax or regulatory
oversight. As a topic, the rise of Indian gaming has all the ingredients
needed for such a fearless exposé: the exploitation of legal loopholes;
backroom dealings and favor-dispensing among statehouse allies;
friction with labor unions and with neighboring communities convulsed by casino traffic and spillover development; bare-knuckled
tactics employed by tribes that already have casinos against other
tribes that would like to introduce competition; extreme inequalities
between different Indian groups, as some groups enjoy riches while
others persevere in grinding poverty because they live in places
remote from tourist or population centers; and of course the plight
of the sued homeowners and farmers.

It happens, though, that legal academia has tended to tiptoe
around the topic. What literature there is tends to range from
tame to supportive, no doubt because it is so hard to treat the topic
unblinkingly without running afoul of tribal sensitivities.

—⟋⟍—

Underlying it all is the historical premise that Indian land was by
and large stolen by the white man. Obviously many examples could
be offered either way, some of arm's-length and aboveboard sales
and some of duress or gross fraud. But which are more typical and
prevalent in American history?

One person with opinions on that subject was the most protean
and interesting figure to arise in twentieth-century Indian law, the
much admired Yale professor and New Deal official Felix Cohen. In
his younger days Cohen had been a noted icon-smasher as part of

the Legal Realism movement: his "Transcendental Nonsense and the Functional Approach" (*Columbia Law Review*, 1935), still one of the most read and cited of Realist texts, pokes fun at an older generation's formalisms that (he argued) served mostly to obscure underlying social policy questions of what the law should accomplish. From this raucous debut at center stage of elite intellectual lawyerdom, one might not have guessed that Cohen would take a career turn that in later years would make him best known as the author of *Handbook of Federal Indian Law*, the standard work in its field. It is said that, by the time of his premature death, Cohen, a key architect of what came to be known as FDR's "Indian New Deal," had become a revered figure in some of the most remote settlements of the Southwestern desert and Alaskan tundra, a long way indeed from the library carrels of Yale and Columbia. Cohen had this to say in 1947:

The fear that recognizing Indian title, or paying Indians for land, would unsettle land titles everywhere and threaten the Federal Government with bankruptcy, would be well grounded if there were any factual basis for the current legend of how we acquired the United States from the Indians. . . . Fortunately for the security of American real estate titles, the business of securing cessions of Indian titles has been, on the whole, conscientiously pursued by the Federal Government, as long as there has been a Federal Government. The notion that America was stolen from the Indians is one of the myths by which we Americans are prone to hide our real virtues and make our idealism look as hard-boiled as possible. We are probably the one great nation in the world that has consistently sought to deal with an aboriginal population on fair and equitable terms. We have not always succeeded in this effort but our deviations have not been typical.

It is, in fact, difficult to understand the decisions in Indian title or to appreciate their scope and their limitations if one views the history of American land settlement as a history of wholesale robbery.

Contemporaries agree that Cohen (whose politics tended toward the Old Left) was drawn to Indian law in part because of his sympathy for the underdog and his concern for fairness. Somehow it seems unlikely that he would have insisted on denying the honorific *innocent* to small-town farmers and townspeople with their modest landholdings, or that he would have applauded as they were made to suffer gratuitous pain so as to afford more leverage to casino promoters. As the great debunker of the law's elevation of form over substance, it seems even less likely that he would have favored a strategy for Indian betterment premised on the most insufferable sort of legal gamesmanship, in which long-dormant argued flaws in title are triumphantly dug up and proclaimed as if in a Gilbert & Sullivan plot.

In 2005 a young UCLA law professor from outside the Indian-law fraternity, Stuart Banner, published *How the Indians Lost Their Land*, an extensively researched work that does much to correct the portrayal of white-Indian relations as a mere catalog of thefts, conquests, and usurpations. As Banner demonstrates, the actions and attitudes of white Americans and their institutions have shown a full range of shadow and light, from extreme wickedness and ignorance to as much grace, goodwill, and foresight as could have been expected under the circumstances. Tracing the many twists and reverses of federal Indian policy, Banner notes that it was usually anything but obvious which proposed measures would truly serve the interests of aboriginal inhabitants, that nearly all major changes in policy enjoyed support among some Indians and Indian-friendly white reformers, and that most of the major disasters to afflict America's Indian population were either unforeseen or not well controllable by the central government in Washington. Few of these observations would have come as a surprise to scholars of the pre-identity politics era, but the book's largely favorable reception suggests a maturing of the debate.

THE SUPREME COURT RECONSIDERS

For whatever reason, native land claims emerged over this period as a serious phenomenon not just in the United States but also in other former colonial countries, notably Canada and Australia. Canada's courts and administrative tribunals have entertained hundreds of claims, some of them every bit as ambitious as their American counterparts, as in a Mississauga band's bid for compensation for a quarter-million acres including the entire city of Toronto and many suburbs. As with the claims in the eastern United States, the original cession under challenge took place nearly 200 years earlier. Another Indian band won C$92.5 million (US$58 million) in settlement of a claim in North Vancouver. In Australia, litigation over the fate of the capital of the state of Western Australia (population 1.5 million) resulted in the following remarkable headline: "Aborigines given ownership of Perth by judge." Softening the blow was the Australian courts' holding that private landowners could not be dispossessed on such a basis, but the prospect did arise that natives might be accorded a right to turn public lands such as parks into permanent urban encampments.

Back in the United States, cases began taking a turn against the tribes starting in about 2000. In that year something extraordinary happened: an Indian land claim actually went to trial before a jury (of non-Indians). That jury took twelve hours to return a damages figure of a mere $36.9 million, much lower than either side had expected, as compensation for the Cayugas' sale of 64,000 acres two centuries earlier. (The tribe had asked for $2 billion.) To that sum the judge added $211 million to cover the magic of compound interest, bringing the grand total to $247.9 million. In 2002 a federal judge threw out the Senecas' claim to be rightful owners of Grand Island, a middle-class Buffalo suburb of 18,000 residents in the Niagara River, finding "no archaeological evidence that the Senecas ever set foot on Grand Island." Then in 2005 came a U.S. Supreme Court decision that confirmed that the high court's thinking had evolved a good bit over the two decades since *Oneida II.*

The new decision, like its predecessor, involved New York's Oneida tribe. That well-off tribe, like some others, had followed a practice of purchasing parcels of ancestral land on the open market and then unilaterally declaring them sovereign Indian country exempt from local taxation and regulation. The small upstate municipality of Sherrill had challenged this practice, and in the case of

City of Sherrill v. *Oneida Indian Nation* the Court sided 8–1 with the town. Ominously from the tribe's point of view, the Court pointedly applied the equitable doctrine known as *laches*: whatever the original merit of its claim to exert sovereignty over the land, it had simply waited too long to assert it. And although the Court denied that it was disturbing its earlier *Oneida II* ruling, its shift in emphasis was impossible to miss: it had now come around to the view that stale claims by tribes, like those by pretty much everyone else, do expire eventually.

Sectors of legal academia reacted with explosive anger. Fletcher and Singel accused the Court of having embraced "the racist notion of Manifest Destiny" in siding with "those who have benefited from the illegal dispossession of Indian lands." Despite the talk of racism and genocide, the opinion in *City of Sherrill* had been written by Justice Ruth Bader Ginsburg, among the Court's most liberal members, and joined by all her liberal colleagues save John Paul Stevens. The next year the Second Circuit court of appeals, citing *City of Sherrill*, threw out the Cayugas' successful damage award—and the suit itself—as barred by the passage of years. The time had come, suggested Judge José Cabranes—like Ginsburg, a Democratic appointee with liberal credentials—to bring down a final curtain on claims that tribes had waited far too long to press. When the Supreme Court the next year refused to hear the Cayugas' appeal, tribal leaders and legal academics reacted with their usual extravagant hyperbole. A New York chief said the high court's decision "sounds an alarm to all tribes that it's open hunting season on them in the judicial system and that Indian issues have no chance in being fairly resolved if they are taken into the courts." A statement from the Onondaga chiefs called the decision "just another chapter in this shameful history of the genocide against Native peoples in this country."

More losses followed. In 2006 a federal judge threw out the claims of the Shinnecock tribe to some of the nation's priciest acreage in New York's Hamptons. In eastern Pennsylvania, another tribe failed in a bid for the land under the factory that makes Crayola crayons. In 2010 the Oneida claim itself was at last dismissed. Although this particular reparations program had gotten farther than almost any others—redistributing many tens of billions of dollars, if you count the value of casino rights—it was simply too absurd for the courts to let it go forward, at least under the auspices of domestic law. But domestic law was not to be the end of it.

—ɯ—

For more than thirty years, before the modern era of Indian land litigation, the federal government operated a panel by the name of the Indian Claims Commission, whose job was to adjudicate tribes' claims of land dispossession and other grievances. In 1951 members of the Western Shoshone tribe complained to the ICC about the historic loss of their land, which had been overrun by white settlers following the completion of the Transcontinental Railroad in 1869. In 1979, after a slow-even-by-government-standards delay of twenty-eight years, the ICC was to find the grievance valid at its core: it agreed that the tribe had been wrongfully ousted from 60 million acres, comprising much of the state of Nevada as well as parts of California, Idaho, and Utah. Unfortunately for the tribe, established federal law provided that the recompense owed them would have to be based on what the land was worth when it was lost, in this case 1872, not its value in more recent times. As a result, it was decided that roughly $150 million in compensation was owed to the tribe—hardly a princely sum, you would think, considering the latter-day value of the land, on which sit many valuable things including the city of Las Vegas.

Some Western Shoshone rejected the award as insufficient and held out for better terms, but the resulting litigation did not proceed happily for them. While the liberal Ninth Circuit appeals court held out hope for a while with a favorable ruling, both the U.S. Supreme Court (in 1985) and the U.S. Court of Claims eventually were to side largely with the Indian Claims Commission's ruling. In 2004 the U.S. Congress passed and President George W. Bush signed legislation providing for the distribution of money in final resolution of the dispute.

But opponents didn't see things as resolved. With help from the University of Arizona College of Law's Indigenous Peoples Law and Policy Program, tribe members in 2001 appealed to a panel of the

United Nations (the Committee for the Elimination of Racial Discrimination, or CERD, in Geneva), arguing that their treatment by the U.S. government had violated international law. The U.N. panel pronounced in their favor, agreeing that the legal redress the United States had afforded them—including Supreme Court consideration and Congressional reconsideration of their case—fell short. CERD directed the U.S. government to negotiate a settlement with the tribe, and said that in the mean time international law required that mining, industrial, and related activities be suspended on the land. (It did not specify whether the area's most lucrative extractive industry, the slots and blackjack tables of Vegas, would have to be brought to a halt.) The tribal plaintiffs hailed the ruling as the first ruling by a U.N. panel against the United States on Indian affairs. It would presumably not be the last.

"... the movement made global"

WHEN A UNITED NATIONS TRIBUNAL RULED IN FAVOR OF the Western Shoshone land claim complaint in 2006, many who had been following the advance of the international human rights movement were not surprised. For some time Native American advocates had been calling for internationalizing tribal disputes with the U.S. government by identifying international-law grounds for advancing Indian claims, and suitable tribunals before which to bring such cases. In his book *Like a Loaded Weapon*, the Arizona law professor Robert Williams, Jr. had argued for this way of pursuing the tribes' stalled bids for land and sovereignty, and Williams's school, the University of Arizona, had represented the tribe against the United States in its complaints before both the U.N. and the Organization of American States. Many private organizations with a declared mission of promoting human rights, led by the British charity Oxfam and including the famed Amnesty International, had campaigned in favor of the Western Shoshone cause and vocally assailed the U.S. government for its resistance.

By casting their cause as one of international human rights, Indian advocates were joining a movement that was clearly on the march, and in few places more so than in legal academia. Indeed, were you of a mind, you might make it a full-time career to travel the rounds of the nation's law schools attending nothing but conferences, panels, and lectures on international human rights.

Thus Georgetown recently hosted a National Forum on the Human Right to Housing at which conferees were instructed on such topics as "promoting affordable housing using a human-rights-based framework." Loyola-Los Angeles put on a conference rallying interest in the new U.N. Convention on the Rights of Persons with Disabilities, hailed as an "international ADA" and presumably the catalyst for the future construction of sidewalk curb cuts and wheelchair ramps in remote tropical settlements. Numerous groups have united behind the fruitful concept of "poverty as a human rights violation," said to justify proposals for an international guarantee of minimum income. According to the introduction to an NYU symposium, international law now guarantees rights to health, education, and "decent work," not to mention freedom from "severe social exclusion."

Indeed, new universal human rights are identified and proclaimed on a regular basis, including rights to fresh water, corruption-free government, and access to gender-reassignment surgery. Gun control advocates led by the Chicago mayor Richard Daley have called for action in the World Court against U.S. firearms makers on the grounds that under-regulated trade in small arms is a human rights violation. In the European Union, in which new universal human rights are regularly spotted, few blinked when an EU commissioner proclaimed that tourism and vacation travel are human rights that should be subsidized by government if necessary to assure universal access.

Human rights, in short—universal, inalienable, internationally guaranteed human rights—have been proliferating at a bewildering pace. Why shouldn't the right to reclaim an aboriginal homeland be among them? Even if restoring the tourist playground of Nevada to tribal use did risk complicating for others the universal human right of vacation travel.

THE BOOM IN HUMAN RIGHTS

Since World War II the United Nations system has generated nine treaties on human rights topics, with more on the way. Regional bodies preside over others; for example, the Organization of American States, comprised of Western Hemisphere nations, maintains a body called the Inter-American Commission on Human Rights to monitor compliance with a document known as the Inter-American Convention on Human Rights.

At least when ratified by the U.S. Senate (not all have been), treaties of this sort are considered legally binding upon the United States. Yet it seems doubtful that most Senators, let alone most citizens, could give an off-the-cuff account of just what is in them and what their implications are.

Many of the treaties and conventions contain high-flown language whose meaning is not easily pinned down. "All peoples have the right of self-determination," announces the International Covenant on Civil and Political Rights (ICCPR), ratified by the United States in 1992. Does "peoples" include Indian tribes, and if so, does that mean they have some sort of right to sovereignty? Well, maybe, or maybe not. The same document declares the right of each people to dispose of its natural resources and in no event to "be deprived of its own means of subsistence." Would losing your land a century ago count on that score? It's hard to tell.

The ICCPR is a model of clarity compared with the 1976 International Covenant on Economic, Social and Cultural Rights (ICESCR), signed but not (yet) ratified by the United States. It proclaims the right of all persons to "an equitable distribution of world food supplies," to "the enjoyment of the highest attainable standard of physical and mental health," and "the right of everyone to social security, including social insurance," to say nothing of the right to "take part in cultural life" and "to enjoy the benefits of scientific progress and its applications." What exactly do these guarantees mean, and how is government to assure them? At whose expense are they to come? How much and what kind of social insurance or cultural participation or access to scientific applications is needed?

No one really knows. Yet advocates regularly call on the U.S. Senate to ratify the ICESCR without further delay.

— ⟍⟍⟋ —

Thirty years ago *international law* was a sleepy if vaguely prestigious specialty in the legal curriculum. Many law schools did not offer a single course in it. One reason for its peripheral standing was that ordinary persons seldom tended to encounter its workings, even if they crossed national lines regularly in their life or work. That was because it was a body of law primarily concerned with defining the rights and interests of governments, and only in a derivative way those of individuals. Many of its oldest and most durable elements consisted of immunities carved out from the reach of conventional national law for the benefit of diplomats, embassies and so forth. Occasionally, it would take an interest in protecting civilian nationals of Nation A from abuse by Nation B, but hardly ever did it take an interest in protecting persons from their own governments. Its object has been described as "the protection of good relations between states." From this you might conclude that international law was not much concerned about individual liberty, and you would be right. International law was not primarily about liberty; it was about peace.

Today international law is one of the hottest topics in the law curriculum. Some schools require it for graduation or urge it upon first-year students. And its hottest subtopic by far is international human rights. In 1992, by one count, only three law schools offered clinics devoted to that subject; within a decade the number had mushroomed to twelve clinics and twenty centers. Columbia, which posts about a dozen course offerings in the subject each semester, and NYU have two of the best known programs, joined in recent years by Virginia, Texas, Penn, Chapel Hill, and other top schools. Washington, D.C. has a cluster of activity with focal points at George Washington University and American University. Journals, publication series, fellowships, and conferences have proliferated beyond anyone's ability to keep up, and the status of the new specialty was confirmed in 2003 when one of its best-known figures, the liberal stalwart Harold Koh, was named dean at Yale Law. In 2007, acknowledging the field's emergence, the American Association of Law Schools unveiled a new Section on Human Rights.

—ɯ—

International human rights, however, is no mere field of scholarly inquiry. It is a movement. Just as much as fields like Race and the Law or Women and the Law, it tends to inspire a sense of there being (as McGeorge Bundy might have put it) "only one right side." The authors of a pioneering casebook expressed their hope that it would "spark continuing interest *and activism* on these issues" (emphasis added). Columbia, announcing the nation's first endowed professorship in the subject in 1999, frankly avowed its intention (along with others) to "help train the next generations of human rights scholars, professors *and activists*" toward the goal of "the professionalization of the human rights *movement*" (emphasis added): "The struggle for international human rights wages on," the school's dean, David Leebron, said in the announcement. In taking on ambitious dockets of litigation, centers like Columbia's and NYU's make little pretense that their main goal is to polish students' practical skills. In short, the new international rights law is not just something to study, but something to *do*.

Human rights activism came of age in the 1980s, with the rise to prominence of two celebrated groups devoted to the cause of monitoring abusive governments. Amnesty International (AI) had been founded to champion the cause of prisoners "imprisoned, tortured or executed because [their] opinions or religion are unacceptable to [their] government." Human Rights Watch (HRW) traces its origins to Helsinki Watch, formed to monitor the then Soviet Union's compliance with the 1975 Helsinki Accords. Both were to become highly influential pressure groups with enormous credibility and good will among Western reporters and opinion makers. Despite the occasional flareup of controversy—as when the two groups have promoted the prosecution of Israeli officials—the groups continue on the whole to enjoy not just good but celebratory press.

The law school clinics and programs maintain close ties with AI, HRW, and other human rights groups, to the point where it can be hard to tell where the one leaves off and the other begins. In particular, the law school projects partner closely with the private groups to pursue litigation and call attention to it in the public press. Seasoned litigators and other key talent rotate regularly between the two sectors as well as closely associated sectors of philanthropy, journalism, public relations, and so forth.

BEYOND DUNGEONS AND DISSIDENTS

All of which might be only moderately noteworthy were the human rights movement still closely focused on the dungeons-and-dissidents causes that originally brought it to prominence. But the movement has changed since then, and dramatically expanded its scope of concern. The AI and HRW websites continue to feature, as one might expect, reports on the persecution of dissidents in countries around the world. On HRW's site, however, one also finds prominence given to investigative reports on sentencing youthful offenders in California, inadequate medical care for pregnant women, and the problems of gays in small-town America. On AI's site, news of political prisoners is interspersed with articles calling for an intensification of world anti-poverty efforts, deploring the inadequate prosecution of domestic violence in Scandinavia (!), and charging that the Cambodian judicial system is afflicted with bribery.

Gone, too, are the days when a list of human rights groups began with HRW and AI and extended not much further. New groups—hundreds, if not thousands of them—have proliferated. Many are devoted to particular causes or topics: women's rights, hunger and food aid, public health, and so forth. Others monitor domestic or regional conflicts in a given part of the world, watching with care for human rights abuses on both sides (or, as the case may be, for abuses on one side but not particularly the other). In many other cases, existing religious, charitable, or ideological groups have chosen to affix a "human rights" label to missions they had been pursuing all along, as with the religious Left mainstay the American Friends Service Committee, the British-based charity Oxfam International, and the American Civil Liberties Union. In short, observing the high repute and energy of the international human rights movement, many groups wanted in. And as this happened, the demands made in the name of the human rights movement grew considerably more complicated and extensive than in the prisoners of conscience days. The Duke law professor Paul Carrington, writing in a skeptical vein not typical of his peers, notes the result: "While not long ago it was possible to suppose that [claims of universal human rights were] narrowly limited to such matters as genocide and torture, we are now told that the list is not closed [and has] grown to include gender discrimination, religious rights, rights relating to sexual orientation, and the right to be free from 'hate speech.'"

—⟁—

Over the years, countries had signed or ratified—and then proceeded to ignore—all manner of mood-music treaties on human rights. The 1948 Universal Declaration of Human Rights, drafted with guidance from Eleanor Roosevelt, had optimistically declared that henceforth "human beings shall enjoy . . . freedom from fear and want," with similarly elevated sentiments. The ICCPR and ICESCR, drawn up in the 1960s, engaged in similar flights. But what if countries were made to live up to their terms?

Some in the United States had seen this coming. The U.S. Senate, to loud protests from certain humanitarian advocates, had declined to ratify some of the treaties entirely and had hedged about its ratification of others with various "reservations," "declarations," and "understandings" limiting their application. For example, the U.N.'s Committee for the Elimination of Racial Discrimination calls for the prohibition of all "ideas based upon racial superiority or hatred." It claims this does not violate the freedom of opinion and expression "given that the exercise of this right carries special duties and responsibilities, including the obligation not to disseminate racist ideas." Given the First Amendment to our Constitution, the United States in ratifying CERD's underlying treaty adopted reservations disclaiming any willingness to suppress speech or ideas in this manner. Crucially, the United States has also made clear (and in this it is backed up by Supreme Court precedent) that the provisions of international treaties are ordinarily not, in the lawyers' jargon, "self-executing," that is, are not enforceable in U.S. courts unless Congress chooses to adopt implementing legislation.

UNWRITTEN YET BINDING?

Despite much talk of solemn obligation, there was nothing either new or unusual in international law about nations' choosing first to ratify treaties and then to ignore their provisions. Unlike domestic law, treaties lack any obvious method of enforcement. When national interest, reciprocity, or fear of retaliation is at issue, of course, countries do often take pains to comply. So, on the one hand, that accounts for the relative success of "workhorse" treaties over such matters as postal delivery, navigation, and aviation, as well as military treaties between genuine allies. On the other hand, at any given time some swaths of putative treaty obligation go ignored on the correct assumption that other governments will not let any resulting annoyance rise to the level of an incident or confrontation. And even with treaties grounded on tangible self-interest, observance often is at an end (or at least up for renegotiation) when the government-to-government relations that give rise to it—based on fear, dependence, eagerness to curry favor, or whatever—reach a turning point. In any event, experience with workhorse treaties is of little relevance in knowing what to expect with show horse treaties, whose main original reason for adoption was to be trotted around the field for admiration.

This now began to change. One important demand of the new human rights movement is simply that countries begin seriously attempting to comply with the treaties, interpreting their terms so as to have some real bite. Reservations and understandings purporting to limit the effect of human rights treaties should (on this view) be construed narrowly, or even perhaps struck down as inconsistent with the treaties' spirit.

But that was just the start of the new demands. Nations are also obliged (it was argued) to observe rules that arise under what is called *customary international law*, based on certain principles that nations have felt obliged to acknowledge as valid at many different times and places. If a norm is widely enough supported by the international community (so the argument goes) a nation may be obliged to comply with it even if it has *declined* to ratify a treaty embodying the norm. Some advocates argue that the Eleanor-Roosevelt-era Universal Declaration of Human Rights, though admittedly non-binding at the time it was passed, has evolved into customary international law and is therefore binding because of the long and respectful treatment it has been accorded.

—〰—

Which gets back to the problem of vagueness. When the Universal Declaration of Human Rights proclaims "freedom from want," or the ICESCR confers on all persons a right to "take part in cultural life," what do they mean? Are countries obliged to furnish persons with the disposable income, cars, or internet connections they might need to achieve these goals?

The treaties had been agreed to in the first place because their sentiments were pitched at such a high level of generality. At that level, all could agree that every "people" was entitled to self-determination. But even if Canada granted self-determination to the French-speaking majority in Quebec, did Quebec in turn have to grant self-determination to its own English-speaking minority? Given the chilly reception met with by most ethnic secessionist movements around the world, it seemed few countries behaved as if they really believed in a strong version of the "self-determination" proposition. Yet it had been widely ratified.

The various sentiments also tended to contradict each other. Thus in one place Mrs. Roosevelt's Universal Declaration of Human Rights proclaims an unalterable right to freedom of speech, even as it insists at other points that "No one shall be subjected to . . . attacks upon his honor and reputation," and furthermore that all are "entitled" to be protected against "incitement" to discrimination, that is to say, against one type of unwholesome speech.

Even when the issues are narrower, worthy goals often conflict. The global convention banning the hunting of endangered marine mammals can run smack into the global convention protecting the right of indigenous peoples to go on pursuing their traditional means of subsistence.

POWER TO THE "INTERNATIONAL COMMUNITY"

Who was supposed to resolve the contradictions and fill in the blanks on the vague terms? In short, who was supposed to decide? The answer seemed in practice to be something called the *international community.*

There is certainly such a thing as an international community with an outspoken consensus of opinion on any number of controversial topics, even if it in no way happens to track any actual consensus of opinion out in the 200-odd nations of the world. "The international community has agreed that reproductive choice is a basic human right," declares the U.N. Population Fund, implicitly reading out of the international community the majority of U.N. member countries which infringe on such a right, some going so far as to trample it flagrantly as with China and its one-child policy. Preferential treatment for disadvantaged ethnic minorities ("special measures" in U.N. jargon) is another thing the international community looks on with favor, though its popularity in the community of non-international persons is at best mixed. An Amnesty International official says nations that carry out the death penalty are "steadily isolating themselves from the international community," though well over half the world's population in fact lives in countries where the death penalty is lawful. The U.S. government's policy of holding Indian reservation land in trusteeship for tribes has been (according to leading human rights groups) "denounced by the international community as a remnant of colonialism," though it seems unlikely that public opinion in most countries is even aware of that policy, let alone outraged by it.

Sometimes rather few nations, perhaps a handful of social democracies in Western Europe, or even none at all, have actually implemented the views said to be those of the international community. But then the identification of international community norms does not rest on any vulgar nose-counting as to whether a given norm is in fact typical. Its Ouija-like pronouncements are more an aspirational matter, as if to supply the need of a sort of surrogate collective world conscience.

As Carrington has noted, when international panels undertake inquiries into whether a proposed norm ought to be proclaimed as universal, they typically entrust the task to panels for which "the primary sources of information are the academic authors who urge its [the norm's] enforcement." It's all wonderfully circular and self-reinforcing. Not to mention self-congratulatory: "In many ways," the executive director Kenneth Roth of Human Rights Watch has boasted, "this is the civil rights movement of the 1960s made global."

—〜〜—

Just as public interest law confers great power on the litigation groups that file the suits and determine their agenda, so the new international human rights law confers great power on the "international community" that gets to prescribe the newly recognized norms. Canny organizers saw early on the importance of setting up their friends and co-thinkers as part of this charmed circle. Coincident with the emergence of the movement, the Ford and Soros philanthropic networks lavishly funded both nonprofit human rights groups (for which Soros helped popularize the term "civil society groups") and law school projects.

Not just anyone can set up a human-rights non-governmental organization (NGO) with assurance it will be recognized. The U.N. Human Rights Council and related agencies engage in what is in effect a certification process, accrediting human rights groups—including several of the bigger law school projects, like NYU's and Columbia's—as NGOs with "consultative" and participatory rights. NGOs with approved status can exercise considerable influence over the development of the new international law—a substantial insider benefit, whatever sort of outsider image the groups may cultivate. Mavericks and newcomers—one dissident group has proposed a "human right to keep and bear arms," and one can imagine others asserting human rights not to be subjected to, say, confiscatory taxation—may or may not be admitted to the club.

—⁂—

Most Western human rights groups have embraced in all sincerity, or at least put on a good show of embracing, the sorts of *bien-pensant* views summed up in Britain's concept of the "*Guardian* reader," and known in the United States (with a few local modifications) as the voice of *New York Times* editorials. Not all the human rights groups are Western, though. One of the more striking aspects of the international community is the degree to which it comfortably accommodates newer groups and delegations based in repressive countries that smoothly deploy the rhetoric of human rights without running into any apparent friction or difficulty with their home regimes. Thus delegations from countries where only one religion can be openly practiced will mouth the right rhetoric about freedom of worship, NGOs hailing from countries where grown women do not show their faces in public pay lip service to Western feminist formulations, and so forth. Everyone manages to sound the way they imagine the Swedish delegate should sound. As a simulation of global consensus, it's a bit like the little singing figures in the Disney ride "It's a Small World"— they look a little bit different from each other, but they keep on putting out an endless loop of the same tune.

THE U.S. IN THE DOCK

For quite some time, various attempts have been made to obtain international human rights review of domestic controversies arising in the United States. The AFL-CIO has repeatedly gone to the U.N.'s International Labour Organization (ILO) contending that Congress is flouting ILO requirements by declining to liberalize the 1947 Taft-Hartley Act to compel wider employer recognition of labor unions. Environmentalists asked UNESCO to intervene in disputes over land use and visitor restrictions in and around Yellowstone National Park and other sensitive sites. Opponents of the welfare reform enacted during the Clinton Administration filed a human rights challenge before the OAS.

Ford and Soros philanthropy helped fit these scattershot efforts into something more of a sustained strategy. Ford played a central role in the 2002 establishment of the U.S. Human Rights Fund, a group intended to coordinate funding for such a push. Subsequent grants enabled the human rights project at Columbia Law School to launch "Bring Human Rights Home," a campaign aimed at generating more scrutiny and pressure from the international community against U.S. domestic policies. "Grantees use two strategic approaches," noted Ford in a report on its law-related programs, *Many Roads to Justice*. "They argue for the application of international laws in domestic courts and they take cases to international tribunals when domestic options have proved unsuccessful." The title of a 2006 symposium in the *N.Y.U. Review of Law and Social Change* summed up the strategy: "Realizing Domestic Social Justice Through International Human Rights."

The movement has proceeded to take off. Hundreds of controversies arising from U.S. law and policymaking are now taken to international bodies. Advocates routinely accuse federal, state, and local governments in the United States of international human rights violations for not guaranteeing felons a right to vote after they finish their sentences; for immigration policies that turn away too many asylum seekers; for excluding persons with criminal records from public housing; for lack of comprehensive civilian review of police misconduct; for failure to print ballots in minority languages that have few exclusive speakers; and many, many more. Along with other big players, like HRW and AFSC, law school projects like Columbia's and NYU's are among regular complaint-filers.

—⁓—

As part of its official "consultative" recognition of NGOs, the U.N. Human Rights Council recognizes "stakeholder" and "civil society actor" groups to monitor particular countries and report on human rights abuses there. It was therefore to be expected—

especially as human rights charges over U.S. domestic policy mounted up—that groups would get themselves named to monitor the United States. Strikingly, the list of certified monitors includes the law-school human rights programs at Columbia, American, Fordham, and Virginia. In a blurring of accuser and monitor roles that is rather typical of U.N. human rights practice, the groups deputized to watch and report on the United States include many of the groups most active in filing complaints against the U.S.

All the NGOs deputized to watch Uncle Sam seem to agree that he is a recidivist—most would probably add "systematic"—violator who needs to be called more severely to account. On January 9, 2006 the U.S.-watching NGOs submitted a joint statement confirming that "all" of them view the U.S. as falling short of its international human rights obligations. In the pages that follow, the groups offer a long bill of particulars, starting with the Western Shoshone case and going on to include such practices as:

- failure to note drivers' race when conducting local traffic stops, thus making it harder to develop complaints of "racial profiling";
- charging some juveniles as adults in criminal cases;
- funding "marriage promotion" and abstinence-only sex education programs (can "perpetuate harmful sex stereotypes"), and refusing to fund abortions with public money, both domestically and in foreign-aid programs;
- disciplining minority students at higher rates than whites (independently, it seems, of whether underlying rates of misbehavior differ across ethnic groups);
- failing to expand children's health insurance coverage and mandated employer family leave; and
- refusing to transfer transgender inmates to an opposite-sex prison until they actually have their surgery.

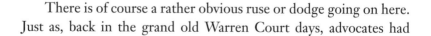

There is of course a rather obvious ruse or dodge going on here. Just as, back in the grand old Warren Court days, advocates had hoped to frame the liberal platform of the moment in terms of a resultant set of rights supposedly conferred by the U.S. Constitution, so, with a bit of care, almost any passionately sought policy goal can be framed in terms of a resultant set of posited international human rights. Indeed, advocates have been quite explicit about their wish to replay this old hand. A 1996 article in the *Harvard Human Rights Journal* laid out the basic plan: if American courts decline the invitation to use Constitutional law to advance particular policies, arguments should be advanced that the policies are alternatively required under principles of international human rights. The author of that article went on to serve as a funding officer in Ford's "human rights in the U.S." campaign.

Numerous hopes dashed in the Burger and Rehnquist years have thus been dusted off and refurbished as human-rights causes. Thus it is with the Supreme Court decisions disapproving racial busing across county lines (*Milliken*) and declining to constitutionalize school finance (*Rodriguez*) both of which—it is now being argued—are at variance with the dictates of international human rights. And that old dream of legal liberalism, the constitutional right to a living, is back on the table as well. As one advocate explains, "international human rights norms embrace substantive rights to food, shelter, education, and other basic needs."

Just like the stalled-out Constitutional law campaign, it offers a way to judicialize an inexhaustible list of proposals that advocates have been unable to win through the conventional democratic process. Unfortunately, as a source of legislative authority, the "international community" has even less democratic legitimacy than the federal judiciary. The federal judiciary may not be elected, but at least the U.S. electorate does get to vote for the president who appoints it. Not so with the international community or international judiciary.

—⚏—

Even if a claim does not prevail on the merits, human rights groups sometimes consider it a substantial victory just to get an international tribunal to assert its jurisdiction.

In the 2005 case of *Castle Rock* v. *Gonzales*, for example, the Supreme Court confirmed that it would not interpret federal law or the U.S. Constitution as creating any general right to sue local police forces for damages over avoidable failure to prevent domestic violence. The ACLU, working with Columbia's Human Rights Clinic, took the *Gonzales* case to the Organization of American States' human rights panel, which—perhaps privately amused to turn the tables on the meddlesome Yankees who have so often criticized Latin American rights records in the past—agreed it had jurisdiction to hear the matter.

Likewise, the U.S. Supreme Court ruled in 2002 that while illegal aliens can lawfully sue their employers for work actually done that has gone unpaid, they cannot sue for loss of *future* wages over work not yet performed, given that it was unlawful for them to hold the jobs in the first place. Advocates disappointed by the decision turned for help to the human rights law project at American University and appealed the matter to the OAS and the ILO, both of which obligingly condemned it as contrary to international law.

RATIFY IN HASTE ...

When one or another human rights treaty is proposed for ratification before the U.S. Senate, the ambitious ideas for specific enforcement tend to get tucked in the back drawer and advocates instead emphasize the treaties' high-minded sentiments—Shouldn't we show our national commitment to the rights of older persons, children, the disabled, or some other group?

Advocates also seek to dissuade Congress from adding reservations in the course of treaty ratification and, if possible, to withdraw reservations already made. The late Columbia professor Louis Henkin, a leading figure in the movement, has suggested that some key reservations, in particular those disclaiming the "self-executing" nature of the treaties, are either unconstitutional or inconsistent with the treaties' purpose and should be struck down. The U.N.'s Committee for the Elimination of Racial Discrimination (CERD) regularly urges the United States to withdraw its First Amendment-based reservation against banning "ideas" or speech that express hate.

Many of its NGO allies have joined it in this call, or even floated the idea that the reservation is to be disregarded as in conflict with emerging customary law. (In general, even most purportedly liberal NGOs show less commitment to American-style free speech than one would hope.)

Would American law school opinion push back on behalf of the First Amendment in such a confrontation? Don't count on it. Since the publication of *Words That Wound* a large and active contingent of law professors has been eager to extend regulation of purportedly hurtful speech. (Academics from this camp have repeatedly chaired the AALS's free-speech-and-media section in recent years.) While such views are still far from universal in the legal academy, it is worth noting that the person Harvard Law School selected to deliver its 2009 Holmes Lectures, a triennial honor it describes as "the institution's most prestigious," was NYU's Jeremy Waldron, perhaps the leading advocate of modifying First Amendment doctrine to allow for wider banning of purported hate speech.

—⟋⟋⟍—

Are there perhaps some dangers in yielding up U.S. sovereignty to a new global governance class? The response of the human rights literature is, basically: Quit complaining, you're too late. It's a *fait accompli*, and what is needed now is simply to adopt a proper attitude of compliance. It is (to quote representative samples of the literature) mere "wishful thinking" to propose returning to "a preregulatory planet in which each state is free to act as it wishes." After all, "notions of sovereignty have changed with growing interdependence." The advocates of international human rights have broken the "monopoly that states held over the rules," and once that process is far enough advanced, "the legal fiction of the sovereign state crumbles."

True, some "sovereigntists" continue to fight a rear-guard action against wide-ranging international supervision of each nation's laws and domestic arrangements. But these are "voices calling for a return to an earlier era," nostalgic at best or sinister at worst. Naysayers of this sort are somehow "against international law" (as opposed to being in favor of smaller, more workable versions of it), or even "opponent[s] of the rule of law"—which sounds somehow one step from being themselves in violation of it.

You do have to wonder, though, what became of the proclaimed right of each and every people to "self-determination." Don't Americans have it too?

—⟪⟫—

Talk of "crumbling sovereignty" is not quite accurate; rather than crumble of its own internal decay, sovereignty—and democratic self-rule more generally—has been the subject of relentless assault by the new legal ideologues. First came the push to carry on as much of the public's business as possible through litigation, which steadily transferred power from persons skilled at winning elections to persons skilled at winning lawsuits and eventually to the murky, semi-private "control groups" that formed to direct the public's business as a result of institutional litigation. Then came an even more basic challenge to sovereignty, in which some of the most fundamental and constitutive political decisions in America's history—the terms on which the nation's land was settled, and the terms on which the fratricide of North and South was put behind us—were revisited in litigation designed to minimize the deference paid to the views and sacrifices of earlier generations. Finally there came the ultimate assault on sovereignty: the plan of subjecting the nation to the direction of a new transnational elite exerting their will by way of an unending series of artificially coined new rights, in exchange for which age-old American liberties would be surrendered with no means of appeal.

—⟪⟫—

Some will object that the danger is but a phantom. The new tribunals might hold the United States up to international condemnation as a systematic rights violator, but that's just atmospherics, an imaginary pillory in a symbolic world square. It's not as if the emergent international community has any means of enforcing its pretensions or punishing us for ignoring its demands.

Or does it?

chapter TWELVE

seized and detained

IN OCTOBER 1998 A JUDGE IN SPAIN ISSUED AN ORDER TO prosecute the retired General Augusto Pinochet of Chile, who had been credibly accused of ordering murders and other atrocities during seventeen years of rule as dictator of the South American nation. Two months later, at the request of opponents of Pinochet armed with the Spanish order, British authorities placed the eighty-two-year-old strongman under arrest after he came to London for treatment at a medical clinic. Lawyers for the general petitioned for his release, but the British government sided with his adversaries, who urged that he be detained while a decision was made whether to hand him over to Spain for trial.

In the diplomatic flap that followed, everyone agreed that new precedent was being set. Pinochet's reported crimes did have some relation to Spain, because his victims had included some Spanish nationals, but they had little if any relation to Great Britain. Instead his opponents were asserting a new principle that would come to be known as *universal jurisdiction*, under which some crimes are so heinous as to render a perpetrator the common enemy of humanity, entitling any nation or court around the world to seize his person and potentially put him on trial. Chile—a nation that declared its sovereign independence from Spain in the year 1810—happened to oppose Pinochet's arrest and prosecution, but (the argument continued) the views of a malefactor's home country must not be given veto effect over the workings of universal justice.

Universal jurisdiction is a sufficiently novel idea that the 1990 edition of *Black's Law Dictionary* contained no entry for the term. Within a few years thereafter it had burst out to become the best-known demand of the international human rights movement. Backers of the idea—who suddenly seemed to be everywhere in the legal academy, amid the widespread ferment of human rights activism there—argued that it was not wholly without precedent. In the Nuremberg trials that followed World War II judges from the triumphant Allied powers put Nazi leaders in the dock not just for crimes committed against Allied nationals but for their crimes more generally, including those committed against German nationals. And going back further, international law had long treated pirates on the high seas as enemies of the human race that any nation might capture and put on trial at will.

There were of course serious problems with both analogies. Germany had unconditionally surrendered following the biggest war in history and had ceased to exist as a functioning state capable of adjudicating atrocity charges. Pirates on the high seas were by convention regarded as being at war with all established states (they "sailed against all flags"). Neither Nuremberg nor the piracy rules did much to undercut international law's longstanding assumption that before you could punish the leaders of a foreign government you first were obliged to see that government removed from power, either by defeat in a war or by domestic overthrow. By contrast, neither Spain nor Great Britain had the least inclination to declare war on Chile. Indeed, Chile had long since been readmitted to the family of respectable nations, having returned to democracy under liberal leadership. (Even as the Andean nation distanced itself considerably from Pinochet's rule, it continued to accord him immunity from prosecution as a sitting member of its Senate.)

The Pinochet case ended somewhat anticlimactically: the British government took jurisdiction but at length released him, on grounds of his age and infirmity. To proponents of universal jurisdiction, the new principle had been set down. A home government's opposition to prosecution—often grounded in amnesties or pardons issued in the wake of a regime change or civil war—might result in hard feelings, but that was just too bad: crimes against humanity could hardly be pardoned by a single nation. Besides, it's not as if Chile was likely to send gunboats or paratroopers to the shores of Spain or Great Britain. What was it going to do, withhold exports of grapes?

It soon emerged that retired officials were not the only ones who might need to worry about being placed under arrest over alleged human rights violations while on state visits or routine personal travel. Many advocates of universal jurisdiction argued for seizing and detaining current holders of high national office as well. Some warned that chaos might result as countries began seizing each others' leaderships, but not to worry, law professors and others said reassuringly: the exercise of universal jurisdiction would be reserved for things like state-sanctioned murder, genocide, torture and war crimes—offenses of "exceptional gravity."

EXTRATERRITORIALITY: THE U.S. CONTRIBUTION

Just as the United States, given its long history of meddling in the affairs of smaller nations, is not ideally situated to read the rest of the world lofty lectures about self-determination, so it is not in the best position to launch a critique of one of the most controversial elements of universal jurisdiction, namely *extraterritoriality*, the projection of a nation's law enforcement power to events, persons, and controversies outside its own borders. For many years American lawmakers, prosecutors, and courts had been irritating other nations around the world through ambitious assertions of extraterritorial authority on topics ranging from tax compliance to antitrust enforcement to the regulation of online gambling. U.S. officials were uneasy at best about the extraterritorial criminal prosecutions that began to spring up in the wake of the Pinochet affair, especially since many of them targeted U.S. allies or nationals. But the fact is that at the same time—egged on by human rights activists and the legal professoriate—the United States had itself been taking a place at the adventurous forefront of analogous developments in *civil* law.

In 1789 Congress passed what is today known as the Alien Tort Statute, conferring jurisdiction on federal courts to hear cases in which a defendant is accused by an alien of violating the "law of nations." After two centuries in which the obscure provision had lay on the statute books almost unused, a federal court revived it in 1980 to allow a suit to go forward over human rights abuses in Paraguay, against a police chief from that country who like his victim had moved to the United States. Since then a busy sector of litigation has arisen under the statute, much of it demanding large sums from deep-pocket businesses that have allegedly aided or abetted abusive police and national authorities on other continents. In 2004 the U.S. Supreme Court ratified much of the development of the statute, ruling that it could be used as a basis for lawsuits over violations of customary international human rights law anywhere in the world. In addition, Congress in recent years has enacted various other laws allowing damage suits against foreign persons, organizations, and even governments charged with aiding and abetting certain types of crime, terrorism in particular.

Like universal-jurisdiction prosecutions, Alien Tort Statute and abetting-of-terrorism lawsuits commonly go forward against the wishes of the government of the foreign nation in which the alleged events took place. Even when it does not result in an adverse judgment, legal action against foreign entities often involves onerous demands for deposition attendance and document production, threats of contempt sanctions and so forth, not to mention the infliction of high legal bills. The attitude of Congress and the courts has generally been that any resulting strain on diplomatic relations with friendly countries—or sworn adversaries, for that matter—is for the State Department to worry about.

THE U.S. IN THE DOCK (CONT'D)

Another enforcement mechanism for international human rights likely to assume greater visibility in coming years is the U.N.-supervised process known as *universal periodic review.*

The United Nations system includes standing committees whose mission is to oversee the implementation of various human rights treaties; among them are CERD (the Committee on the Elimination of Racial Discrimination) and CEDAW (the Committee on the Elimination of Discrimination Against Women). While the rulings of these bodies are ordinarily not viewed as binding, at least for the present, their findings may influence other tribunals that do have binding authority. Some of the oversight committees are empowered to hear complaints against countries over alleged human rights violations, whether individualized (by, say, a particular inmate complaining of treatment) or generalized (as with a challenge to an overall prison practice).

In 2006, responding in part to complaints from countries who felt they were being unfairly singled out for human rights scrutiny, and in even greater part to pressure from NGOs and their associates, the U.N. adopted what is known as "universal periodic review," in which all its member states (192 at last count) submit to review of their human rights records on a rotating schedule every four years. These reviews function in effect as audits: the country files its periodic self-critical review, groups critical of the country's record submit their own critiques of its record, and the U.N. panel then responds by asking for further information, congratulating the state for its action on a certain point, declaring its dissatisfaction on another, and so forth.

How this process works can be seen in a recent scheduled review by the U.N.'s Committee on the Elimination of Racial Discrimination (CERD) of the U.S. government's latest periodic report on its human rights progress. In a series of terse, peremptory pronouncements, the panel expressed its favorable or unfavorable opinions at the actions of the U.S. Congress in enacting or failing to enact certain new statutes. It announced its decided disapproval of a U.S. Supreme Court decision that did not go as far as some had hoped in allowing race-conscious assignment of students in schools, and its even more decided disapproval of ballot initiatives by which the electorates of California and Michigan had by wide margins voted to end race-based preferences at public universities. In fact it suggested that the voters of California and Michigan by passing the initiatives might have placed their states in violation of international law. And it went on to deliver itself of opinions—in all cases, opinions associated broadly with the Left—on a dozen other hot topics in American governance. No one involved with this process—not the committee members, hailing from various countries; not the U.S. government itself, variously adopting apologetic and proud-of-our-progress tones in defending its record; and of course not the NGOs demanding stronger condemnation of the U.S. for its ways—seemed to think this process was in any way unusual, presumptuous, or outrageous. All accept it as the new normal.

—⟋𝔪⟍—

In recent years there has flared up a heated public discussion of the degree to which the U.S. Supreme Court should refer to foreign legal materials in arriving at its decisions. Justices including Anthony Kennedy, Stephen Breyer, and Ruth Bader Ginsburg have in various opinions cited approvingly to European human rights law, the U.N.'s International Convention on the Elimination of All Forms of Racial Discrimination, and various national courts including those of Jamaica, India, and Zimbabwe. In *Roper v. Simmons* (2005), Justice Kennedy's majority opinion struck down the death penalty for juvenile offenders amid numerous references to foreign conceptions of human rights. In *Graham v. Florida* (2010), the Court struck down life-without-parole for juvenile offenders, with Kennedy (again writing the majority opinion) citing the "climate of international opinion" and even the U.N. Convention on the Rights of the Child, a human rights treaty that the United States has pointedly *refused* to ratify. Meanwhile, conservative Justices Antonin Scalia, Clarence Thomas, and John Roberts were highly critical of the appearance of a growing reliance on foreign legal views, and Scalia spoke out publicly as well, debating Justice Breyer on the topic before a public audience.

Much of the public commentary on the subject missed the point. As all the justices agreed, the Supreme Court since the earliest days of the republic has consulted foreign legal sources for a variety of uncontroversial purposes. At the same time, Kennedy and some other justices were careful to note that by citing foreign practice they did not necessarily intend to hold it out as of obligatory or binding effect on the United States. So does everyone agree then that foreign ideas of rights can sometimes be illuminating as an advisory matter, but are no more than that? Well, no. As sophisticated commentators had reason to know, much of the "international community"—specifically, much of the human rights movement at law schools, NGOs, and elsewhere—*does* consider the evolving content of international human rights norms to be binding upon the United States, whether or not the American public or Congress are yet ready to accept it as so. Many of these advocates are visibly frustrated that the U.S. sometimes declines to embrace or ratify the norms or make them enforceable in its courts, and they hope the Supreme Court will bypass this problem by incorporating the norms directly into its jurisprudence. Indeed, many NGOs have been active in calling the foreign law to the attention of the Supreme Court, through amicus briefs or otherwise. When the debate broke out, however, many in the international human rights movement kept mum, apparently not thinking the time ripe to publicly declare the full scope of their ambitions.

THE DOSSIER CHASE

The heyday of universal jurisdiction arrived when some European governments began enacting laws explicitly throwing open their courts to human rights cases from around the world. Current and former officials from many nations were soon being indicted (and less often detained) on a regular basis. A particularly sweeping 1993 law made Belgium the scene of prosecutorial investigations of a varied cast of figures ranging from obscure African potentates to sitting U.S. presidents and even, not without a certain irony, the country's own foreign minister, charged with improprieties in an arms deal with Nepal. In Great Britain, a crisis unfolded on the Heathrow tarmac when an Israeli general aboard an El Al plane learned that

London police had been issued a warrant to arrest him over his actions on behalf of the Israeli military; after some tense hours the plane was allowed to depart with him on it. Other targets included Arab leaders including the Libyan dictator Moammar Qaddafi.

Spain continued active as a venue too, entertaining charges against former officials of the Argentinian and Guatemalan governments. In 2006 its high court announced that it was considering whether to charge high officials of China with genocide in Tibet. That exception aside, many dictators whose ideological origins could be traced to the Left, such as Cuba's Fidel Castro and the rulers of North Korea, seemed to go about their world travels with little fear of arrest, however much blood they might have on their hands. But perhaps that too might change in time.

The prosecutions of course did not emerge from thin air, and seldom did they have their ultimate origin within the country where the papers were served. Instead a pattern was seen: adversaries would assemble a dossier alleging crimes by national officials and then begin shopping it to prosecutors and judicial departments in various countries, customizing it as needed to suit the countries' local legal requirements (and perhaps political leanings), all the while quietly studying officials' travel plans if a detainment was part of the scheme. The affidavits and charges making up the dossier might be drawn in whole or part from groups with intense ideological commitments against the regime or government in question; indeed, it was not unheard-of for the charging groups themselves to have participated as guerrillas or other combatants in local conflicts and themselves to have been accused of atrocities. That was no bar to employing their affidavits in a universal-jurisdiction prosecution; if the complainants were themselves suspected of atrocities (so the argument went) the proper answer was for someone to develop a separate dossier against them and thus enable a second prosecution.

It came to be known as *lawfare*: aiming human rights charges at a target country and its officials, whether on solid or dubious legal and factual grounds, could be an effective way of hampering that country's defense and foreign policy efforts, damaging its image abroad, and tying up its officialdom. The charge might also compel the release of sensitive documents, introduce frictions into national relationships such as those between NATO allies, and discourage risk-averse persons from entering or remaining in some types of government service in target countries. If it went well, it could lead to a show trial beamed to a worldwide audience accusing the hated officials of human rights violations, something not likely to be forgotten even if they escaped conviction.

—⟢—

Despite early assurances that only crimes of "exceptional gravity" affecting the "fundamental interests of the international community" would give rise to universal jurisdiction, the relevant boundaries turned out to be rather more elastic. Charges of *war crimes*, for example, often turn out to hinge on questions of targeting and proportionality: Could a military objective have been gained with less harm to nearby civilians? Might a less forceful response have quelled a given uprising? Moral lapses on targeting and proportionality have been credibly alleged against leaders on both sides of many conflicts through history; as regards World War II, for example, many respectable historians have condemned the Allied command (and ultimately the American presidents Truman and Roosevelt and the British prime minister Churchill) over the policy of bombing German and Japanese civilian populations with more ferocity than was probably needed to win the war. In addition to bearing the reproach of history, should the three men also have been put on trial for war crimes? Under the new dispensation, it was hard to see why not. Concerns about proportionality—sometimes decried by respondents as attempted "micro-management" of war conduct—underlay complaints against U.S. officials over NATO air strikes in the former Yugoslav civil war and against Great Britain over the sinking of an Argentine warship in the Falklands War, among many other requested prosecutions.

The definition of *torture* became a major issue in U.S. politics after revelations that American leaders had authorized waterboarding and other barbarous practices in the Iraq conflict and the War on Terror. But many human rights groups define torture far more broadly than that. They argue, for example, that civilian penal sanctions common in many American states, such as solitary confinement, life imprisonment without possibility of parole, and the death penalty, should be deemed torture because of their harsh psychological effect on inmates. State officials who have taken part in the implementation of these practices, in other words, might stand accused of international human rights crimes. The catchall *crimes against humanity* category has been interpreted to include practices that involve an "attack on human dignity or grave humiliation or a degradation of one or more human beings," such as Israel's decision to allow civilian settlement in some portions of occupied Arab territory. The practice of slavery is also ordinarily labeled a crime against humanity; while not controversial in itself, that has led some to argue that reparations for slavery, even in the no longer recent past, are called for under principles of international human rights law.

"Exceptional gravity" or no, by the time you added up all the different practices that have been deemed fundamental violations of human rights, a very large share of the nations of the world, large or small, Western or non-Western, outwardly peaceful or torn by civil war, present possible targets for prosecution. European courts became the scene of a large docket of complaints filed against top officials of the United States, France, Germany, and so forth, with perhaps the most celebrated case waged against the Israeli prime minister Ariel Sharon. Among many high-ranking U.S. officials named in papers demanding prosecution were the Secretaries of State Colin Powell and Henry Kissinger, the Gulf War general Norman Schwarzkopf, and Presidents George H.W. Bush and George W. Bush. Other voices demanded the prosecution of the British prime ministers Tony Blair and Margaret Thatcher. Advocates expressed pleasure and excitement over the prospect of a big score in the form of the seizure and detention of a former or sitting president, prime minister, or high cabinet minister of the United States or another major power.

TIME FOR AN INTERNATIONAL CRIMINAL COURT?

Even to their supporters, it was increasingly apparent that the new universal jurisdiction procedures were fraught with problems. Providing defendants with due process protections, for example, could be a highly challenging affair, even aside from the failure to provide trial in the locality of the alleged offense (as many time-honored conceptions of due process have held to be vital). Evidence submitted by the private group seeking the prosecution can be of uncertain reliability, especially if underlying events had taken place in a distant land years earlier. Vital witnesses for one or both sides were often unable or unwilling to appear for examination. Key information bearing on, e.g., the state of mind of an accused official was often in the possession of a foreign government which might refuse to divulge it, even if exculpatory, lest it expose state or military secrets, inculpate other officials, or lend perceived legitimacy to the proceeding. The vaunted detachment and objectivity of host-country prosecutors and judges might also be interpreted as an entire lack of accountability to the polity where the alleged crimes took place, perhaps even tinged with an imperialist-style willingness to impose the host country's values.

Then there were the constant jolts to relations between nations, made worse by the mouse-and-cat thriller games that unfolded as human rights groups tracked target officials through changes of planes and speaking venues to prepare for an attempted collar. The United States began exerting pressure on its putative allies in Western Europe, even threatening to support the removal of NATO military headquarters from Belgium because of its repeated prosecutions of U.S. officials. Belgium did indeed back off its pioneering law, for that and other reasons, and other European governments likewise pared back their laws, adding as a prerequisite for prosecution, for example, that some misdeed of a defendant be linked to their own territory. In other instances national authorities intervened to seek the dismissal of particular troublesome cases, or courts excused themselves from hearing the cases on narrow or technical legal grounds. Significantly, the International Court of Justice, a body within the U.N. system whose rulings are influential if not necessarily binding, in

2002 found it improper to prosecute a government's sitting officials under principles of universal jurisdiction. Prosecutions of retired (as opposed to sitting) officials continued, and they seriously complicated the ability to travel abroad of some former officials of Israel and other countries. But the momentum was slowing.

Just in time, then, came a proposal that would do away with the unruly sport of chasing targets through multiple national courts. International tribunals had already been convened to confront atrocities committed in notorious "failed states": Rwanda, Sierra Leone, and the former Yugoslavia. What was needed now, or so it was argued, was one big new transnational court to take jurisdiction over crimes against humanity wherever committed. In 1998, after a round of negotiated compromise, there was unveiled the plan for a permanent new International Criminal Court. Initially it would be given authority to hear claims over war crimes, genocide, and crimes against humanity, but further expansions of its jurisdiction were contemplated in the future. As of 2010 negotiations were under way to expand its jurisdiction to cover the proposed crime of "aggression," a charge that over the years has been flung around rather casually against many a combatant power.

—◊◊◊—

Accredited human-rights NGOs were deeply involved in the successful campaign for an International Criminal Court, just as they were counted as the most vocal advocates of universal jurisdiction, the revival of the Alien Tort Statute in the United States, and the universal periodic review process at the U.N., in each case working with allies in U.S. law schools. And as advances were made on each front, the NGOs also were managing to accumulate unto themselves quite an impressive variety of roles and functions. In practice they are the ones who ordinarily marshal complaints of rights violations before the tribunals, the ones who help the treaty panels develop the agenda for universal periodic review and point out what they consider violations, and the ones officially deputized to watch one or more target countries on an ongoing basis. They file many civil actions under the Alien Tort Statute (although private lawyers seeking dollar payouts have been a larger and larger factor on this front as time has gone on.) They commonly compile and submit the dossiers that result in prosecutions under universal jurisdiction. And they are very much invovled in developing the agenda for the new ICC: in its early operation, 99 percent of the cases referred to the new court for possible prosecution came from NGOs.

It all adds up to a lot of power for NGOs, which may or may not be accountable to any particular constituency (some are membership organizations, others not) and which in effect derive their favored position from their acceptance by other players within the "international community" itself—a community that sometimes seems to consist in large part of perhaps a few tens of thousands of persons who spend a lot of time talking to each other.

As NGOs have emerged as ambitious players in the new system, they have begun striking up working relationships and ententes with other NGOs, which in turn has tempted them to expand their portfolios: it is now common for women's-rights NGOs to agitate on racial issues, for health advocates to develop positions on war proportionality, for environmental groups to lend support to labor causes, and so forth. Indeed, as it has been realized that reframing a longstanding concern as a human rights issue is a way to catch the world's attention while seizing the moral high ground, NGOs themselves have begun to be (in effect) lobbied by groups eager to secure the human rights imprimatur for their various causes. In the political ecology of Washington, D.C. or other national capitals, there are at any given time hundreds, even thousands of overlooked causes seeking attention, higher funding, or changes in government policy. By heading for Geneva or Brussels or New York, these groups can now in effect marshal international muscle and prestige to put pressure on their own home governments.

ARRESTING U.S. OFFICIALS?

For some human rights groups, the goal of all goals is the prosecution and detainment of United States officials. Among the more prominent U.S.-based NGOs is the New York City-based Center for Constitutional Rights (CCR), founded by the legendary radical lawyer William Kunstler and others as a more explicitly Left alternative to the American Civil Liberties Union. Upon the departure of the George W. Bush administration in 2009, CCR launched a noisy campaign calling for its top officials to be put on trial for war crimes, naming vice president Dick Cheney, national security advisor Condoleezza Rice, defense secretary Donald Rumsfeld, and CIA director George Tenet. ("We already know the truth . . . what we need is a PROS-ECUTOR!" its headline screamed.) CCR had earlier been known for its legal onslaughts aimed at Israel; in perhaps its best-known case, it unsuccessfully sued Caterpillar Tractor under the Alien Tort act for having sold tractors to the Israeli government, which supposedly made the company responsible for the later death of the pro-Palestinian activist Rachel Corrie, crushed by a bulldozer at a protest.

Far from finding itself marginalized within the human-rights community, CCR has been accorded an honored place in it. It filed the original lawsuit that in 1980 broke open the old Alien Tort Statute for use by human rights litigants, and has taken the lead in many other noteworthy suits as well. It is of course fully accredited by the U.N. and richly funded by the usual foundations. Among its extensive connections, it maintains close, extensive ties with the nation's two leading law school human rights projects, the ones at Columbia and NYU, with whom it often cooperates in suit-filing.

—m—

Arresting foreign dignitaries against the wishes of their home governments, while on medical visits or otherwise, was very much the sort of thing international law was developed to prevent. That is why official and diplomatic immunities always loomed so large in traditional international law: insults, injuries, and denials of safe passage to these persons had been an important reason why countries took up arms down through the ages, from the Second Punic War to the assassination of Archduke Ferdinand in 1914. In 2002 the U.S. Congress passed an "American Servicemembers' Protection Act" authorizing the president "to use all means necessary and appropriate" to retrieve "any American national" detained by or at the request of the International Criminal Court. To put it more bluntly, Congress authorized acts of war to rescue Americans caught up in ICC jurisdiction. (The bill was nicknamed the "Hague Invasion Act," after the seat of the ICC and some other international courts.) The leading British judge Nicolas Browne-Wilkinson gave a prescient warning about universal jurisdiction:

> If the law were to be so established, states antipathetic to Western powers would be likely to seize both active and retired officials and military personnel of such Western powers and stage a show trial for alleged international crimes. . . . It is naïve to think that, in such cases, the national state of the accused would stand by and watch the trial proceed: resort to force would be more probable.

Miscalculations as to how far countries will go to defend their nationals have been at the root of wars both large and small, as in 1982 when Argentina seized the Falkland Islands, not expecting that Britain would send a flotilla halfway around the world to reclaim the thinly populated isles. By encouraging, even glamorizing, the seizure of officials the new international law has much increased the likelihood of such miscalculations in future—suggesting that indulging the international community's sense of righteousness may not always come for free.

Conspicuously lacking as it is in a reliable peaceful means of enforcement, international law has long seemed to circle back to the playground taunt: Yeah? You and what army? We may still get a chance to find out.

chapter THIRTEEN

conclusion

IRVING KRISTOL FAMOUSLY DISCERNED IN MODERN American society the emergence of a *new class*, its standing founded more on educational achievement and cultural fluency than on older forms of wealth or social position, its specialty the manipulation of ideas and symbols rather than physical labor or the ownership of the means of production. Estranged from and suspicious of the world of property and business, the new class (Kristol argued) is instead friendly toward the continued expansion of governmental activity, in part because it is itself relatively successful in influencing the actions of government. In particular, it is skilled in argument, and it often achieves (whether in its voting patterns or in its likes and dislikes generally) a kind of class solidarity at least as cohesive and impressive as that of, say, business managers or factory workers.

According to Kristol and others who took up his analysis, the characteristic redoubts of the new class include the universities, journalism, and the media, the public sector itself, and the professions, especially law. But has ever an institution been developed that is as powerful an engine of the new class ethos as the one that sits astride all four of these sectors—the modern elite law school?

Many have observed that the new class is fully as attuned to status distinctions as any class to come before it, but simply draws on a different set of status signifiers, with the right educational and cultural cues counting for more than the traditional trappings of wealth or breeding. Surely some version of class thinking is at work when the dean of Yale Law School refers to his institution as "the Republic of Conscience," or when a law professor refers to a "broad consensus among members of the elite, thinking class and like-minded folk" as underlying constitutional change. Unlike "they," with their grubby politics, who are always trying to catch the ears of lawmakers with their self-interested requests, "we" are distinguished not merely by our superior understanding but by our purity of mind and motive.

—⧆—

That the law schools churn out so many bad ideas is notable enough. But equally notable is that they predictably churn out certain *kinds* of bad ideas.

Overall, the ideology of law schools is biased toward the expansion of law and its uses, and away from a recognition of the inevitable costs, limitations, and inaccuracies of law. Countless law review articles propose new causes of action, lay out wider theories of damage recovery, or otherwise call for giving courts and lawyers more to do. Relatively few recommend changes that reduce the average citizen's fear of being caught up in legal process or the time he must spend thinking about law. Each new change generates more demand for lawyers' services and makes them more powerful and salient in society, while constricting the range of freedom in which other persons can act without fear of legal consequences.

Much has been said about legal academia's penchant for what Harvard law professor Mary Ann Glendon has called "rights talk"— its couching of demands and preferences in terms of purportedly fundamental rights, asserted as if timeless and universal but in fact proliferating and evolving on a restless, unending, ad hoc basis. The old "negative" rights to be left alone, we are told, must give way to assertions of new "positive" rights to government action. Being a matter of rights, the demands must be implemented without delay, protests of high cost or inconvenience are to be rejected, and calls for compromise are to be suspected as morally dubious. But the advance of rights talk has shrunk not only the old "negative" realm of individual liberty but also the bounds of democratic choice, as more and more spending and programmatic decisions are put off base to the give and take of the legislative process and public budgeting. As advocates win expansions of government through legal assertion that they could not have won (or won as fast) by appealing to majority sentiment, conventional politics itself begins to atrophy, and a new road to power in society opens up: stop trying so hard to appeal to the median voter, and take up instead as a professional arguer-about-rights. And if that is the career path you choose to pursue, you will almost certainly do well to begin at an elite law school.

FROM "RIGHTS TALK" TO INTERNATIONAL HUMAN RIGHTS TALK

The growth of the new international law is the perfect logical culmination of fifty years' worth of bad ideas from legal academia.

The personnel, to begin with, are familiar. In the NGOs' "international community," with its heavy contingent of law professors, we see a clubby near-replica of the faculty meeting, with its obligatory moralistic cant, its distrust or incomprehension of sectors of society such as the military, and its patented uniformity-in-difference in which nominally diverse people follow each other at the microphone to express identical sentiments.

There is the same idealization of judicial processes and litigation. Through much of the twentieth century, if people considered the idea of a world government at all, they tended to think of some global legislative body, such as the U.N. General Assembly, perhaps supplemented by an executive-branch arm of global regulators or blue-helmeted U.N. police. But the new international law instead faithfully follows the preferences of contemporary law school opinion by entrusting power to judges, lawyers and tribunals. With the partial exception of the European community, transnational legislative bodies have not achieved the expected prominence; the real energy and appetite has been in the growth of international judicial commissions and panels. Given the gradual escalation of rights-talk into international-human-rights talk, this is just what one would have expected.

—⟁—

The new push for transnational rights law was also the crowning and ultimate expression of the legal academy's longstanding taste for access to centralized power.

It is worth noting that one of the defining characteristics of an elite law school is that it is "national." (To be a "regional" school is by definition not to have attained first rank.) To attend one of the best law schools is to join a community not greatly defined by locality; at an intellectual and academic level, the law school experiences at (say) Berkeley and Columbia, or Northwestern and Penn, would be altered in only minor ways if the schools were required to pick up and move to each others' parts of the country for a while. In the pecking order of topics in legal scholarship, federal topics outrank state-court topics such as torts and employment law, which in turn outrank local government law. And one reason for the long decline of property from a pillar of the law school curriculum to something less than that is that it has always seemed so irredeemably . . . local.

Across much of America local self-governance—on schools perhaps above all, but also on land, property and resource law, local taxation and finance, police and corrections, roads and transportation, voting and election practice, and so on—is still passionately valued. But it is much less passionately valued in high-end legal academia, which is one reason institutional reform litigation, with its relentless pressure toward uniformity and top-down governance, its homogenization of once-distinctive local government cultures, has tended to be vastly more popular in legal academia than in the outside society. The ventures into symbolic litigation over reparations and historical land tenure aroused fury not just because they menaced residents' tangible interests, but because they seemed to call into question the legitimacy of the particular communities they lived in and to which they felt loyalty. Academic backers of the litigation, by contrast, were more likely to view it through a national lens: we as a nation had failed to give blacks and native Americans a decent shake, and the suits would force us to confront our collective shortcomings as a people.

Those who favor the preservation of local and state autonomy are usually well aware that locally chosen authorities will make some errors and allow some disparities that might have been corrected or ironed out in a more centrally governed system. Similarly, the much maligned "sovereigntists" in international law are usually well aware that policy will sometimes be made wrongly by national and local authorities that might have been made rightly by international tribunals. That does still not convince them that it is a good idea to hand over wide-ranging control of domestic U.S. policy to international jurists, no matter how well-credentialed or civilized the participants in the faculty meeting might seem.

—⁂—

Do the new modes of governance work?

They certainly fail at many of their advertised objectives. Institutional reform litigation on topics from prisons to homelessness to mental health care has been fraught with unintended, occasionally tragic consequences. Citizen suits allow strategic objections to many good projects yet fail to succeed at blocking many bad ones. The unending expansion of education law has correlated with no very favorable trend in student or school performance. The early payouts in a few land claims and reparations cases were not repeated.

And yet in a different sense the suits clearly *have* worked. They have redistributed power and wealth to the class of lawyers and interest groups who can master the techniques of suing. Whether or not they advance the ultimate objectives of the clients of public programs, the suits have served government employees, unions, and other provider groups by tying the hands of budget-cutting lawmakers. They have served activists and pressure groups by keeping their cause in the papers, raising the profile of their demands, and giving them a subpoena-punched window through which to observe the inside operations of institutions they wish to influence. The private lawyers who file the suits can not only make out fabulously well on a fee level but can also become Very Important People in the governance of whole sectors of public life, all with no need to worry about re-election. They will outlast the new mayor and governor, and they know it. Is this an unplanned consequence? Or is it the secret behind the durability of public interest law? And if the latter, is it any reason law schools vie with each other to stake out a presence in that field and steer their students toward it?

There is every reason to believe international human rights law will develop along a similar path. It is already lawyer-driven and opaque to outsiders, and getting more so. It has not yet developed consent decrees as a way of moving power off-books to private litigants, but NGOs already exercise considerable power in ways not visible to the public, and profit-minded private counsel—such as tort lawyers putting the Alien Tort Statute to use—are rapidly moving into the field. In the best tradition of public interest law, none of these groups are in the habit of answering to the public or to much of anyone else.

TEACHERS, OR LAWGIVERS?

Every so often, an academic field of study will grow in confidence to the point that it announces itself as the rightful queen of the political and social disciplines, possessing the key to all riddles of governance. History and political philosophy were among the first to make such bids; there later followed political science, sociology, social psychology, schools of government and administration, and above all economics. Perhaps law was bound to have its turn.

Economics aside, none of the other contenders have managed to keep up the pretensions: we do not think of turning over the last word on political questions to political philosophers or political scientists the way we are more or less willing to turn the last word on physics over to academic physicists or on medical therapy over to the practitioners of academic medicine. Are law professors and legal intellectuals the rightful arbiters of what the law should be? Probably not. Whatever the distinctive insights they can contribute, and they are many, they are hardly the only ones trained in thinking about human motivations and incentives, fairness and practicality, problems of proof, probability, and evidence, or a dozen other aspects of the problem. Like judges and lawyers generally, law professors ordinarily express opinions in language that falls much short of the precision or exactitude of scientists or high-level economists, and their judgments fall back on a substantial admixture of intuition, guesswork, and art. Partiality, arbitrariness, and contradiction come with the territory. Because of the lawyer- and lawsuit-driven nature of law, legal scholarship finds it even harder than many other fields of scholarship to shake off the role of handmaiden to advocacy. Even less plausible is the premise that legal scholars form an elect of moral purity with consciences more finely honed than those of the rest of us. Their record as participants in the litigation system—let alone the emergence of legal ethics as a field in which opinions may be obtained for a price—suggests instead that they are just as exposed to temptation as ordinary mortals and not really much better at resisting it.

—◇◇◇—

If law schools ought generally not to set up in the business of trying to govern the rest of us, what good can they do? Potentially a great deal. To begin with, training students in the skills and knowledge they will need in legal practice is no mean function and no small challenge. Training future lawyers to respect the legitimate interests of their future clients, and to recognize the dignity of the kind of everyday legal work that the world will always need, is not half bad either. Training them to do all this in an ethically grounded, appropriately humble way is potentially noblest of all. We neither need nor want more philosopher-monarchs. But we could use more good lawyers.

endnotes

CHAPTER ONE   THE HATCHERY OF BAD IDEAS

They also hire clerks: on the influence wielded by judges' clerks at the Supreme Court and elsewhere, see, e.g., David Garrow, "The Brains Behind Blackmun," *Legal Affairs*, May/June 2005; Bob Woodward and Scott Armstrong, *The Brethren: Inside the Supreme Court* (Simon & Schuster, 1979); Stephen Choi and Miti Gulati, "Which Judges Write Their Opinions (And Should We Care?)," 32 Fla. St. U. L. Rev. 1077 (2005); Paul Wahlbeck, James F. Spriggs II and Lee Sigelman, "Ghostwriters on the Court?: A Stylistic Analysis of U.S. Supreme Court Opinion Drafts," *American Politics Research*, Vol. 30, No. 2, pp. 166–192 (2002) (applying literary authorship analysis to find that Justice Marshall's opinions fell into five distinguishable styles of authorship during a term in which he employed five clerks).

What is taught in the law schools in one generation: Chris Goodrich, *Anarchy and Elegance: Confessions of a Journalist at Yale Law School* (Little, Brown, 1991), p. 116 (quoting Yale's Grant Gilmore).

Democratic party at the lectern: John O. McGinnis and Matthew Schwartz, "Conservatives Need Not Apply," *Wall Street Journal*, Apr. 1, 2003.

Chimpanzee: Jim Robinson, "Beastly Behavior? A Law Professor Says It's Time to Extend Basic Rights to the Animal Kingdom," *Washington Post*, Jun. 5, 2002 (quoting Steven Wise).

Silly titles, opaque passages, antic proposals: Richard A. Posner, "Legal Scholarship Today," 45 Stanford L. Rev. 1627 (1993).

Relativity: Laurence Tribe, "The Curvature of Constitutional Space: What Lawyers Can Learn From Modern Physics," 103 Harv. L. Rev. 1 (1989).

Sanism: Michael L. Perlin, "'Baby, Look Inside your Mirror': The Legal Profession's Willful and Sanist Blindness to Lawyers with Mental Disabilities," 69 U. Pitt. L. Rev. 589 (2008).

French-derived high theory: A.P. Farley, "The Black Body as Fetish Object," 76 Ore. L. Rev. 457 (1997); A.P. Farley, "Lacan and Voting Rights," in Austin Sarat, Jonathan Simon *et al.*, *Cultural Analysis, Cultural Studies and the Law* (Duke, 2003), p. 323.

Sued by less-empowered: Leslie Bender, "Feminist (Re-)Torts: Thoughts on the Liability Crisis, Mass Torts, Power, and Responsibilities," 1990 Duke L. J. 848 (1990); Walter Olson, "Theory-Addled Lawyers," Across the Board, Feb. 1994.

Tort of sexual fraud: Jane E. Larson, "'Women understand so little, they call my good nature "deceit"': a feminist rethinking of seduction," 93 Colum. L. Rev. 374 (1993).

Interviews held behind screens: See Walter Olson, *The Excuse Factory: How Employment Law Is Paralyzing the American Economy* (Free Press, 1997), p. 27; "There Oughta Be A Law," *Time* magazine "Swampland" blog, Mar. 19, 2007 (on career of Adam Cohen). See also Deborah L. Rhode, *The Beauty Bias: The Injustice of Appearance in Life and Law* (Oxford U. Press, 2010) (Stanford law professor argues for "appearance bias" laws).

"I haven't opened up a law review in years": Aaron Twerski, "Legal scholarship: It should be relevant again," *National Law Journal*, Sept. 3, 2007 (quoting Dennis Jacobs and reporting that at recent Cardozo School of Law symposium in New York "dealing with the waning influence of law reviews, nearly all the judges in attendance agreed that law review articles had a minimal impact on jurisprudence.")

Sobered-up: Jeffrey Toobin, "Bench Press," *The New Yorker*, Sept. 21, 2009.

CHAPTER TWO   THE FORCES OF UNANIMITY

Yale's own special kind of school spirit: Adam Liptak, "Yale Law Frets Over Court Choices It Knows Best," *New York Times*, Nov. 13, 2005 (quoting Owen Fiss).

There is only one Yale Law School and it is us: Harold Koh, "Welcome Address to New Students," Sept. 1, 2005 (reprinted at YLS website).

81–15 split: Adam Liptak, "If the Law Is An Ass, The Law Professor Is a Donkey," *New York Times*, Aug. 28, 2005 (citing *Georgetown Law Journal* study by John McGinnis, Matthew Schwartz and Benjamin Tisdell of federal campaign contributions by professors at leading schools). For similar findings, see Paul Caron, TaxProf blog, Sept. 10, 2008 (95–5 split in lawprof contributions Obama-McCain); David Bernstein, Volokh Conspiracy blog, Jan. 7, 2008 (10–1 split); Andrew Peyton Thomas, *The People Versus Harvard Law* (Encounter, 2005), p. 115 (citing 74–16 D-R split in 2003 *Wall Street Journal* survey).

Diversifying their points of view: Peter Schuck, "Law Schools: Diverse in All But Viewpoint?" *The American Lawyer*, Dec. 2005. For an argument that professors' politics does not have much influence on students', see Patricia Cohen, "Professors' Liberalism Contagious? Maybe Not," *New York Times*, Nov. 2, 2008.

Try to hire the smartest: David Horowitz, *The Professors: The 101 Most Dangerous Academics in America* (Regnery, 2006), p. xl (quoting Robert Brandon). Follow-up: "Philosophy Professor Robert Brandon Clarifies Comments," Duke Office of News & Communications press release, Feb. 12, 2004. Intelligence and ideology: see Instapundit blog, communication from Jim Lindgren, Feb. 11, 2004. Not all ideologies have merit: Leiter Reports blog (Brian Leiter), Nov. 23, 2004 and Aug. 28, 2005 ("affirmative action for conservatives").

Every constitutional law casebook, treatise and handbook: Steven Teles, *The Rise of the Conservative Legal Movement: The Battle for Control of the Law* (Princeton U. Press, 2008), p. 45 (quoting critic). Teles's book includes much illuminating detail about ideological trends among law school faculties, including pp. 23–26 (tracing shifts to New Deal period).

Most influential faculty as measured by citation counts: LeiterRankings.com blog, Nov. 12, 2007.

Law-and-race centers: often the institution selects a veteran civil rights plaintiff's attorney to direct the center, as at Harvard, Ohio State, and North Carolina.

GW animal law program attempts to change attitudes: Neil Buchanan, Dorf on Law blog, Jul. 31, 2008. Descriptions of other schools' offerings are taken from the programs' websites.

Northeastern: see Robert Granfield, *Making Elite Lawyers* (Routledge, 1992) pp. 169 *et seq.* (on school's "leftist reputation" and affinity for values of "1960s social activists"). Antioch: Joel Seligman and Lynne Bernabei, *The High Citadel* (Houghton Mifflin, 1978), p. 174. Trial lawyer's generosity to Irvine: Spencer DeBrosse, "New UCI Law School Offers Another High Scholarship," NewUniversity.org, Jan. 10, 2010.

Dohrn: Ben Smith, "Obama once visited '60s radicals," Politico blog, Feb. 22, 2008 (Dohrn and husband Bill Ayers "flatly unrepentant"). See Joshua Elder, "Dohrn 'defiles' NU, alum says," *Northwestern Chronicle*, Feb. 15, 2002.

Angela Davis: Walter Mosley, "Angela Davis speaks at HLS," *Harvard Law Record*, Apr. 28, 2005 (standing ovation); Molly Hennessy-Fiske, "Activist Angela Davis Addresses BSA, BLSA," *Harvard Crimson*, Feb. 1, 1997 (another appearance).

Lynne Stewart at Stanford: Michael Tremoglie, "Terrorist Law School Mentor," FrontPage blog, Nov. 18, 2003. At Hofstra: Walter Olson, "Over the Edge," *City Journal*, Oct. 5, 2007.

Solomon Amendment: *Rumsfeld* v. *FAIR*, 547 U.S. 47 (2006). In a rare note of dissent, the dean and two professors at George Mason, the maverick public Virginia law school, submitted a brief on the other side arguing the measure's constitutionality.

Disdain for business law: see Dave Hoffman, Concurring Opinions blog, Apr. 9, 2008; Stephen Bainbridge, Business Associations blog, Apr. 8, 2008. See also Stephen Bainbridge: "Reflections on Twenty Years in Law Teaching," 56 U.C.L.A. Law Review "Discourse," 2008.

Scholarly associations: Daniel Klein, "Why So Few Conservative and Libertarian Professors?" Minding the Campus, Jan. 27, 2010. Self-selection of left-leaning lawyers into academic law: Richard Posner, *Overcoming Law* (Harvard U. Press, 1995), p. 87.

History department can transform itself: see Robert KC Johnson, "The Cole Thesis," Cliopatria blog, Nov. 28, 2004. Shared assumptions, connections and comfort levels: Stephen Bainbridge, Professor Bainbridge blog, Jan. 8, 2010.

Objective standards for quality of work vs. club structure: Liptak, "If the Law Is An Ass" (quoting Northwestern dean David Van Zandt). More of themselves: Andrew Peyton Thomas, *The People Versus Harvard Law* (Encounter, 2005), pp. 126–27 (quoting Alan Dershowitz).

Like locusts every seven years: private communication to author.

Accreditation: see David Bernstein posts, Volokh Conspiracy blog, Jul. 13–20, 2006; David Barnhizer, "A Chilling of Discourse," 50 St. Louis U. L. J. 361 (2006); U.S. Commission on Civil Rights, "Affirmative Action in American Law Schools, Briefing Report" (Apr. 2007), statement of Commissioner Gail Heriot joined by Chairman Gerald Reynolds, pp. 175–185; Gail Heriot, "Affirmative Action in American Law Schools," 17 J. of Contemp. Leg. Iss. 237 (2008); Stephen Bainbridge blog, Oct. 26, 2007 (calling for ending ABA's role in law school accreditation).

OCU suit: Jay F. Marks, "Memo to Oklahoma City University attorney details gender issues," *The Oklahoman*, Dec. 21, 2008.

A very ideological screen: Daniel Polsby, dean, George Mason University School of Law (interview with author). Animal rights grants: Lynne Marek, "U.S. Attorneys Flock to Animal Law," *National Law Journal*, Jun. 7, 2007; Overlawyered blog, Jul. 5, 2001; "HLS Receives Gift To Study Animal Rights Law," Harvard press release, Jun. 13, 2001.

Ford attitude toward research: Mary McClymont and Stephen Golub, eds., *Many Roads to Justice: The Law-Related Work of Ford Foundation Grantees Around the World* (Ford Foundation, 2000), pp. 14, 316.

CHAPTER THREE   CAREERISM SAVES THE DAY

RateMyProfessors.com: all quoted reviews visited February 17, 2010. For some pertinent cautions on the limitations of student evaluations, see Stanley Fish, *New York Times* "Opinionator," Jun. 21 and Jun. 28, 2010.

Stiles: see William R. Johnson, *Schooled Lawyers: A Study in the Clash of Professional Cultures* (NYU Press, 1978).

Ames: Paul Carrington, *Stewards of Democracy* (Westview, 1999), p. 181.

School of fencing or dancing: Thorstein Veblen, *The Higher Learning in America* (B.W. Huebsch, 1918), p. 211.

March of accreditation: Herbert Packer and Thomas Ehrlich, *New Directions in Legal Education* (Carnegie Commission on Higher Education and McGraw-Hill, 1972), pp. 25–28; Steven Teles, *The Rise of the Conservative Legal Movement: The Battle for Control of the Law* (Princeton, 2008), pp. 25–26 (hereinafter Teles, *Rise*) Roger Cramton, "Demystifying Legal Scholarship," 75 Georgetown Law Journal 1 (1986), at footnote 45.

Constituency on the ground for academic law doubled in the fifteen years to 1977: Teles, *Rise*, p. 42.

Critiques of law reviews: Harold Havighurst, "Law Reviews and Legal Education," 51 Northw. U. L. Rev. 22, 24 (1956); Fred Rodell, "Goodbye to Law Reviews," 23 Va. L. Rev. 38 (1936). For a modern echo, see Richard Posner, "Against the Law Reviews," *Legal Affairs*, Nov./Dec. 2004.

1914 AALS address: Wesley Hohfeld, "A Vital School of Jurisprudence," 14 AALS Handbook, 76–139, p. 88, cited in Laura Kalman, "Professing Law:

Elite Law School Professors in the Twentieth Century," in Austin Sarat *et al.*, eds., *Looking Back at Law's Century* (Cornell U. Press, 2002).

Corporation lawyer must give way to public counsel: Laura Kalman, *Yale Law School and the Sixties* (Chapel Hill, 2005) (hereinafter Kalman, *YLS*), 36 (citing Charles Clark).

Fie on Bills and Notes: Harold D. Lasswell and Myres S. McDougal, "Legal Education and Public Policy: Professional Training in the Public Interest," 52 Yale L.J. 203 (1943).

Training in policy analysis a demanding business: Thomas Bergin, "The Law Teacher: A Man Divided Against Himself," 54 Va. L. Rev. 637–57 (1968).

Worst of all worlds: Roger Cramton, "Demystifying Legal Scholarship," 75 Georgetown L. J. 1, 15 (1986).

Predictions on future legal demand: see, for example, Herbert Packer and Thomas Ehrlich, *New Directions in Legal Education* (Carnegie Commission on Higher Education and McGraw-Hill, 1972), pp. 7–9 (auto no-fault, group and prepaid legal service plans foreseen).

Yale virtually only school not to require Property: Kalman, *YLS*, p. 48.

Yale Law School anthem: circulating in oral tradition by the 1980s, as heard by the author.

No idea how to get a TRO: Kalman, *YLS*, p. 211 (Dean Pollak).

Domestic employees: Zoe Baird nomination transcript, Committee on the Judiciary, United States Senate, Jan. 19 and 21, 1993.

Tiered system: for a contrasting discussion of the much lower importance of prestige ranking in the medical school context, see HalfMD blog, Oct. 21, 2008 (citing article in Academic Emergency Medicine finding that ranking of graduates' medical schools was only the 14th most important factor in determining access to competitive residency opportunities).

Prestige is dominant objective even at religious law schools: Roger Cramton, "Demystifying Legal Scholarship," 75 Georgetown L. J. 1 (1986).

Traffic law unprestigious: see University of Chicago Law Faculty Blog, Jan. 28, 2007 (Lior Strahilevitz speech); Luke Gilman blog, Mar. 4, 2007.

Law review circulation numbers: Ross E. Davies, "Law Review Circulation 2009: The Combover," *The Green Bag* (GMU law review), 2010.

More attention to transgender Wicca than to uninsured motorist coverage: Quoted at Joerg Knipprath, Token Conservative blog, Feb. 18, 2010.

Anthony Kronman, *The Lost Lawyer: Failing Ideals of the Legal Profession* (Belknap/Harvard, 1993); Walter Olson, "Theory-addled lawyers," Across the Board, Feb. 1994 (review). For a more recent view, see Jack Balkin (Yale), Balkinization blog, Mar. 19, 2007 (citing "interdisciplinarity and high theory as the markers of scholarly seriousness and the keys to upward mobility in the profession").

Daniel Farber and Suzanna Sherry, *Beyond all Reason: The Radical Assault on Truth in American Law* (Oxford, 1997). See Walter Olson, "The Law on Trial," *Wall Street Journal*, Oct. 14, 1997 (review). John Marshall versus Roberto Unger: Suzanna Sherry, "The Canon in Constitutional Law" in J. M. Balkin and Sanford Levinson, eds., *Legal Canons* (NYU Press, 2000), p. 380.

Zany passion for novelty: Mary Ann Glendon, "What's Wrong With the Elite Law Schools," *Wall Street Journal*, Jun. 8, 1993. See Mary Ann Glendon, *A Nation Under Lawyers: How the Crisis in the Legal Profession Is Transforming American Society* (Farrar, Straus & Giroux, 1994).

Widely noted speech: Harry T. Edwards, "The Growing Disjunction Between Legal Education and the Legal Profession," 91 Mich. L. Rev. 34 (1992)

Had Professor A. stifled his yearning to strike back: The results of his failure to do so can be found at "Evaluating Evaluations: How Should Law Schools Judge Teaching?," 40 J. Leg. Ed. 47 (1990).

CHAPTER FOUR   THE HIGHER VOLUMES

Millions of consumers have had their hearing put at risk: Ina Fried, "Apple faces suit over iPod-related hearing loss," CNet, Feb. 2, 2006.

Revolution in consumer law: *Greenman v. Yuba Power Products*, 59 Cal.2d 57 (1963).

Future law clerks read casebooks: Alex Kozinski, "Who Gives a Hoot About Legal Scholarship?" 37 Hous. L. Rev. 295 (2000).

Prosser rates his own progress: William Prosser, "The Assault on the Citadel (Strict Liability to the Consumer)," 69 Yale L. J. 1099 (1960); William Prosser, "The Fall of the Citadel (Strict Liability to the Consumer)," 50 Minn. L. Rev. 791 (1966); John Hasnas, "What's Wrong With a Little Tort Reform?," 32 Idaho L. Rev. 557 (1996). On the stylized dance of mutual self-promotion between legal academics and judges who both wish to push the law in a certain direction, see also Judge Kozinski, "Who Gives a Hoot About Legal Scholarship?"

Battlefield of social theory: Christopher J. Robinette, "The Prosser Notebook: Classroom as Biography and Intellectual History," 2010 U. of Ill. L. Rev. 577 (2010).

Distributed among the public as a cost of doing business: *Escola* v. *Coca-Cola Bottling*, 150 P.2d 436 (Cal. 1944).

Implied reasonable assumption of risk should not be allowed to reduce: Chase Van Gorder, "Assumption of Risk Under Washington Law" (Eau Claire, Wis.: Professional Education Systems, Inc.) (1995).

Standard-form contracts: Friedrich Kessler, "Contracts of Adhesion–Some Thoughts About Freedom of Contract," 43 Colum. L. Rev. 629 (1943). See chapter 10, "No Exit: The Death of Contract," in Walter Olson, *The Litigation Explosion* (Dutton/Truman Talley Books, 1991).

New Jersey Supreme Court went first: *Henningsen* v. *Bloomfield Motors*, 161 A.2d 69 (N.J. 1960).

Even if lawsuits must be multiplied: William Prosser, *Handbook of the Law of Torts* (West, 1941), p. 202, quoted in Hasnas, "What's Wrong With a Little Tort Reform?"

The article that was to lay out the rationale: Harry Kalven, Jr., and Maurice Rosenfield, "The Contemporary Function of the Class Suit," 8 U. of Chi. L. Rev. 684 (1941). Kalven went on to become a renowned academic and a leading authority on such topics as the First Amendment and the workings of juries. Rosenfield, a non-academic, practiced civil liberties law and represented *Playboy* in its early years (as well as comedian Lenny Bruce, whose cast of attorneys also included Kalven). Then he switched gears to become an entertainment producer, bringing a succession of Broadway shows to the stage as well as producing the Robert De Niro breakthrough film *Bang the Drum Slowly* (1973).

Kalven and Rosenfield page references: They may never come, 688; come and get it, 691; too exact and complete, 701; paying lawyers handsomely, 717; why not let lawyer go it alone?, 718; virtually every question that is important socially, 698–99. The authors recognized–but did not appear to find terribly troubling–that unlike many official regulators, class action lawyers would as a group prove eager to pounce on purely technical violations, meaning that "the method will result in an insistence upon the harshest results and the most technical interpretations" (p. 719).

James Frey memoir: David Nieporent, "A Thousand Little Refunds, Plus Attorneys' Fees," Overlawyered, Oct. 2, 2007; Walter Olson, "Update: Not a Million Little Refunds," Nov. 24, 2007 (about 1,700 class members requested refunds, which meant legal fees of $783,000 exceeded $400 per disgruntled reader). Milli Vanilli: Amy Stevens, "The Mouthpieces: Class-Action Lawyers Brawl over Big Fees in Milli Vanilli Fraud," *Wall Street Journal*, Oct. 24, 2001.

Palm colors: Elisa Batista, "Palm Handed Suit Over Colors," Wired News, Aug. 24, 2002. Toshiba agreed to pay: Walter Olson, "Gold Bugs," *Reason*, Feb. 2000.

Not one case in a hundred: Prosser, "Assault on the Citadel," p. 1114. Alarm of manufacturers not justified: Prosser, "Fall of the Citadel," p. 842.

Ninth Circuit upheld dismissal of Apple case: Cynthia Lambert, California Civil Justice Blog, Jan. 5, 2010.

Statutes of limitation: Peter Huber, *Liability: The Legal Revolution and Its Consequences* (Basic, 1990), chapter 6. Retroactivity: Daniel E. Troy, *Retroactive Legislation* (American Enterprise Institute, 1998).

Recovered-memory extension: Walter Olson, "Stale Claims," *Reason*, Nov. 2000.

The cry inevitably raised: Prosser, "Assault on the Citadel," p. 1122.

CHAPTER FIVE   THE AUTHORITY BUSINESS

Tobacco settlement: Ch. 1, "The Joy of Tobacco Fees," in Walter Olson, *The Rule of Lawyers* (St. Martin's, 2002).

Daynard-Scruggs dispute: Bob Van Voris, "Tobacco Road Not Gold for All," *National Law Journal*, Dec. 28, 1998; Overlawyered blog, Apr. 21–23, 2000; Myron Levin, "Tobacco Wars' Huge Legal Fees Ignite New Fight," *Los Angeles Times*, May 20, 2001 ("a bit more mercenary," "stupefying," Daynard never quoted as a private litigator). House testimony: House Judiciary Committee hearing, Jul. 21, 1999, on H.R. 1875 and H.R. 2005, Interstate Class Action Jurisdiction Act of 1999 and Workplace Goods Job Growth and Competitiveness Act of 1999. Even afterward: reporting in *Boston Globe*, Aug. 9, 2001, *L.A. Times*, Aug. 10, 2001; Associated Press, Oct. 21, 1999 and Apr. 1, 2000. See Overlawyered blog, Apr. 21–23, 2000 and Aug. 13–14, 2001.

Tardily rectifying omission: "Correction: Tobacco litigation worldwide," *British Medical Journal*, Oct. 6, 2001. See Richard Daynard *et al.*, "Tobacco litigation worldwide," *British Medical Journal*, Jan. 8, 2000, and editorial, "Beyond conflict of interest: Transparency is the key," *British Medical Journal*, August 1, 1998. Soft drinks the next tobacco: Michael Blanding, "Hard on soft drinks," *Boston Globe* magazine, Oct. 30, 2005.

Authoritative voice of Olympian prescriptiveness: Laura Kalman, "Professing Law: Elite Law School Professors in the Twentieth Century," in Austin Sarat *et al.*, eds., *Looking Back at Law's Century* (Cornell U. Press, 2002), p. 359.

Wendy Murphy: Rachel Smolkin, "Justice Delayed," *American Journalism Review*, Aug./Sept. 2007; Mark Obbie, LawBeat blog, Jul. 18, 2007; KC Johnson, Durham in Wonderland blog, Dec. 31, 2006.

Harvard plagiarism scandals: see, e.g., Joseph Bottum, "The Big Mahatma," *Weekly Standard*, Oct. 4, 2004; Marcella Bombardieri and David Mehegan, "Ogletree admits lifted passages," *Boston Globe*, Sept. 9, 2004 (no deliberate wrongdoing, says Bok); Steven Marks, "Ogletree Faces Discipline for Copying Text," *Harvard Crimson*, Sept. 13, 2004 (Ogletree told Crimson he hadn't read Balkin passage); Sara Rimer, "When Plagiarism's Shadow Falls on Admired Scholars," *New York Times*, Nov. 24, 2004.

Roster of big names: National Legal Scholars website (http://nationallegalscholars.com/who.html); see also Bill Childs, TortsProf Blog, Oct. 9, 2007.

Halo effect: Leigh Jones, "More Law Professors Consult at Firms," *National Law Journal*, February 9, 2007 (quoting Bill Urquhart of Quinn Emanuel).

One day a week for outside work "standard" but "hard to enforce": Derek Bok, *Universities in the Marketplace: The Commercialization of Higher Education* (Princeton, 2003), p. 61. Very important day among their days: Deborah L. Rhode, *In Pursuit of Knowledge: Scholars, Status, and Academic Culture* (Stanford University Press, 2006), p. 21 (quoting Charles Sykes).

Dershowitz and tobacco: Jon Burstein, "Lawyer wants $34 million for working 118 hours on Florida's case against tobacco companies," *Fort Lauderdale Sun-Sentinel*, July 14, 2000; Cindy Krischer Goodman, "Harvard prof suing lawyers over tobacco settlement," *Miami Herald*, Aug. 2, 2000. See Overlawyered blog, Aug. 8–9, 2000.

Drug companies and the university: see, e.g., Eyal Press and Jennifer Washburn, "The Kept University," *The Atlantic*, March 2000. Shift of research activity from basic science: Bok, *Commercialization of the University*, pp. 58–59. See also Mark Luce, "Academia, Inc: Bartering Brains for Bread," *Salon*, 1999.

Chicago study: Cass Sunstein, Reid Hastie *et al.*, *Punitive Damages: How Juries Decide* (U. of Chicago Press, 2002), publisher's online material at press. uchicago.edu. Sunstein "pre-eminent legal scholar of our time": "Renowned legal scholar to join Harvard Law faculty," *Boston Globe*, Feb. 19, 2008 (quoting Elena Kagan). On the controversy, see Alan Zarembo, "Funding

Studies to Suit Need," *Los Angeles Times*, Dec. 3, 2003; W. R. Freudenburg, "Seeding science, courting conclusions: Reexamining the intersection of science, corporate cash, and the law," *Sociological Forum*, v. 20 (1), pp. 3–33 (2005); Sheldon Krimsky, "Exxon Funds Litigation Research, Gets Reduced Damages," The Pump Handle (blog), Jan. 16, 2007; Jon Haber (American Association for Justice), "Manipulating science," *National Law Journal*, Jul. 23, 2007. Piquantly, one article calls Krimsky "a leading authority" on conflicts of interest in academia: Eyal Press and Jennifer Washburn, "The Kept University," *The Atlantic*, March 2000. Earlier (Rustad) studies on punitive damages: see Olson, *The Rule of Lawyers*, pp. 278–279.

Legal research that isn't linked to interested party: see also William G. Childs, "The Overlapping Magisteria of Law and Science: When Litigation and Science Collide," 85 Neb. L. Rev. 643 (2007) (expert reports from litigation recast as scholarly articles). See also Childs, Torts Prof blog, Apr. 4, 2006 (suggesting that "while defense-funded studies are not unheard of, most such research is performed on behalf of plaintiffs' counsel").

A lot of judges just wilt: author's interview with Lawrence Schonbrun, Feb. 25, 2008.

Cendant fees: Karen Donovan, "Legal Reform Turns a Steward Into an Activist," *New York Times*, Apr. 16, 2005. On Miller's longstanding relationship with the Milberg Weiss firm, see, e.g., Robert Lenzner, *Forbes*, Feb. 16, 2004.

Enron fees: Josh Gerstein, "Judge To Mull $695 Million Legal Fee," *New York Sun*, Feb. 29, 2008; "Texas Objects To Enron Fees," Mar. 13, 2008.

NASDAQ fees: Diana B. Henriques, "In Landmark Settlement, a Question of Fees," *New York Times*, Sept. 13, 1998, and "Lawyers Are Awarded $144 Million From Class-Action Stock Suit," Nov. 10, 1998.

Brickman: author's interview with Lester Brickman. See Lester Brickman, *Lawyer Barons: What Their Contingency Fees Really Cost America* (Cambridge University Press, forthcoming 2011).

Skunk arrives at garden party: William Simon, "The Market for Bad Legal Advice: Academic Professional Responsibility Consulting as an Example," 60 Stan. L. Rev. 1555 (2008). See Roger Parloff, "Blowing the Whistle on Unethical Lawyers," *Fortune*, Jun. 4, 2008 (ethics opinion that went out under name of Prof. Geoffrey Hazard was drafted by law-firm client). What the market will bear: Simon, "Market for Bad Legal Advice," at footnote 36.

Fieger Trial Practice Institute: "Fieger's $4 Million Gift To Law College at MSU Establishes Nation's First Trial Practice Institute for Law Students,"

Michigan State University news release, Nov. 27, 2001; "$4 million gift to MSU-DCL funds trial practice institute," MSU News, Dec. 6, 2001; "Fieger's gift," *Lansing State Journal*, Nov. 29, 2001 (defense of grant); letter from concerned alumnus, *Detroit Free Press*, Nov. 28, 2001.

Obscenity-laced tirade: "Fieger Under Fire For Alleged Swearing Fit," MSNBC, Apr. 17, 2001. "Nazis" and "creeps": Jennifer Sullivan, "Attorney, judge in war of words," *Manatee* (Fla.) *Herald-Tribune*, Apr. 2, 2002. "Severe and reprehensible": Associated Press, Nov. 16, 2005 (quoting David Gorcyca).

Jury wins later overturned: Dawson Bell, "Fieger's wins lose luster in appeals," *Detroit Free Press*, May 29, 2001 (noting that although Fieger claims a political "conspiracy to get me" accounts for reversals, the partisan and philosophic makeup of appeals panels doesn't seem to make a marked difference in his chances of success). Insinuates sexual tryst: "Appeal reverses malpractice award," *Detroit News*, Aug. 24, 1999; editorial, Aug. 25, 1999; "Briefly", Aug. 25, 1999 (Fieger's response). Unapologetic about bullying charges: Dawson Bell, "Fieger's wins lose luster in appeals." See also Tim Jones, "Renowned attorney trying to bring some L.A. into law," *Chicago Tribune*, Mar. 31, 2004.

Renaming for donors: Robert Jarvis, "A Brief History of Law School Names," 56 J. Legal Educ. 388 (2006). See Paul Caron, TaxProf blog, Jul. 19, 2007. See also Ann Bartow, "Trademarks of Privilege," 40 Davis L. Rev. 919, 933 (Florida).

Texas Tech: Kara Altenbaumer, "Tech School of Law close to obtaining $15 million present," *Lubbock Avalanche-Journal*, Mar. 16, 2000; "Donor remains generous after donation 'not enough,'" AP/ AmarilloNet.com, Sept. 12, 2000 (school holds out for higher donation); "Tough Questions: Taking the High Road," *National Jurist*, Oct. 2000. See Linda P. Campbell and John Moritz, "Lawyers who led Texas' assault on the tobacco industry awarded $3.3 billion," *Fort Worth Star-Telegram*, Dec. 11, 1998.

University of Mississippi School of Law naming campaign: see http://www. umlawcampaign.com/donor.html

Cy près, Vanderbilt: see Walter Olson, Point of Law blog, Dec. 5, 2005 (citing words of Vanderbilt professor Richard Nagareda as quoted in *Nashville Tennessean*). West Virginia: Walter Olson, Point of Law blog, May 9, 2008. New Mexico: Scott Sandlin, "Class action leftovers aid UNM law school," *Albuquerque Journal*, Feb. 16, 2009. Hausfeld's Center for Competition Law: George Washington University press release, Sept. 6, 2007. Prayers answered: Loyola-Chicago press release, Feb. 14, 2008; Antitrust and Competition Policy Blog, Jul. 31, 2007 (University of Missouri lawprof D. Daniel Sokol describes Loyola center as "plaintiff friendly in its programming").

CHAPTER SIX THE CLASSROOM OF ADVOCACY

Yale clinic helped win Connecticut 2010 school finance case: Christian Nolan, "Supreme Court Says Students Guaranteed 'Suitable' Education," *Connecticut Law Tribune*, March 22, 2010 (YLS Education Adequacy Clinic). Students fight for Social Justice at Sexuality and Gender clinic: *Columbia News* (university publication), Dec. 10, 2007. Other boasts of social justice achievements are taken from the websites of the schools involved.

Clinics' track record: Heather Mac Donald, "This is the Legal Mainstream?" *City Journal*, Winter 2006.

Rapid rise in number of clinical programs: Steven M. Teles, *The Rise of the Conservative Legal Movement* (Princeton, 2008) (hereinafter Teles, *Rise*), p. 37.

Merely ameliorative: Waldemar A. Nielsen, *The Big Foundations* (Twentieth Century Fund study; Columbia U. Press, 1972), p. 406 (quoting Taconic Foundation executive John Simon). Nielsen's influential book, reflecting the views of its day, is full of slighting references to foundations whose benefactions are oriented toward local improvement, assistance to impoverished children and old people, or uncontroversial medical, university, or scientific causes, as opposed to social-change causes.

Johnny Appleseeds of litigation liberalism: even aside from its successful launch of the "public interest law" movement and clinical legal education, Ford's role in shaping the development of law in the United States and elsewhere deserves a book in itself. For an official overview, see Mary McClymont & Stephen Golub, eds., *Many Roads to Justice: The Law Related Work of Ford Foundation Grantees Around the World* (Ford Foundation, 2000) (hereinafter *Many Roads*). In the twenty years to 1970, Ford committed more than $70 million in 150 grants to the law and legal field. (1970 Ford "President's Review"; Teles, *Rise*, p. 30). For Ford's role in welfare litigation, see *Many Roads*, p. 91 (helped establish Center on Social Welfare Policy and Law in 1965); Heather Mac Donald, "The Billions of Dollars That Made Things Worse," *City Journal*, Autumn 1996. On Ford's support of a project on law and development that became the seedbed of Critical Legal Studies, see Laura Kalman, *Yale Law School and the Sixties* (UNC Press Books, 2005) (hereinafter Kalman, *YLS*), p. 262; Mark Tushnet, "CLS: A Political History" 100 Yale L.J. 1515 (1991) at 1533, 1531. See also, e.g., Richard Magat, *The Ford Foundation at Work* (Plenum, 1978), p. 86 (foundation supports "organized media campaigns" as well as changes in school curricula in hope of obtaining "right-minded citizenry").

Big Establishment blitz on behalf of tax exemption for litigation groups: Teles, *Rise*, pp. 49 *et seq.*; *Time*, Nov. 16, 1970.

Reich, Bittker, and the founding of the NRDC: Kalman, *YLS*, p. 223.

Pneumatic tubes: The Ford Foundation is headquartered at 320 E. 43rd Street in Manhattan. The New York Times was long based at 229 W. 43rd.

Ford furnished Harvard: Lester Brickman, "CLEPR and Clinical Education: A Review and Analysis," in *Clinical Education for the Law Student: Legal Education in a Service Setting* (CLEPR, 1973), p. 87, fn 32.

William Pincus opposition to law reformers' efforts to limit caseload of ordinary representation: CLEPR newsletter, Dec. 1969 (v. II, no. 4).

Most does not rise to the level of "cause" lawyering: David Luban, "Taking Out the Adversary: The Assault on Progressive Public Interest Lawyers," 91 Calif. L. Rev. 209 (2003).

Clinic client turned out to be the abusive parent: "Clinical Education: The Student Perspective," CLEPR newsletter, Jul. 1974 (v. VII, no. 1).

Rooming house fire: Kalman, *YLS*, p. 131 (quoting Avi Soifer).

Beleaguerment: environmental clinics have been the main exception to the rule that clinics hardly ever run into serious political opposition no matter how disputable their views. Luban, "Taking Out the Adversary," collects several other examples.

Reclamation of Southern Assets (ROSA) project: Mary Mitchell, "Reclaiming land may be bigger than reparations," *Chicago Sun-Times*, Jun. 5, 2005; "Shady down-South stuff," Feb. 20, 2005; Karen E. Pride, "Southern land reclamation project set to help 90 Chicago families," *Chicago Defender*, reprinted at website of Rep. Bobby Rush (D-Ill.), Jul. 29, 2005.

Revolving door: thus Martha F. Davis, "The Pendulum Swings Back: Poverty Law in the Old and New Curriculum," 34 Fordham Urban L. J. 1391, 1413–1414 (2007) cites the "active pipeline between academia and legal services practice" at law schools such as Columbia, whose Environmental Law Clinic (e.g.) is directed by an "activist and scholar" long associated with New Jersey's Public Interest Research Group.

Accreditation pressure on Louisiana State: Martha Neil, "LSU May Create Much-Desired Clinical Education Program," ABAJournal.com, Apr. 22, 2008.

Soros initiative: for an approving account, see Davis, "The Pendulum Swings Back."

Upsets altruistic students, two sides: Robert Granfield, *Making Elite Lawyers: Visions of Law at Harvard and Beyond* (Routledge, 1992), pp. 41 and 7–8.

CHAPTER SEVEN   POOR PITIFUL GULLIVER

Endangered species: "Agency: Lawsuits Stymie Conservation," AP/ FindLaw, Nov. 21, 2000; "Tribe says sheep habitat designation derails development plans," AP/*North County Times* (Calif.), Apr. 5, 2005.

Walter-Logan bill: Franklin D. Roosevelt, "Veto of a Bill Regulating Administrative Agencies, Dec. 8, 1940," at American Presidency Project (University of California, Santa Barbara website): http://www.presidency. ucsb.edu/ws/print.php?pid=15914

Daydream of liberation: Charles A. Reich, *The Greening of America* (Random House, 1970). The book sold fabulously well, but as the Sixties spell wore off it was sometimes treated roughly by critics. See R. Z. Sheppard, "Peter Pantheism," *Time*, Nov. 22, 1976 (calling it "the most profoundly naïve bestseller of the period" and saying its author "wafts nonsensical generalizations like dandelion seeds").

Most-cited article: Charles A. Reich, "The New Property," 73 Yale L. J. 733 (1964).

In the air: Milton Friedman, *Capitalism and Freedom* (U. of Chicago Press, 1962).

On the role Reich's work played in litigation against welfare program limits, and his work with the Field Foundation, see Steven M. Teles, *Whose Welfare? AFDC and Elite Politics* (Kansas, 1996); Martha Davis, *Brutal Need: Lawyers and the Welfare Rights Movement* (Yale, 1993); Charles A. Reich, "Midnight Welfare Searches and the Social Security Act," 73 Yale L.J. 1350 (1963).

Rights revolution in the Supreme Court: see, e.g., *Goldberg v. Kelly*, 397 U.S. 254 (1970) (welfare); *Morrissey v. Brewer*, 408 U.S. 471 (1972) (parole); *Goss v. Lopez*, 419 U.S. 565 (1975) (school discipline). See Teles, *Whose Welfare?*, p. 55 (courts' "revolution in welfare policy . . . caused the percentage of eligible persons actually receiving welfare to more than double in a matter of a few years").

Took a genuinely aggrieved single person: Thomas O'Brien, "Classroom Bullies: New York's Abusive School-Finance Litigation," Point of Law blog, Sept. 7, 2005.

WLBT case: *Office of Communication of the United Church of Christ* v. *FCC*, 359 F.2d 994 (1966); *Office of Communication of the United Church of Christ* v. *FCC*, 425 F.2d 543 (1969). See Milton Mueller *et al.*, "Reinventing Media Activism: Public Interest Advocacy in the Making of U.S. Communication-Information Policy, 1960–2002," Syracuse University Convergence Center School of Information Studies, Jul. 15, 2004.

Tougher scrutiny: *Citizens to Preserve Overton Park* v. *Volpe*, 401 U.S. 402 (1971).

One advocate's candor: Joseph L. Sax, *Defending the Environment* (Knopf, 1971) (hereinafter Sax, *Defending*). Cited passages: pp. 45 (Potomac construction, cloud on title, no one knows exactly what the lawsuit achieved); pp. 70, 115 (danger from cranks and delay minimized; thoughtful, "far more limber" agency decision-making foreseen); 148 (warns against excessive deference); 110 (judges' greatest strength is lack of expertise); 83, 108, 110 (other officials as favor-trading "insiders" vs. judges who take no phone calls and have no budget to balance); 128–29 (expressway loses on pettifogging grounds); 131, 135 (great bulk of litigation has been on procedure, merits seldom reached); 70 (probably not a development plan that couldn't be attacked for failure to study). On Ford Foundation support for the book, see Richard Magat, *The Ford Foundation at Work* (Plenum, 1978), 24.

Build the bad project after all: on environmentalists' disillusion with what could be accomplished under NEPA, see, e.g., Gerald Rosenberg, *The Hollow Hope* (Chicago, 1991), 277, 283 (temporary enjoining of projects was "most readily observed impact"); David M. Trubek and William J. Gillen, "Environmental Defense II," in Burton A. Weisbrod *et al.*, *Public Interest Law* (Univ. of Calif. Press 1978), pp. 196–7, 211 (victories for environmental litigators "fewer in number and more Pyrrhic in nature" as time went on).

Suing = "citizen participation": see, e.g., Sax, *Defending*, p. 232.

Naïve legality: Jeremy Rabkin, *Judicial Compulsions: How Public Law Distorts Public Policy* (Basic, 1989), p. 86.

CAA citizen standing slipped into bill at last minute, Rabkin, *Judicial Compulsions*, p. 284, footnote 26.

Affluent will lead the way for everyone: Sax, *Defending*, p. 245.

Taxpayer standing: *Frothingham* v. *Mellon*, 262 U.S. 447 (1923) (9–0, Sutherland opinion). Exception opened up for suits against expenditures advancing religion: *Flast* v. *Cohen*, 392 U.S. 83 (1968).

Disease of politics: Sax, *Defending*, p. 82 (Hudson River Expressway controversy). Ski tramway episode: Sax, p. 184 (quoting William Tague, "The

Rise and Evaporation of the Mount Greylock Tramway," *Berkshire Review*, Summer 1967).

Hired hands: Sax, *Defending*, p. 240.

CHAPTER EIGHT   THE PERMANENT GOVERNMENT

New York City homeless litigation: This account is based largely on articles in the Manhattan Institute publication *City Journal* including Peter Hellman, "Justice Freedman v. New York," Spring 1997, and Sol Stern, "The Legal Aid Follies," Autumn 1995. See also Randall K. Filer, "What Really Causes Family Homelessness?," Autumn 1990; Susan V. Demers, "The Failures of Litigation as a Tool for Developing Social Welfare Policy," 22 Fordham Urban Law J. 1009 (1994) (hotel cooking facilities); "Justice Helen Freedman needs to make a decision on Homeless position," *New York Daily News*, Sept. 4, 2007.

Rikers Island: David Schoenbrod and Ross Sandler, "Prison Break," *City Journal*, Summer 1996.

Unofficially called Board of Special Ed: Sol Stern, "New York's Fiscal Equity Follies," *City Journal*, Spring 2004.

Prevent a meditated wrong: John Willard and Platt Potter, *A Treatise on Equity Jurisprudence*, p. 434 (Banks & Brothers, 1875).

Exhaustive critique: Felix Frankfurter and Nathan Greene, *The Labor Injunction* (Macmillan, 1930). On particular criticisms, see, e.g., pp. 54–59 (confides excessive discretion to judge), 81 (overbreadth of remedy "terrorizes innocent conduct"), 80 (tactical use; "even if we win, we lose"), 190 (power of single judge). Compare Owen Fiss, *The Civil Rights Injunction* (Indiana, 1978), p. 6 (repudiating Frankfurter & Greene view). On collusive suits, see, e.g., Frankfurter & Greene, pp. 14–15 (employer plaintiffs); *Chicago and Grand Trunk Railway* v. *Wellman*, 143 U.S. 339, 345 (1892).

Injunctions against New Deal legislation: Donald Horowitz, "Decreeing Institutional Change: Judicial Supervision of Public Institutions," 1983 Duke L. J. 1265, 1268. See also Josiah Henry Benton, *What Is Government By Injunction?* (Rumford Press, 1898).

Contumelious or intransigent defendants long a prime target of injunction power: Theodore Eisenberg and Stephen Yeazell, "The Ordinary and the Extraordinary," 93 Harv. L. Rev. 465 (1980).

Brown viewed as so legitimate: Fiss, *The Civil Rights Injunction*, 5.

Wide sweep of new court orders: Samuel J. Brakel, "Prison Reform Litigation: Has the Revolution Gone Too Far?," 70 Judicature 5 (1986); Square footage of cells, wattage of light bulbs, every state affected: Malcolm M. Feeley and Edward L. Rubin, *Judicial Policy Making and the Modern State* (Cambridge, 1998). Child welfare systems in 35 states: Ross Sandler and David Schoenbrod, *Democracy by Decree* (Yale, 2003), p. 122. Serrano: *Serrano* v. *Priest*, 5 Cal. 3d 584 (1971). This decision later came to be known as *Serrano I* and was followed by cases under the same name reported at 18 Cal. 3d 728 (1976) (*Serrano II*) and 20 Cal. 3d 25 (1977) (*Serrano III*).

Owen Fiss enthusiasm: see "The Forms of Justice," 93 Harv. L. Rev. 1 (1979); *The Law As It Could Be* (NYU Press, 2003), p. 244 ("Second Reconstruction").

Abram Chayes, "The Role of the Judge in Public Law Litigation," 89 Harv. L. Rev. 1281 (1976).

Narrow court orders against governments give way to broad: Horowitz, "Decreeing Institutional Change," at pp. 1266, 1294–95. Vincent M. Nathan, "The Use of Masters in Institutional Reform Litigation," 10 U. Tol. L. Rev. 419, 421 (1979).

Named defendants stand in: compare Frankfurter and Greene, *The Labor Injunction*, p. 83 (criticizing "equitable doctrine of suit by representation," with Fiss, *The Civil Rights Injunction*, p. 49 (approving virtual representation of nonparties despite criticisms of fairness).

Expanding role of masters: Horowitz, "Decreeing Institutional Change," p. 1274 (had been used predominantly for fact finding); Nathan, *The Use of Masters*, p. 424 (previously "exceptional," citing U.S. Supreme Court's 1912 Rules of Practice in Equity); David Kirp and Gary Babcock, "Judge and Co.: Court Appointed Masters, School Desegregation and Institutional Reform," 32 Ala. L. Rev. 313 (1981).

"Equity will not issue a decree it cannot enforce": Nathan, "The Use of Masters," p. 419.

Judge Freedman's husband: the Center for Social Welfare Policy and Law at Columbia is now known as the National Center for Law and Economic Justice.

CFE does not bother to hide ties to NYC teachers' union: Thomas C. O'Brien, "Classroom Bullies: New York's Abusive School-Finance Litigation," Point of Law blog, Sept. 7, 2005.

Evolution of school finance litigation to cut unions and wealthy districts into the coalition: Marilyn Gintell, ed., *Strategies for School Equity* (Yale U. Press, 1998), pp. 87–88.

Crisis strategy on welfare: Richard Cloward and Frances Fox Piven, "A Strategy to End Poverty," *The Nation*, May 2, 1966. See Steven M. Teles,

Whose Welfare? AFDC and Elite Politics (Kansas, 1996), pp. 5–6 (Cloward/ Piven's strong ideological views), pp. 86–89; Martha Davis, *Brutal Need: Lawyers and the Welfare Rights Movement* (Yale U. Press, 1993), pp. 47–50; Sol Stern, "The Legal Aid Follies," *City Journal*, Autumn 1995.

Welfare rights litigation: aside from Teles, *Whose Welfare?*, and Davis, *Brutal Need*, sources include R. Shep Melnick, *Between the Lines: Interpreting Welfare Rights* (Brookings, 1994). See also R. Shep Melnick, "The Politics of the New Property: Welfare Rights in Congress and the Courts" in Ellen Paul and Howard Dickman, *Liberty, Property, and the Future of Constitutional Development* (SUNY Press, 1990).

Prison crisis strategy: See, e.g., Margo Schlanger, "Civil Rights Injunctions Over Time: A Case Study of Jail and Prison Court Orders," 81 N. Y. U. L. Rev. 550 (2006), p. 560, citing David Goldman, California Law Review, 1973; Feeley and Rubin, *Judicial Policy Making*, p. 376 ("drive up the costs of prisons").

Convenience of clients not consulted: Feeley and Rubin, *Judicial Policy Making*, p. 377; Ross Sandler and David Schoenbrod, *Democracy by Decree*, pp. 8, 124–25.

Texas prisoners not happy to lose their jobs: Carroll Pickett with Carlton Stowers, *Within These Walls: Memoirs of a Death House Chaplain* (St. Martin's, 2002), pp. 135–50 (scathing critique of Texas court decree). Horowitz, "Decreeing Institutional Change," some prisoners plainly worse off, p. 1306.

Tenants hire lawyers to fight their "own" lawyers: Sandler and Schoenbrod, *Democracy by Decree*, p. 129. See also Sol Stern, "The Legal Aid Follies," *City Journal*, Autumn 1995.

"Defendants who would like to lose": Horowitz, "Decreeing Institutional Change," p. 1294. Prison officials "cussed" but secretly welcomed suits: Schlanger, "Civil Rights Injunctions Over Time," p. 563 (quoting Mark Kellar); see also Feeley and Rubin, *Judicial Policy Making*, pp. 139, 363, 366, and Sandler and Schoenbrod, *Democracy by Decree*, p. 122. A classic article on collusive and sweetheart injunction litigation is Michael McConnell, "Why Hold Elections? Using Consent Decrees to Insulate Policies from Political Change," 1987 U. Chi. L. Forum 295, 315–16. McConnell cites cases including *U.S. v. Board of Ed of City of Chicago*, 588 F. Supp. 132 (N.D. Ill. 1984), vacated and remanded, 744 F. 2d 1300 (7th C. 1984) (defendant agrees to lobby for more funds), and *Dunn v. Carey*, 808 F. 2d 555, 560 (7th Cir. 1988) (court of appeals speculates that local officials had been "frustrated at their inability to win political approval for the construction of a new city hall," so they agreed in a consent decree to construct one). See "Consent of the Governors," *Regulation*, Mar/Apr. 1981 (unsigned piece written in part by the author). On New York City officials' negotiated disposition of a "friendly suit" on the conduct of the city's foster care programs in such a way as to exclude input from Roman Catholic and Jewish agencies that had been active in carrying on the program, see Richard Epstein, "*Wilder* v. *Bernstein*: Squeeze Play By Consent Decree," 1987 U. Chi. L. Forum 209. For the later, disastrous effects of the long-running Wilder foster care decree, see Sandler and Schoenbrod, *Democracy by Decree*, pp. 1–6; Nina Bernstein, *The Lost Children of Wilder* (Pantheon, 2001).

Collusion between parties to school finance litigation: this is abundantly documented in the literature. On Alabama plaintiffs' "early and important alliance" with nominal defendants, see Helen Hershkoff, "School Finance Reform and the Alabama Experience," in Marilyn Gintell, ed., *Strategies for School Equity* (Yale U. Press, 1998), p. 27. San Antonio case: *San Antonio Independent School District* v. *Rodriguez*, 411 U.S. 1 (1973). State lawmakers secretly pleased at excuse to raise taxes: Matthew H. Bosworth, *Courts as Catalysts: State Supreme Courts and Public School Finance Equity* (SUNY Press, 2001), pp. 128, 156–157. See also Gerald Rosenberg, *The Hollow Hope* (Chicago, 1991), 34, at note 23 (author's conversation with Gary Orfield); Bosworth, *Courts as Catalysts*, p. 96 (Texas); Frank Easterbrook, "Civil Rights and Remedies", 14 Harv. J. L. Pub. Pol. 103, 108 (1991) (in Kansas City case, "school board favored the district court's remedy"); Thomas C. O'Brien, "Classroom Bullies: New York's Abusive School-Finance Litigation," Point of Law blog, Sept. 7, 2005; Sol Stern, "Campaign for Fiscal Equity and New York: the March of Folly," in Eric Hanushek, ed., *Courting Failure: How School Finance Lawsuits Exploit Judges' Good Intentions and Harm Our Children* (Hoover/Education Next Books, 2006).

Results of busing crusade: see Stephen P. Powers and Stanley Rothman, *The Least Dangerous Branch? Consequences of Judicial Activism* (Praeger, 2002), pp. 37 *et seq.*, 48 (campaign led to mix of successes and failures in South, almost unmitigated failure in North). Mickey Kaus, *The End of Equality* (Basic, 1995); Richard E. Morgan, *Disabling America* (Basic, 1984), pp. 46 *et seq.* On the spectacular failure of the Kansas City (Jenkins) order, see Paul Ciotti, "Money and School Performance: Lessons from the Kansas City Desegregation Experiment," Cato Policy Analysis #298, Mar. 16, 1998; Abigail Thernstrom and Stephan Thernstrom, *No Excuses: Closing the Racial Gap in Learning* (Simon & Schuster, 2003), pp. 164–65; John Derbyshire, "Everything's up the Spout in Kansas City," *National Review*, Sept. 18, 2009 (spend-more-money theory "tested to destruction" in Jenkins orders); Alfred A. Lindseth, "The Legal Backdrop to Adequacy," in Hanushek, ed., *Courting Failure*, pp. 38–39; *Jenkins* v. *Missouri*, 216 F. 3d 720 (2000) (Beam, J., dissent).

Mental illness: Powers and Rothman, *The Least Dangerous Branch?*, p. 133. Also: Heather Mac Donald, "Have We Crossed the Line?," *City Journal*, Winter 1993 (decrees created incentives for "indiscriminately discharging patients").

Inmate violence increased: Powers and Rothman, *The Least Dangerous Branch?*, pp. 100 and 181; Kathleen Engel and Stanley Rothman, "Prison Violence and the Paradox of Reform," 73 Pub. Int. 91, 100–01 (1983). On the Texas experience, see Feeley and Rubin 90–91, and the work of John J. DiIulio, Jr., including "Prison Discipline and Prison Reform," 89 *Public Interest* 71–90 (1987), and "The Old Regime and the Ruiz Revolution: The Impact of Judicial Intervention on Texas Prisons," in John J. DiIulio, Jr., ed., *Courts, Corrections, and the Constitution: The Impact of Judicial Intervention on Prisons and Jails* (Oxford U. Press, 1990). Staff morale a casualty in prison suits: Rosenberg, *The Hollow Hope*, pp. 305–310.

Philadelphia crime spree: Sandler and Schoenbrod, *Democracy by Decree*, p. 186.

Results of school finance litigation: Hanushek, ed., *Courting Failure*; Bosworth, *Courts as Catalysts*; Martha Derthick and Joshua Dunn, "Who Should Govern? Adequacy Litigation and the Separation of Powers," in Martin West and Paul Peterson, eds., *School Money Trials: The Legal Pursuit of Educational Adequacy* (Brookings Institution Press, 2007). More: William A. Fischel, "How Judges Are Making Public Schools Worse," *City Journal*, Summer 1998. New Jersey's Abbott case: Winnie Hu, "In New Jersey, System to Help Poorest Schools Faces Criticism," *New York Times*, Oct. 30, 2006.

California and Proposition 13: William A. Fischel, "Did Serrano Cause Proposition 13?" *National Tax Journal*, December 1989; Caroline M. Hoxby, "All School Finance Equalizations Are Not Created Equal," 66 Q. J. of Econ. 1189 (2001). See also Caroline Hoxby and Ilyana Kuziemko, "Robin Hood and His Not-So-Merry Plan: Capitalization and the Self-Destruction of Texas' School Finance Equalization Plan," National Bureau of Economic Research Working Paper, Sept. 2004; Virginia Postrel, "A Public Policy Failure," *New York Times*, Oct. 7, 2004.

Grab the dumb ones, not the lawyer's kid: Richard Arun, *Judging School Discipline: The Crisis of Moral Authority* (Harvard U. Press, 2003), 127, citing Ellen Jane Hollingsworth et al., *School Discipline: Order and Autonomy* (Praeger, 1984). See also Richard E. Morgan, *Disabling America* (Basic, 1984), pp. 46 *et seq.*, 63 *et seq.* The schools' shift toward discretionless "zero tolerance" policies, often with absurdly harsh results, is a later and arguably related story.

Education suit diverted resources to sophisticated complainants: Jeremy Rabkin, *Judicial Compulsions: How Public Law Distorts Public Policy* (Basic, 1989), pp. 168–69. See also Jeremy Rabkin, "Captive of the Court," *Regulation*, May/Jun. 1984.

Welfare aftermath: Teles, *Whose Welfare?*, p. 44 (public opinion strongly pro-welfare in 1961, after early 1970s sentiment never repeated); pp. 115, 118 (eventually most welfare gains were rolled back, often by Congress). Court declines to constitutionalize welfare rights: see, e.g., *Dandridge* v. *Williams*, 397 U.S. 471 (1970); *New York State Department of Social Services* v. *Dublino*, 413 U.S. 405 (1973).

Failure of prison crisis strategy, public support for prison building boom: Schlanger, "Civil Rights Injunctions Over Time," p. 560–61; Horowitz, "Decreeing Institutional Change," p. 1306.

Latitude necessary for dispatch of own internal affairs: *Rizzo* v. *Goode*, 423 U.S. 362 (1976). In a case the next year, Justice Brennan (of all people) argued in dissent against locking in government defendants: *U.S.* v. *Trust Co. of New Jersey*, 431 U.S. 1, 45 (1977). "The Framers fully recognized that nothing would so jeopardize the legitimacy of a system of government that relies upon the ebbs and flows of politics to 'clean out the rascals' than the possibility that those same rascals might perpetuate their policies simply by locking them into binding contracts."

Double bunking of pre-trial detainees not due process violation: *Bell* v. *Wolfish*, 441 U.S. 520 (1979).

Defendants should be able to adapt, easier to get decrees lifted: *Frew* v. *Hawkins*, 540 U.S. 431 (2004). See Ross Sandler and David Schoenbrod, "The Supreme Court, Democracy and Institutional Reform Litigation," 49 N.Y.L.S. L. Rev. 915 (2005).

Continued vitality of institutional reform litigation: see Margo Schlanger, "Beyond the Hero Judge," 97 Mich. L. Rev. 1994, 2035 (1999); Schlanger, "Civil Rights Injunctions Over Time." Cincinnati police: Kevin Osborne, "Blame game," CityBeat.com, Aug. 13, 2008. California prison health: "Judge could seize $8 billion," AP/*San Diego Union Tribune*, Aug. 13, 2008; Mike Zapler, "California prison health overseer demands $8 billion for medical facilities," *San Jose Mercury News*, Aug. 13, 2008. Veterans' mental health: Kelly Kennedy, "Judge: VA care falls outside his authority," *Navy Times*, Jun. 27, 2008.

Broadening of decree as horse trading results in extra commitments: Sandler and Schoenbrod, "From Status to Contract and Back Again: Consent Decrees in Institutional Reform Litigation," *Review of Litigation*, Fall 2007.

On the episode in New York City's special-education litigation in which the plaintiff's lawyers insisted on "preventive" services which thrust them deeply into non-special education, see Sandler and Schoenbrod, *Democracy by Decree*, p. 70. Can grow to hundreds of pages' worth: see Sandler and Schoenbrod, "The Supreme Court, Democracy and Institutional Reform Litigation," at footnote 47.

Nontransparency: Sandler and Schoenbrod, *Democracy by Decree*, p. 125 ("neither the decree" in Jose P. case nor any amendments "were ever published, even in periodicals on special education litigation"); Sandler and Schoenbrod, "Status to Contract," Fall 2007 (sessions closed to public). "Public" treated as interloper: Rabkin, *Judicial Compulsions*, p. 280, at note 52 (recounting experience in trying to get pleadings and documents from pending Public Citizen suit against FDA).

They "own" areas of litigation: Sandler and Schoenbrod, *Democracy by Decree*, p. 135.

CHAPTER NINE "RESPONSIBILITIES FLOW ETERNAL"

We want a change in America: Paul Shepard, "Lawyers Plan Slave Reparations Suit," AP/*Washington Post*, Nov. 4, 2000. Randall Robinson, *The Debt: What America Owes To Blacks* (Dutton, 2000).

Forman episode: "A Black Manifesto," *Time*, May 16, 1969; *New York Review of Books*, Jul. 10, 1969; "Reparations Up To Date," *Time*, May 3, 1971; Lawrence H. Williams, "Christianity and reparations: revisiting James Forman's 'Black Manifesto,' 1969," *Currents in Theology and Mission*, Feb. 2005; Bayard Rustin, "The Failure of Black Reparations," *Harper's*, Jan. 1970.

Inspired a Yale law professor: Boris I. Bittker, *The Case for Black Reparations* (Random House, 1973). Bittker's Old Left background: Laura Kalman, *Yale Law School and the Sixties* (Chapel Hill, 2005), p. 63. Reduce the emotional temperature: Bittker, p. 68. On Bittker's latter-day relevance, see also Jonathan Rauch, "Blacks deserve reparations–but not for slavery," *Reason*, Sept. 1, 2001.

Targeted toward the disadvantaged rather than blacks-as-blacks: Graham Hughes, "Reparations for Blacks?" 43 N.Y.U. L. Rev. 1063 (1968).

Changed centuries of precedent to ensure a win in this case: Margaret A. Little, "A Most Dangerous Indiscretion: The Legal, Economic, and Political Legacy of the Governments' Tobacco Litigation," 33 Conn. L. Rev. 1143 (2001) (quoting Thomas V. ("Mike") Miller, Jr.).

They're going to come after us with guns: John Henry Schlegel, "Notes Toward an Intimate, Opinionated, and Affectionate History of the Conference on Critical Legal Studies," 36 Stan. L. Rev. 391, 403 (1984) (quoting Mark Tushnet).

Legal suppression of hurtful speech: Mari Matsuda, Charles Lawrence, Richard Delgado, and Kimberlé Williams Crenshaw, *Words That Wound: Critical Race Theory, Assaultive Speech, and the First Amendment* (Westview, 1993). A predecessor piece collected in that volume was Richard Delgado, "Words That Wound: A Tort Action for Racial Insults, Epithets, and Name-Calling," 17 Harv. C.R.-C.L. L. Rev. 157 (1982). On Critical Race Theory, note also W. F. Twyman, Jr., "The Lightness of Critical Race Theory," *The Intellectual Conservative* (Dec. 6, 2005) (noting that many of the black law professors to make the most impact in the outside world, such as Stephen Carter (Yale), William Gould (Stanford), and Barack Obama (Chicago), tended to keep their distance from CRT).

Critical Race Theory manifesto: Mari J. Matsuda, "Looking to the Bottom: Critical Legal Studies and Reparations," 22 Harv. C.R.-C.L. L. Rev. 323 (1987). Special voice of those who have experienced discrimination: 324. Quotes Prosser & Keeton on policy, 382. Continues as long as there is stigma: 385, 397. Group, not individual rights: 394.

The many components of Wachovia: Jeff Jacoby, "The slavery shakedown," *Boston Globe*, Jun. 9, 2005.

Ropemakers and caulkers: Robinson, *The Debt*, p. 209.

More a political than a historical question: Brian DeBose, "NAACP to target private business," *Washington Times*, Jul. 12, 2005 (quoting James Lide).

Requested the return of donated archives: see Overlawyered blog, June 10, 2005 (historian John Steele Gordon).

Not about the money: Michael Tremoglie, "Reparations — 'It's Never About Money,'" FrontPage blog, Mar. 4, 2002 (quoting Alexander Pires); Kelley Vlahos Beaucar, "Lawsuit Chases Companies Tied to Slavery," FoxNews.com, Mar. 25, 2002 (quoting Manning Marable). $97 trillion: *Harper's*, Nov. 2000.

Just because slavery ended over a hundred years ago doesn't excuse them: see Walter Olson, "Reparations, R.I.P.," *City Journal*, Autumn 2008 (quoting Deadria Farmer-Paellmann). Wrongs flow eternal: Robinson, *The Debt*, p. 230.

Should have been available: Alfred L. Brophy, "Reparations Talk: Reparations for Slavery and the Tort Law Analogy," 24 Boston College Third World L. J. 81, 92 (2004). State legislators may be willing: Ibid., at footnote 29.

I think we're being conservative: Matt O'Connor, "Suit seeks $1 trillion from Japan for war," *Chicago Tribune*, Sept. 6, 2001 (quoting Anthony D'Amato).

Take your money today and sue you tomorrow: Greg Barrett and Kelly Brewington, "Interim Chief Defends NAACP's direction," *Baltimore Sun*, Dec. 13, 2004 (quoting Dennis Hayes).

Trust fund for political advocacy: Robinson, *The Debt*, p. 246. Free college tuition: Ibid., p. 244–45. Corporations should be required to give shares of stock: Alfreda Robinson, "Corporate Social Responsibility and African American Reparations: Jubilee," 55 Rutgers L. Rev. 309, 381 (2003). Suing history book makers: Amy Martinez, *Palm Beach Post*, Oct. 23, 2000 (reporter's phrasing summarizing plans of Dennis Sweet).

Black radio and black press couldn't get enough of the issue: see Juan Williams, "Get a Check? No, Thanks," *GQ/FrontPage*, Sept. 2001.

Only 4 percent of whites supported: Harbour Fraser Hodder, "The Price of Slavery," *Harvard Magazine*, May/Jun. 2003 (2000 Harvard/Chicago poll). Among those rallying resistance to the idea was ex-radical David Horowitz, who gave speeches on college campuses and bought ads in campus newspapers with an uncompromising anti-reparations message. See David Horowitz, *Uncivil Wars: The Controversy Over Reparations for Slavery* (Encounter, 2002).

Dangerous, evil idea: Williams, "Get a Check?" "Marked applause" for Kerry at Howard University: "Kerry opposes slavery reparations," *Washington Times*, Apr. 15, 2004.

Courts threw out: for a list of reparations cases dismissed, see Brophy, "Reparations Talk," at footnote 7.

National project of racial reconciliation: Charles J. Ogletree Jr., "Tulsa Reparations: The Survivors' Story," B.C. Third World L.J. 13 (2004). Rides on hopes of racial healing: Emily Newburger, "Breaking the Chain," *Harvard Law Bulletin*, Summer 2001.

Learning experience in self-discovery: Robinson, *The Debt*, pp. 220, 247.

Alabama poll: Sam Hodges, "Slavery payments a divisive question," *Mobile Register*, Jun. 23, 2002 (quoting Alabama pollster/professor Keith Nicholls).

CHAPTER TEN   FOREVER UNSETTLED: THE RETURN OF INDIAN CLAIMS

Mashpee: Paul Brodeur, *Restitution: The Land Claims of the Mashpee, Passamaquoddy, and Penobscot Indians of New England* (Northeastern U. Press, 1985) (adaptation of *New Yorker* articles), p. 6.

Cayuga tribe vs. "trespassers": Walter Olson, "Give It Back To the Indians?," *City Journal*, Autumn 2002 (quoting Clint Halftown).

It's in total violation: Matthew Purdy, "Tribal Justice? They'd Settle for Syracuse," *New York Times*, Jan. 30, 2000 (quoting Irving Powless). See also John Caher, "New York State May Be Solely Liable for Indian Land Claims," *New York Law Journal*, Apr. 2, 2002.

One Typical Indian Law Article: on the tendency of outside funders to favor radical formulations, see Vine Deloria, *We Talk, You Listen: New Tribes, New Turf* (Macmillan, 1970), pp. 71–72 ("The chief method of distinguishing good guys from bad guys [among liberal religious grantmakers in 1967–68] was whether or not they believed in 'confrontation.' If an Indian swore he believed in 'confrontation' and promised to burn the agency when he got home, he was eligible for funds. If he was uncertain about assassinating the Secretary of the Interior, then he was classified as a 'conservative racist' and was not funded.")

Widely noted article: Francis J. O'Toole and Thomas N. Tureen, "State Power and the Passamaquoddy Tribe: 'A Gross National Hypocrisy?'" 23 Maine L. Rev. 1 (1971). On Tureen, see also Brodeur, *Restitution*, 79–82; Kim Isaac Eisler, *Revenge of the Pequots* (U. of Nebraska Press, 2002).

So-called innocent landowners hold void title: Wenona T. Singel and Matthew L.M. Fletcher, "Power, Authority, and Tribal Property," 41 Tulsa L. Rev. 21 (2005), viewed on SSRN Sept. 4, 2010.

Both legal and just to evict: Robert Odawi Porter, "Feeding America's appetite for land," *Indian Country Today*, Jun. 17, 2005.

"Little Eichmanns": Matt Labash, "The Ward Churchill Notoriety Tour," *Weekly Standard*, Apr. 25, 2005. Genocide: The Indian-law literature includes many respectful and uncontradicted citations of the "genocide thesis" endorsed by Churchill and associated with independent historian David Stannard, who has posited that the collapse of American Indian populations after European contact, generally ascribed to their lack of immunity to Old World diseases, should be construed as the triumph of white society's deliberate policy of killing as many Indians as possible. See David E. Stannard, *American Holocaust: The Conquest of the New World* (Oxford U. Press, 1992), p. 146. Many historians have dismissed the thesis as a feverish fancy: see, for example, Guenter Lewy, "Were American Indians The Victims of Genocide?," *Commentary*, Sept. 2004.

Uniquely American form of racial dictatorship: Robert A. Williams, *Like a Loaded Weapon: The Rehnquist Court, Indian Rights, and the Legal History of Racism in America* (U. of Minnesota Press, 2005).

Simply an imperial nation: Porter, "Feeding America's appetite for land."

1971 article: O'Toole and Tureen, "State Power and the Passamaquoddy Tribe."

Meetings going on in the Cabinet room: Olson, "Give It Back To the Indians?"; Brodeur, *Restitution*, p. 97.

Most important: *Oneida County v. Oneida Ind. Nation*, 470 U.S. 226 (1985) (Oneida II).

Mashantucket Pequots: see Brett Fromson, *Hitting the Jackpot: The Inside Story of the Richest Indian Tribe in History* (Grove Press, 2004); Eisler, *Revenge of the Pequots*.

Archibald Cox helped out: Brodeur, p. 101.

Wasn't the Kickapoos' to sell: Walter Olson, "Give It Back to the Indians?" See also Walter Olson, "My Kingdom for a Casino," *Forbes*, May 8, 2006.

Golden Hill Paugussett: Sam Libby, "Another Chance for Golden Hill Paugussett," *New York Times*, Dec. 12, 1999.

This is all about power: Walter Olson, "Stale claims," *Reason*, Nov. 2000 (quoting Ray Halbritter).

Probably the one great nation of the world: Felix S. Cohen, "Original Indian Title," 32 Minn. L. Rev. 28 (1947), pp. 33–34.

Maturing of the debate: Stuart Banner, *How the Indians Lost Their Land: Law and Power on the Frontier* (Harvard U. Press, 2005).

Canadian claims: Ruth Walker, "Indian land claims flood Ottawa," *Christian Science Monitor*, Mar. 20, 2001.

Perth: Kathy Marks, *The Independent* (U.K.), Sept. 21, 2006; "Native title could lock up parks: Ruddock," AAP/*The Australian*, Sept. 22, 2006; Chris Merritt and Patricia Karvelas, "Title win boosts capital city claims," *The Australian*, Sept. 21, 2006.

Melbourne: Ben Packham, "Native title claim looms," *Herald-Sun*, Sept. 21, 2006.

Magic of compound interest in Cayuga suit: Margaret Cronin Fisk, "200-Year-Old Land Dispute Nets $247.9 Million," *National Law Journal*, Oct. 17, 2001.

Senecas and Grand Island: Dan Herbeck and T.J. Pignataro, "Sigh of relief," *Buffalo News*, Jun. 22, 2002.

High court's thinking had evolved: *City of Sherrill v. Oneida Indian Nation*, 544 U.S. 197 (2005). Manifest Destiny, illegal dispossession: Singel and Fletcher, "Power, Authority."

Reactions to Cayuga dismissal: Jim Adams, "Supreme Court drops Cayuga land claim case," *Indian Country Today*, May 19, 2006. In August 2010 a panel of the Second Circuit, citing developing precedent, dismissed the Oneida tribe's 35-year-old claims.

CHAPTER ELEVEN   " . . . THE MOVEMENT MADE GLOBAL"

Called for internationalizing tribal disputes: Robert A. Williams, *Like a Loaded Weapon: The Rehnquist Court, Indian Rights, and the Legal History of Racism in America* (U. of Minnesota Press, 2005). It should be noted that in 2007, just as the Indian land-claims movement had begun running into seriously adverse rulings, there came a new U.N. Declaration on the Rights of Indigenous Peoples (DRIP), with provisions unusually favorable toward the assertion of tribal land claims.

Right to housing: forum held Nov. 8–9, 2009 at Georgetown Law Center (http://www.nlchp.org/2009Forum.cfm). Severe social exclusion: Cathy Albisa and Sharda Sekaran, "Realizing Domestic Social Justice Through International Human Rights: Foreword," 30 N.Y.U. Rev. L. & Soc. Change 351, 353– 54 (2006).

Action against firearms: David Kopel, Volokh Conspiracy blog, Apr. 28, 2010. Right to tourism: Ilya Shapiro, Cato at Liberty blog, May 6, 2010 (quoting EU commissioner for enterprise and industry Antonio Tajani).

One of the hottest topics in the curriculum: see, e.g., Martha F. Davis, "The Pendulum Swings Back: Poverty Law in the Old and New Curriculum," 34 Fordham Urban L. J. 1391 (2007) (hereinafter Davis, "Pendulum"), at p. 1406 ("current curricular wildfire"). On the rapid growth of clinical programs, see Deena R. Hurwitz, "Lawyering for Justice and the Inevitability of International Human Rights Clinics," 28 Yale J. Int. L. 505 (2003). For a sampling of human rights programs, see "Human Rights Survey", Association of American Law Schools Human Rights Section, law.villanova.edu/.

Spark continuing interest and activism: Jeanne M. Woods and Hope Lewis, *Human Rights and the Global Marketplace: Economic, Social and Cultural Dimensions* (Nijhoff, 2004), at p. xviii, quoted in Davis, "Pendulum," at p. 1414. Professionalize movement: John Kelly, "Law School Creates Nation's First Chair in International Human Rights, Named for Louis Henkin," *Columbia Daily Record*, Mar. 29, 1999 (quoting David Leebron).

Human Rights Watch and Amnesty International websites: visited summer 2010.

No longer limited to genocide and torture: Paul D. Carrington, *Stewards of Democracy: Law as a Public Profession* (Westview, 1999), p. 190. See Jack Goldsmith and Curtis Bradley, "Customary International Law as Federal Common Law: A Critique of the Modern Position," 110 Harv. L. Rev. 815 (1997).

Unwillingness to suppress speech: Article 20 of the U.N. Covenant on Civil and Political Rights prescribes that "Any advocacy of national, racial or religious hatred that constitutes incitement to discrimination, hostility or violence shall be prohibited by law."

International community has agreed that reproductive freedom is a human right: "Family Planning: Improving Reproductive Health," UNFPA website, visited Sept. 11, 2010.

Steadily isolating themselves on death penalty: "World is 'Winning' Battle Against Death Penalty Despite Setbacks," Amnesty International website, Feb. 25, 2010 (quoting AI Interim Secretary-General Claudio Cordone).

The primary sources of information are the academics: Carrington, *Stewards of Democracy*, p. 190.

Movement of the 1960s made global: Karen W. Arenson, "New Soldiers in the Fight for Human Rights," *New York Times*, Apr. 14, 2002 (quoting Kenneth Roth).

Yellowstone: Jeremy Rabkin, *Why Sovereignty Matters* (AEI Press, 1998), pp. 46–47, quoted by David Davenport, "The New Diplomacy Threatens American Sovereignty and Values," in Robert H. Bork, ed., *A Country I Do Not Recognize: The Legal Assault on American Values* (Hoover Institution Press, 2005).

Grantees use two strategic approaches: Mary McClymont and Stephen Golub, eds., *Many Roads to Justice: The Law-Related Work of Ford Foundation Grantees Around the World* (Ford Foundation, 2000), p. 292. More information on the U.S. Human Rights Fund can be found at its website, www.ushumanrightsfund.org. On the institutional background, including foundations' role, see Davis, "Pendulum," p. 1414 (Ford a "central player" in founding USHRF as umbrella funding group); Scott Cummings, "The Internationalization of Public Interest Law," 57 Duke L. J. 891 (2008). Title sums up strategy: Albisa and Sekaran, "Realizing Domestic Social Justice Through International Human Rights."

U.S.-watching NGOs: "Memorandum To: Members of the U.N. Human Rights Committee; From: U.S. Civil Society Organizations and Advocates; Re: List of concerns for the review of the U.S. Second and Third Periodic Report," dated Jan. 9, 2006, available at www.equaljusticesociety.org/petition/US_NGO_Submission%20_FINAL.pdf (declaring that "all of the signatories" share "strong concerns about the U.S. failure to comply fully with its international human rights obligations".) The memo followed a request for advice by UNHRC. For a listing of "civil society organizations and advocates" recognized/assigned to watch the United States, see Aug. 29, 2005 UNHRC submission (listing Human Rights Watch, Center for Constitutional Rights, American Friends Service Committee, and various others, including law school projects at Columbia, NYU, Virginia, Fordham, and American).

Laid out the basic plan: Dorothy Q. Thomas, "Advancing Rights Protection in the United States: An Internationalized Advocacy Strategy," 9 Harv. Hum. Rts. J. 15, 19–20 (1996).

Even less democratic legitimacy: see John McGinnis and Ilya Somin, "Should International Law Be Part of Our Law?" 59 Stan. L. Rev. 1175 (2007).

Sue local police for failing to prevent domestic violence: *Castle Rock* v. *Gonzales*, 545 U.S. 748 (2005). An earlier, better-known case in which the U.S. Supreme Court declined to recognize such a right was *DeShaney* v. *Winnebago County*, 489 U.S. 189 (1989). On the bringing of international human rights law to bear on the case, see Caroline Bettinger-Lopez (Columbia), "Time to Set a New Standard," *National Law Journal*, Oct. 22, 2007. For some underlying policy issues regarding government liability for failure to protect citizenry, see Walter Olson, "Lawsuit Reform in Washington," *Wall Street Journal*, Dec. 24, 2005.

Illegal aliens' suit for loss of future wages: *Hoffman Plastic Compounds* v. *NLRB*, 535 U.S. 137 (2002). See Walter Olson, "A Wink Too Far," *National Review*, Apr. 3, 2002.

Self-executing: Louis Henkin, *Foreign Affairs and the U.S. Constitution* (Oxford U. Press, 1996), pp. 198 *et seq.*

Wider banning of purported hate speech: Jeremy Waldron, "Dignity and Defamation: The Visibility of Hate (2009 Holmes Lectures)," 123 Harv. L. Rev. 1596 (2010).

Quit complaining, you're too late: see, e.g., Philippe Sands, *Lawless World: America and the Making and Breaking of Global Rules from FDR's Atlantic Charter to George W. Bush's Illegal War* (Viking, 2005), pp. xvii, xviii, xix, 15, 17 (notions of sovereignty changed with growing interdependence, wishful thinking for preregulatory planet, voices calling for a return to an earlier era, breaking states' "monopoly" over rules, legal fiction of sovereign state crumbles).

CHAPTER TWELVE   SEIZED AND DETAINED

No 1990 entry for "universal jurisdiction" in Black's: Henry Kissinger, "The Pitfalls of Universal Jurisdiction: Risking Judicial Tyranny," *Foreign Affairs*, Jun/Jul. 2001.

Nuremberg and piracy history: see Lee A. Casey and David B. Rivkin, Jr., "The Dangerous Myth of Universal Jurisdiction," in Robert H. Bork, ed., *A Country I Do Not Recognize: The Legal Assault on American Values* (Hoover Institution Press, 2005).

Offenses of exceptional gravity: the "Princeton Principles on Universal Jurisdiction," a widely cited declaration drafted in 2001 by a group of scholars who met at Princeton, N.J., declared universal jurisdiction to apply to "crimes of such exceptional gravity that they affect the fundamental interests of the international community as a whole." See Stephen Macedo, ed., *Universal Jurisdiction: National Courts and the Prosecution of Serious Crimes Under International Law* (U. of Pennsylvania Press, 2006); G. John Ikenberry, "Princeton Principles on Universal Jurisdiction," *Foreign Affairs*, Jan.-Feb. 2002.

Federal court revived it in 1980: *Filártiga v. Peña-Irala*, 630 F.2d 876 (2d Cir. 1980). Supreme Court ratified Alien Tort developments: *Sosa v. Alvarez-Machain*, 542 U.S. 692 (2004). For reactions to *Sosa*, see Jonathan Adler, "Sosa Justice," *National Review*, July 21, 2004; James R. Copland, Point of Law blog, Jul. 22, 2004 (some Alien Tort suits driven by "cowboy law professors" who want to "exploit U.S. courts to get their preferred policies implemented without having to worry about the State Department or Congress.") On extraterritoriality, see also Austen Parrish, "The Effects Test: Extraterritoriality's Fifth Business," 61 Vand. L. Rev. 1455 (2008); "Reclaiming International Law from Extraterritoriality," 93 Minn. L. Rev. 815 (2009).

Recent scheduled review: CERD (United Nations Committee for the Elimination of Racial Discrimination) observations adopted Mar. 5, 2008 following fourth, fifth and sixth periodic reports from the United States.

Justice Kennedy: *Roper* v. *Simmons*, 543 U.S. 551 (2005).

Big score in the form of seizure or detention: for enthusiasm regarding the arrest of Western world leaders, see, e.g., Philippe Sands, *Lawless World: America and the Making and Breaking of Global Rules from FDR's Atlantic Charter to George W. Bush's Illegal War* (Viking 2005), p. 28 (Thatcher, Blair, Bush).

ICC jurisdiction over aggression: Kenneth Anderson, "The ICC and Crime of Aggression," Volokh Conspiracy blog, Jun. 13, 2010; Brett D. Schaefer, "The U.S. Loses on Aggression in Kampala," National Review Online "The Corner," Jun. 14, 2010; Jeremy Rabkin, "Aggression Outlawed!," *Weekly Standard*, Aug. 23, 2010. Incidentally, Article 20 of the U.N. Covenant on Civil and Political Rights, the same article that calls for banning advocacy of hatred that incites to discrimination, also prescribes that "Any propaganda for war shall be prohibited by law." Some NGOs have argued that this should be understood to render unlawful various pronouncements made by the White House and Executive Branch in the United States, and perhaps more generally to prohibit the dissemination of hawkish views by some wider class of persons. See also Michael G. Kearney, *The Prohibition of Propaganda for War in International Law* (Oxford University Press, 2007) (proposing that "direct and public incitement to aggression" be answerable to criminal charges before the International Criminal Court); Richard B. Collins, "Propaganda for War and Transparency," 87 Denver U. L. Rev. 819 (2010).

"What we need is a PROSECUTOR!": Center for Constitutional Rights website, visited Mar. 8, 2008. Among many other examples of CCR's close ties to legal academia, CCR president Ellen Chapnick went on to be appointed "Dean for Social Justice Initiatives" at Columbia (Columbia faculty webpage, Ellen B. Chapnick).

Prescient speech: see Stephen Macedo, "Introduction," in Macedo, ed., *Universal Jurisdiction*, p. 6 (quoting Nicolas Browne-Wilkinson). Browne-Wilkinson wrote the House of Lords decision approving the extradition of Pinochet to Spain, but, alone among conferees at Princeton, dissented from the text of the Princeton Principles.

CHAPTER THIRTEEN   CONCLUSION

New Class: Irving Kristol, "Business and the 'New Class," in *Neoconservatism: The Autobiography of an Idea* (Simon & Schuster, 1995), p. 205. For background, see B. Bruce-Briggs, *The New Class?* (Transaction, 1979).

Mary Ann Glendon, *Rights Talk: The Impoverishment of Political Discourse* (Free Press, 1991).

acknowledgments

I am grateful for generous support to the Cato Institute and likewise to the Manhattan Institute, where I did much of the research and early writing on the book over several years. Portions of chapters nine and ten appeared in earlier form in the Manhattan Institute's publication *City Journal*; earlier versions of some material also appeared at MI's blog *Point of Law* and at my own blog *Overlawyered*. Encounter Books has done an outstanding job on the book's production and promotion, with the Cato Institute doing invaluable service on the latter front as well. For corrections, updates and supplements to the book, check SchoolsForMisrule.com and Overlawyered.com.

The law library at Pace University School of Law in White Plains, N.Y. and its staff were unfailingly helpful in my research. Thanks in particular to Vicky Gannon and Prof. Marie Stefanini Newman. The Ford Foundation in New York City generously let me examine archives from its rich history of involvement in legal education and the state of the courts and legal profession.

Many others both in and out of legal academia shared their expertise or corrected my misimpressions. I will mention only Marc Arkin, Dave Boaz, Lester Brickman, Bill Childs, James Copland, Richard Epstein, Ted Frank, Gail Heriot, Heather Mac Donald, Peggy Little, Daniel Polsby, Roger Pilon, Aaron Powell, Jeremy Rabkin, Lawrence Schonbrun, Ilya Shapiro, and John Steele. As always, thanks go to my family.

index